Tsunami in the Head – Better Understanding and Coping with Burnout

Rebecca Petersen

Tsunami in the Head – Better Understanding and Coping with Burnout

New Approaches for a Resilient Society

 Springer

Rebecca Petersen
Zürich, Switzerland

ISBN 978-3-658-49736-1   ISBN 978-3-658-49737-8   (eBook)
https://doi.org/10.1007/978-3-658-49737-8

Translation from the German language edition: "Tsunami im Kopf – Burnout besser verstehen und bewältigen – Neue Zugänge für eine resiliente Gesellschaft" by Rebecca Petersen, © Der/die Herausgeber bzw. der/die Autor(en), exklusiv lizenziert an Springer Fachmedien Wiesbaden GmbH, ein Teil von Springer Nature 2025. Published by Der/die Herausgeber bzw. der/die Autor(en), exklusiv lizenziert an Springer Fachmedien Wiesbaden GmbH, ein Teil von Springer Nature. All Rights Reserved.

This book is a translation of the original German edition "Tsunami im Kopf – Burnout besser verstehen und bewältigen" by Rebecca Petersen, published by Springer Fachmedien Wiesbaden GmbH in 2025. The translation was done with the help of an artificial intelligence machine translation tool. A subsequent human revision was done primarily in terms of content, so that the book will read stylistically differently from a conventional translation. Springer Nature works continuously to further the development of tools for the production of books and on the related technologies to support the authors.

This Springer imprint is published by the registered company Springer Fachmedien Wiesbaden GmbH, part of Springer Nature.
The registered company address is: Abraham-Lincoln-Str. 46, 65189 Wiesbaden, Germany

If disposing of this product, please recycle the paper.

Foreword von Dr. Klaus Sejkora

There are countless psychological specialist publications and self-help books on the subject of burnout, and just as many personal accounts from those affected have been published. Rebecca Petersen unites both aspects in her person. She is a psychological counselor and a teaching transactional analyst PTSTA — and she experienced a severe burnout herself, both physically and emotionally. This makes this book something truly special.

When I met Rebecca in person in the spring of 2023 after some written correspondence, I encountered a smart, cheerful, and lively young woman. No one would have spontaneously guessed what a difficult path she had recently traversed and how successfully she had managed it. She told me about her book project, her theoretical reflections on burnout disorders, and her personal experiences with them. I was immediately captivated by what I heard, especially by the powerful metaphors that were to guide the book: "Tsunami in the head" perfectly captured what many of my patients described about their experiences during their burnout episodes. "Tidal wave," "sea," "driftwood," "house on the coast," "lighthouse," "the great wide world"—all these images that Rebecca described to me made me impatiently await the first part of her manuscript.

Now I have read it and am impressed by this comprehensive compendium, which is aimed at those affected, relatives, managers and colleagues, as well as treating and consulting professionals. Rebecca combines, in an engaging mix, personal experience with a theoretical map drawn from occupational psychology, burnout research, and above all, transactional analysis. Her book will also be a valuable resource for me in my psychotherapeutic work, and I will be happy to recommend it further.

Make use of this book as well. It will be a great help to you in love, appreciation, and respect for yourself and for other people.

Linz (Austria)

Linz (Österreich)   Dr. Klaus Sejkora

Foreword von Dr. Barbara Hochstrasser

Rebecca Petersen, principal in the field of special education, psychological counselor, coach, consultant, and transactional analyst, presents a courageous personal account of her own experience with burnout and the insights and consequences she has drawn from it in this book. However, as a personal narrative, this book does not claim scientific rigor.

Overcoming and recovering from burnout can only succeed if the affected person accepts this crisis, reflects on it, explores the personal and professional triggering factors, honestly examines themselves, and draws consequences from this in terms of changes in attitudes, values, potentially obstructive cognitive constructs, as well as in their behavior.

This is exactly what Rebecca Petersen does. She uses her experiences, personal analysis, and conclusions about the nature, development, and healing process of burnout, together with her professional expertise as a coach and transactional analyst, to develop and present in this book a model of the emergence and recovery process of burnout, alongside her personal narrative. As a counterpoint to burnout, she introduces the concept of resilience. She describes seven phases of this process, which form the individual chapters of the book—premonition, illness, recovery and setbacks, being supported and allowing good things, reflection/gaining security, categorizing uncertainty, and integration both internally and externally. Each chapter contains an account of personal experiences and a description of the characteristics of that phase. This is very helpful for both those affected and those interested.

What makes her book truly special, however, are undoubtedly the suggestions and questions for (self-) reflection listed in each chapter for four groups of target audiences. These are (potential) affected individuals, relatives and (work) teams, managers, and people inclined toward self-reflection. These suggestions and questions can provide highly valuable impulses for the respective audiences, making it easier to engage with burnout and its various facets. However, the questions and suggestions are not only valuable for those affected by or interested in burnout, but also for anyone who wishes to engage more deeply with themselves and their current (life) situation in general.

M.P.H, President of the Swiss Expert Network for Burnout

Dr. med. Barbara Hochstrasser

Foreword von Dr. Martin Keck

Burnout is a phenomenon that has developed into a serious problem in recent years in Switzerland, Austria, and Germany as well. Despite its enormous significance, burnout is often recognized too late or inadequately treated. Burnout is a risk factor for the onset of depression, heart attack, stroke, osteoporosis, and diabetes. If left untreated, burnout shortens life expectancy. It is defined as a state of emotional exhaustion, depersonalization, and reduced performance capacity, which is widespread in the working world and can lead to serious health problems—one of which is exhaustion depression. Burnout occurs particularly in occupational groups with high demands and stress. Especially affected are professions with high intrinsic motivation, such as physicians, nurses, teachers, or social workers. A study by the German Trade Union Confederation (DGB) from 2017 found that about 10% of all employees in Germany suffer from burnout symptoms. Although the weekly working hours are longer and the number of public holidays is lower, a similar prevalence of burnout symptoms has also been found in Switzerland. A study from 2018 shows that 10–15% of employees are affected.

In its new classification system ICD-11, the World Health Organization (WHO) does not classify burnout as an independent disease, but rather, appropriately, as a risk factor that can impair health. The feeling of being burned out results from chronic workplace stress, according to part of the definition. Previously, burnout had been included without a clear definition. Now, the term is listed with this description in the catalog of approximately 55,000 diseases and symptoms.

A combination of psychotherapeutic interventions, stress management, and of course also organizational approaches such as workplace interventions and preventive measures can help reduce the risk of burnout and improve the mental health of those affected. A specific medical distinction between burnout, depression, and other conditions that can also lead to symptoms of exhaustion is very important to ensure appropriate treatment. An interesting example of a measure to prevent burnout in Germany is the project "Health Promotion at Work—GIB" by the Federal Institute for Occupational Safety and Health. As part of this project, various prevention programs were developed and tested for different occupational groups. An evaluation study from 2018 shows that these programs can help reduce the risk of burnout and improve the mental health of participants. The Swiss recommendations for the prevention and treatment of burnout also emphasize the importance of individual and organizational intervention and identify a variety of risk factors that can contribute to burnout, including working conditions, personality traits, and social relationships.

There is much to be done! I therefore warmly congratulate Rebecca Petersen on her book, which makes an important contribution to the understanding, prevention, and management of burnout.

Prof. Dr. Dr. med. Martin E. Keck, Chief Physician, Rehabilitation Clinic Seewis/GR, Professor Keck Practice, Stäfa/ZH, Specialist in Psychiatry and Psychiatry FMH/ Neurology FMH/Psychosomatics and Psychotherapy (D).

Dr. Martin Keck

References

DGB Good Work Index (2017). Psychological stress and strain. Results of the DGB Good Work Index. Berlin: Hans Böckler Foundation.

Buddeberg-Fischer, B., Klaghofer, R., Buddeberg, C. (2018). Burnout and stress—Results of the Swiss Working Conditions Study 2016. Swiss Medical Journal, 99(20), 659–664.

Federal Institute for Occupational Safety and Health (2018). GIB—Workplace Health Promotion: Prevention of burnout and other work-related mental illnesses. Project report F 2398. Dortmund: Federal Institute for Occupational Safety and Health.

Hochstrasser, B. (22.06.2016). Burnout Treatment Part 1: Fundamentals., M.E. Keck, Swiss Medical Forum 2016; 16(25): 538–541.

Hochstrasser, B. (22.06.2016). Burnout Treatment Part 2: Practical Recommendations., M.E. Keck, Swiss Medical Forum 2016; 16(26-27): 561–566.

Preface

Rebecca Petersen has worked for several years as a manager in the field of special education and is self-employed as a trained psychological counselor, systemic coach and consultant, as well as a teaching transactional analyst (PTSTA). Despite her extensive expertise in counseling and coaching, as a school principal she suffered from burnout and was incapacitated and unable to work for several months.

Burnout is a current and socially relevant issue that is rarely discussed. It is often accompanied by feelings of shame and guilt. Everyone has their own image of what burnout is—but does this actually correspond to reality? And if so, why does it seem to affect so many people without being noticed?

With her book and the approaches it contains, the author aims to change this situation for organizations, teams, leaders, consultants, as well as those affected and their families and friends, and to foster a new awareness of social responsibility. In doing so, she builds a bridge to a new perspective on resilience and health, thereby making an active contribution to prevention and education. Her book provides access and ease to a topic that must be taken seriously, thus enabling an open, healthy approach to a complex, insidious, and life-changing illness.

Rebecca Petersen

Acknowledgments

I dedicate this book to my mother, who contributed greatly to my strong will to achieve and survive, and who inspired me never to give up believing in the possibility of healing and to make the best of each situation and circumstance, even when it was often truly difficult to endure my own weakness and limitations.

I would also like to take this opportunity to especially thank my family, particularly my mother and my siblings. During the time of my burnout illness, I was unable to confide in them due to intense anxiety as well as feelings of shame and guilt. I did not have the strength to face the questions that would arise. I wanted to solve my problems on my own. I have achieved this goal. And yet, I am grateful that deep down I always knew my family would have been there for me unconditionally, had I needed and allowed it.

I still feel a deep connection to each and every one of them, and it is truly a gift to be part of such a family.

Our interactions are characterized by appreciation, openness, and impartiality, which allow each family member to express their individuality. Here, my maternal grandparents laid a strong foundation and made it possible for us to establish deep roots in life. I am very grateful for that as well!

I would like to extend special thanks to my partner, who has consistently supported me with great dedication by proofreading my work and who has met me with hope and understanding during stressful times. I would also like to express my personal gratitude to my many truly wonderful friends, who have accompanied me in various ways along my path to recovery and have not held it against me that I confided in some of them only very late. Here, too, I can say with joy and deep gratitude that all my close, in some cases long-standing, friends are themselves strong individuals who are always willing to join me in the adventure of life, self-reflection, and personal development, and who are prepared to face whatever life brings with courage, openness, and honesty, without judging themselves or others. I truly appreciate that!

At this point, I would like to extend my sincere thanks to all those who have actively supported me in recent years as coaches, mentors, consultants, and transactional analysts, etc., and who have repeatedly provided me with appreciative yet critical feedback for my personal development and the achievement of various milestones in my life.

Many thanks also to Dr. Klaus Sejkora, Dr. Barbara Hochstrasser, and Dr. Martin Keck, who have agreed to introduce my book with a foreword. I am very pleased that they, too, are actively engaged in their respective professional fields in the area of burnout prevention and education.

And last but not least, I would like to thank all those who have been appreciative, open, and respectful companions on my journey in writing and realizing this book, as well as in my life in general! I am grateful for all the encounters and acquaintances that have shaped me into the person I am today. And in this sense, I am also thankful for my own strength and personality, which enable me to face life openly and courageously time and again, to dare to take new paths, and to embrace change!

From the heart

Rebecca Petersen

Introduction

"There is a way out! There is hope!
Healing is possible! Even if it doesn't always feel that way
and the path back seems hopeless, dark, and endless. Everyone
can emerge from it as a winner! You already carry everything
you need within you!"
Rebecca Petersen

The experience of burnout has profoundly and lastingly changed me. I was completely unprepared when I was torn from working life for over half a year, until I was able to start again with a therapeutic work trial. During this time, I was personally very challenged by social isolation, anxiety, existential fears, feelings of shame and guilt, as well as physical symptoms and complaints. The incredibly intense physical and emotional exhaustion, severe back pain, and persistent sleep disturbances were three of the main features during this period. On my way back to a normal life, I had to acquire parts of a new identity as well as new behaviors and ways of thinking in order to reclaim and sustainably strengthen my physical and mental health. This was a long and arduous journey that ultimately led me closer to myself and to a new inner clarity and strength, and it has lastingly strengthened my confidence in myself and my abilities. Burnout is as diverse as people themselves. In addition to my expertise as a consultant, coach, transactional analyst, and manager, I can now offer my own perspective and experiences to foster better understanding and awareness. This creates a holistic approach and an honest perspective.

This book offers an intimate insight into my personal experience during my burnout illness. It is a personal concern of mine to provide a basis for discussion and to advance awareness and education about burnout. I want to support others affected by sharing my experiences and encourage them, but also make an active contribution to prevention. That is why I am writing this book.

Accordingly, the book is intended for all those who are generally interested in the topic of "burnout." People who fear that they themselves may be affected. It is intended for people who know someone dear to them who, in their view, might be affected by burnout or is already suffering from it. If you haven't experienced it yourself, you can't really imagine what it's like! And even if you have experienced it, it may have felt completely different for another person affected. Burnout is as varied and diverse as people themselves. And it is precisely this that makes diagnosis and early detection so challenging.

With new and diverse approaches, I aim to improve the distorted, unclear picture of burnout disorder and lift the veil from the unknown. My book is intended to be an easily digestible read that nonetheless informs about a serious topic and offers direct insight into the experience.

It was precisely this unclear, distorted image of burnout that, among other things, led me to refuse to accept for far too long that I was suffering from burnout. And this, too, is typical for so many affected individuals.

With my openness, I want to reach out to other people who may secretly suspect that they are suffering from burnout or recognize a tendency toward it within themselves. I also want to encourage family members, friends, and acquaintances to take their personal assessments seriously and to address their observations with the person concerned—courageously and perhaps repeatedly, but always mindfully and respectfully. This requires a great deal of sensitivity and a certain level of know-how. Directly addressing the issue can lead to defensiveness and may further intensify confusion, distortion, and/or denial in the affected person.

What is needed is a well-defined yet determined and mindful approach toward one another, a calm, trusting space for interaction, and a safe atmosphere, as well as an encounter at eye level, so that an affected person can even summon the courage and feel the necessity to admit to their current weaknesses and problems, and subsequently become active and seek help. Fortunately, some people react with great relief when they finally receive an honest, supportive, and appreciative suggestion from outside regarding a possible burnout condition. This can be the decisive moment and help to realistically assess the situation and recognize the seriousness of the situation early enough.

Burnout is a serious, multifaceted, and complex illness that can be treated! Recovery and healing are all the more successful the earlier it is recognized. From my perspective, in the long term, it can even turn out to be an opportunity and represent a kind of transformation into a new, happier life with greater clarity and joy—for those affected, families, leaders, teams, and organizations. This is possible when everyone courageously faces the circumstances and dares to take responsibility for their part within the system.

In this spirit, I wish you an exciting journey into a new, unfamiliar world. By delving into this topic personally, you are already making an important initial contribution to prevention and education. For this, I sincerely thank you!

With best regards
Rebecca Petersen

About the Structure of This Book

The book is divided into eight chapters, each of which, following an initial introduction and overview, describes a phase of burnout illness and recovery. The author based the division of the phases on her own experiences in order to create a personal and direct approach. At the beginning, in the first chapter "Initial Situation," you will find important general information to clarify terminology, which is intended to help you understand the author's initial situation as well as possible and to facilitate entry into the topic and mutual understanding.

Each of the seven chapters offers different insights into a phase of burnout and follows a recurring structure with eight differently designed approaches in each case. The phases of burnout are presented here subjectively, based on the author's personal experience.

- Access A: Each chapter begins with a feeling and the description of a corresponding image.

- Access B: Under "My Story," the author recounts her experiences during each phase of the burnout illness. The reader is drawn in directly and relives the burnout phases from destruction and catastrophe to hope, confidence, and new beginnings.
- Access C: In "Burnout Diary," the author's experiences and impressions are briefly described as isolated snapshots, providing direct insight into the experience of burnout. These experiences and impressions are independent of Access B and do not follow any chronology.
- Access D: "Figuratively Speaking" offers a creative approach through a comic series specially designed by the author, characterized by clarity and optimism.
- In the following four approaches, the author directly addresses different system groups:
- Access E: This section provides advice for (potential) affected individuals on self-reflection and learning resilience.
- Access F: The next section offers relatives, friends, and colleagues helpful insights for each phase of the illness and recovery from burnout. The main focus here is to stimulate systems thinking and to make existing resources within the system (family, circle of friends, team) more visible and accessible.
- Access G: The author now addresses leaders in the context of "Corporate/Social Responsibility." Key insights are highlighted that provide relief and support in each phase and foster mutual understanding.
- Access H: With a variety of targeted questions for (self-)reflection, as steps toward self-awareness in both professional and private life, new approaches are once again created. These enable the identification of restrictive (thinking, feeling, and behavioral) patterns and beliefs, and the discovery and further development of new personal insights and abilities in connection with

one's own wisdom and intuition. In the final approach, goal-oriented concepts from theory and transactional analysis are presented.

• The following concepts and theories are described: in Phase 1) resilience, in Phase 2) script, in Phase 3) autonomy, in Phase 4) integrating Adult Ego State and intuition, in Phase 5) basic positions and permissions, in Phase 6) drivers and injunctions, and in Phase 7) basic psychological needs and symbiotic relationship patterns.

For the sake of completeness, the author recommends reading all chapters of the book from beginning to end in order to gain a comprehensive and in-depth understanding of the topic of burnout and to delve into the individual phases in a structured and targeted manner. At the same time, thanks to its clear structure and various approaches, the book also offers the opportunity for those seeking a brief overview to engage with the topic in sections, thereby gaining short insights and impressions. This, too, can represent an engaging and meaningful way to approach the subject.

Although the topic and terminology of burnout are widely discussed, burnout is not classified as a distinct medical diagnosis according to ICD-10, but rather as a syndrome that often overlaps with other health conditions, especially psychological disorders (e.g., depression). The ICD-11 describes burnout as a qualifying diagnosis that further characterizes a defined illness such as depression [1]. There are also various definitions of burnout, formulated by different authors based on differing assessment methods and measurement instruments [1].

Nevertheless, in severe cases, burnout has the value of an illness and, according to Hochstrasser [1], can be treated as a disease requiring treatment and therapy. In this book, the term burnout disorder is used, or for simplicity, the isolated term burnout (as a syndrome) is employed. This book makes no claim to completeness whatsoever!

Any recommendations in this book cannot replace medical and (psycho-)therapeutic treatment! This work is primarily a personal account by the author, from which guidance for (self-)reflection is derived. All descriptions address female, male, as well as gender-neutral individuals.

In this sense, the book offers a diverse journey of discovery for all those interested, not only with regard to the topic of burnout, but also in terms of the individual path of personal development and the (re-)discovery of one's own original strength, power, and resilience in the creative interplay between intellect and one's own inner wisdom and intuition—intended for a wide range of applications in organizations, teams, for leaders, and private individuals, always in the spirit of and to promote a systemic perspective and the (further) development toward autonomy, self-efficacy, and awareness.

References

1. Hochstrasser, B. (06/22/2016). Burnout Treatment Part 1: Fundamentals. *Swiss Medical Forum*: 538.

The Essentials at a Glance

Burnout is a multifaceted condition that includes both physical and psychological symptoms and changes. According to ICD-10, it is currently considered a syndrome, but not a disease that can be diagnosed as such [1]. The symptoms and signs of burnout are diverse, complex, and highly individual. In the early stages, they can therefore often be misinterpreted or overlooked.

As the condition progresses, it is characteristic that those affected, due to the increased release of stress hormones, are no longer able to properly perceive themselves. This results, quite literally, in a "tsunami in the head."

The elevated hormone levels (stress hormones) influence the plasticity of the nervous system and can affect concentration and cognitive performance [2].

It is often not visible how a person is feeling internally. Depending on the individual, those affected may be experts at skillfully concealing their true state from others and/or downplaying or denying it to themselves.

Although burnout primarily refers to the professional context, for example, young people and parents can also experience burnout, as prolonged stress can certainly arise in private life as well [3].

Burnout is curable! Just as the course of the condition is individual, so too can, may, and should the path to recovery be individually tailored.

Depending on the severity of a burnout condition, recovery can take several months to over a year. In most cases, a gradual return to work, depending on individual capacity, is recommended and should be carried out with careful support [4]. This process can also take several months to more than a year, and many affected individuals report that it was only after several years that they truly overcame what they had experienced and its consequences, and were finally able to leave the burnout behind them.

References

1. Hochstrasser, B. (22.06.2016). Burnout Treatment Part 1: Fundamentals. *Swiss Medical Forum*: 538.
2. Hochstrasser, B. (22.06.2016). Burnout Treatment Part 1: Fundamentals. *Swiss Medical Forum*: 539.
3. Hochstrasser, B. (February 2023). Burnout and Exhaustion Depression. *Journal of Psychiatry and Neurology*, pp. 2–7: 4.
4. Hochstrasser, B. (22.06.2016). Burnout Treatment Part 1: Fundamentals. *Swiss Medical Forum*: 541.

Contents

About the Author

Rebecca Petersen is the founder of Triflect GmbH. For several years, she has been effectively supporting people in their personal and professional development, enabling sustainable change with greater clarity, focus, and perspective through her professional work and impact. Rebecca Petersen is recognized in Switzerland as a systemic coach, supervisor, and organizational consultant, as well as a psychological counselor and teaching transactional analyst

PTSTA-C. She was also trained by internationally renowned coaches in Los Angeles (USA) and is internationally certified as a Transformative Coach. For many years, Rebecca Petersen has successfully worked as a lecturer, trainer, consultant, coach, and advisor with private individuals, teams, executives, and organizations, as well as serving as a manager in the field of special education. During this time, she herself suffered from burnout, which prompted her to write this book. Since then, she has been committed to burnout prevention and education, supporting people in strengthening their autonomy, self-awareness, resilience, mindfulness, inner strength, and (self-healing) power.

Rebecca Petersen

Website/Email: www.triflect.ch, info@triflect.ch

Location: Zurich (Switzerland)

Initial Situation

Abstract The author provides insight into the current state of knowledge on burnout and resilience and delivers important factual information. Furthermore, she describes her initial situation regarding her professional role as a principal in the field of special education at the time she experienced burnout. To enhance understanding, the author offers an introduction to the field of transactional analysis, its scope of impact, and various areas of application.

Burnout

According to ICD-10 (medical nomenclature), burnout is not classified as a disease, but as "burnout (burnout syndrome)" [1].

In the current ICD-11 [2], the burnout syndrome is characterized by three dimensions:

1. Feelings of exhaustion or energy depletion
2. Increased mental distance from work or feelings of negativism or cynicism related to work
3. A sense of ineffectiveness and lack of accomplishment

ICD-11 [2] lists burnout as a diagnosis associated with employment and unemployment [1]. Burnout continues to be defined as a syndrome resulting from chronic workplace stress that has not been successfully managed.

However, according to Barbara Hochstrasser, the restriction to the occupational context is problematic in that stress can also arise in private life and prove just as harmful to health. Increasingly, one also reads and hears about parental or student burnout [1].

The term burnout was coined in the 1970s by Herbert Freudenberger in a medical and psychoanalytic context [3]. He defined the condition as a "process of exhaustion caused by excessive demands on the energies, strengths, and resources of the affected person" [3].

Since then, various researchers have addressed the burnout phenomenon. The definitions vary depending on the theories used.

Maslach and Jackson [4] found a symptom pattern similar to Freudenberger's in various professional groups in the health and education sectors, which they also referred to as burnout. To capture this phenomenon, they developed the Maslach Burnout Inventory [5], which describes burnout in three dimensions:

1. emotional exhaustion,
2. cynicism or demotivation, as well as
3. the subjective assessment of being less effective.

The Maslach Burnout Inventory-General Survey (MBI-GSS) [6], adapted for studies in the general population, subsequently became, according to Hochstrasser [1], the most widely used questionnaire for assessing burnout.

A burnout disorder encompasses severe physical, psychological, and cognitive exhaustion, which occurs together with autonomic symptoms, loss of motivation, and reduced performance [7].

According to Hochstrasser, five symptom domains [8] can be distinguished:

1. **Psychological symptoms:** Irritability; nervousness; restlessness; low mood; anxiety; jumpiness; brooding; self-doubt; panic; hypersensitivity; vulnerability
2. **Physical and autonomic symptoms:** Exhaustion; inability to recover; reduced resilience; headache; tachycardia; dizziness; sensory hypersensitivity; susceptibility to infections; gastrointestinal disturbances; difficulty falling or staying asleep; sweating
3. **Cognitive symptoms:** Concentration difficulties; memory disturbances; attention deficits; executive function impairments (e.g., loss of ability for multitasking)
4. **Motivational symptoms:** Loss of interest in work or personally rewarding activities; inability to engage with others; cynicism; devaluation of other people and previously positive situations
5. **Behavioral abnormalities:** Hyperactivity or reduced activity; social withdrawal, self-observation, self-focus; inattentiveness; tendency toward mistakes and accidents, reduced performance; loss of stress tolerance

The spectrum of possible symptoms for an initial and progressive burnout disorder is diverse. This makes early detection of burnout so difficult, because the symptoms are usually considered and treated individually, and in sum are not recognized as the onset of a burnout disorder. In addition, those affected often downplay or do not want to acknowledge them. In the appendix of this book, under "Letters for Those Affected—Part 3" you will find a supplementary list of possible early signs and symptoms, which provides an initial impression of the complexity of possible physical, psychological, and autonomic symptoms. This is intended as support so that burnout can be recognized and treated before a breakdown occurs. The fact is that constant stress and overload have a negative impact on the entire human system. However, it can still happen that this state of stress is endured for years as an apparent normal state, and the symptoms and changes in the body develop insidiously and, according to Nelting, remain partially or completely unrecognized [9]. The autonomic nervous system, however, often reacts much more quickly than we are aware. This is clearly explained by Buchenau and Nelting in their book.

According to Nelting [9], persistent stress ultimately leads to an imbalance between the two nervous systems—the sympathetic nervous system (responsible, for example, for activating many physiological and metabolic processes) and the parasympathetic nervous system (responsible for calming and recovery). This can, among other things, lead to high blood pressure. If this remains high even at rest, it may also indicate an imbalance of the autonomic nervous system.

According to Nelting [9], measuring heart rate variability can also provide an indication of autonomic imbalance. As already mentioned, prolonged stress, which can promote the development of burnout, has negative effects on the activity of the sympathetic nervous system. The parasympathetic nervous system is increasingly incapacitated. The experience of rest and recovery becomes less and less accessible.

Nelting [9] explains heart rate variability as the heart rate flexibly adapting to the respective demands in a healthy state. With prolonged stress, heart rate variability at rest may be lower because the parasympathetic nervous system is less active. If the autonomic balance deteriorates over a longer period due to ongoing stress and overload, the risk of a heart attack also increases, according to Nelting [9].

For the phenomenon in which individuals affected by burnout often underestimate or misjudge their own situation and, despite severe physical and emotional exhaustion and a growing sense of meaninglessness, fail to recognize what they are actually heading toward, Nelting [9] identifies, in addition to a high willingness to perform and favorable personality traits (see Phase VI—The Lighthouse—Classifying Uncertainty) of the affected person, two further explanations:

1. The persistent state of stress and alarm mode affects our creativity. New thoughts cannot truly be conceived. According to Nelting, self-deception occurs more frequently as the burnout process progresses [9].
2. Moreover, the heavy strain on the autonomic nervous system blocks self-perception. We become less aware of what our body and soul truly need and, as a result, are increasingly unable to respond to these needs in daily life. This leads to a decoupling of perception, which in turn can cause us to even forget to drink when we are thirsty, to no longer get enough sleep and rest overall, or to be suddenly overwhelmed by feelings such as sadness, listlessness, or disillusionment, according to Nelting [9]. He further describes that the increasing inability to perceive oneself, one's own body, and one's own needs is, in itself, a protective mechanism of the organism from ancient times, so that we would not be

disturbed by such perceptions in the struggle for survival. According to Nelting [9], this self-protection arises through the release of stress hormones and other substances that, for example, make us less sensitive to pain.

Accordingly, it is worthwhile to respond early, and to be mindful and honest with oneself, in order to recognize a possible burnout as early as possible, to treat it appropriately, and, if possible, to halt its progression before self-perception is too clouded by stress hormones and the negative spiral, as a "self-perpetuating process," pulls the affected person inexorably downward. Seeking support can already make sense in cases of increased and prolonged stress, (mild) depressive moods, diminished emotional awareness, or a feeling of "no longer being able to find rest," but also in the presence of diffuse physical symptoms or an increased need for social withdrawal and recovery.

There are good options and helpful resources online for an initial self-assessment. Many psychological practices offer self-tests based on the "Maslach Burnout Inventory-General Survey" (MBI-GSS) mentioned above [6], which can provide initial indications regarding risk. However, there is always the danger that the affected person will downplay or try to ignore the result. This, too, would be another possible warning sign according to the mechanisms described above. Mindful and honest self-reflection is therefore truly the best prevention against an unwanted breakdown and the risk of falling into a protracted burnout, from which there is then no looking away, let alone a self-determined choice or a way back.

In addition to symptoms, burnout can also be described by the sequence of various phases. According to Freudenberger, burnout can be divided into twelve different phases [10]:

1. The compulsion to prove oneself
2. Increased effort
3. Subtle neglect of one's own needs
4. Repression of conflicts and needs
5. Reinterpretation of values
6. Increased denial of emerging problems
7. Withdrawal
8. Observable behavioral changes
9. Depersonalization/loss of sense of one's own personality
10. Inner emptiness
11. Depression
12. Complete burnout exhaustion

These phases can overlap or merge seamlessly into one another. It is also possible for individual stages to be shorter, very prolonged, or to recur. The symptoms and their intensity can vary depending on the stage and may require different amounts of emotional or physical energy or trigger varying levels of stress.

According to Freudenberger, the manifestations depend on the individual's situation, personality, inclinations, history, and ability to cope with stress [10].

Many affected individuals report in retrospect that they found it difficult to actively break out of the hamster wheel. Although implementation may seem challenging, it always makes sense to take initial active steps to reduce stress and relieve oneself personally, regardless of how far the burnout process has already progressed.

Preventively, but also in the process of recovering from burnout, mindfulness-based methods and/or approaches to increase stress competence and self-confidence can be helpful. Psychotherapy and psychosocial counseling provide new perspectives and offer professionally qualified support. Through counseling, coaching, and personal development, new insights into inner drivers, limiting belief patterns, and script beliefs can open up new paths to autonomy and self-efficacy. Classic approaches such as regular exercise and sports in the fresh air not only serve to improve general mood but also to physiologically reduce stress (breakdown of stress hormones). In addition, sufficient social interaction and trusting relationships are important building blocks in the prevention and recovery from burnout. Participation in a self-help group can also be a helpful form of support. These are just a few notable ways in which excessive stress and thus a potential burnout can be actively and preventively addressed.

In the next section, you will find further approaches, ideas, and helpful new perspectives on the topic of "resilience."

Resilience

In the context of burnout, resilience is often mentioned as the counterpart to stress. Therefore, I would like to define the term right at the outset. An interesting definition is provided by Welter-Enderlin and Hildebrand: "Resilience is understood as the ability of people to overcome crises in the life cycle by drawing on personal and socially mediated resources and to use them as an opportunity for development. Concepts related to resilience include salutogenesis, coping, or autopoiesis. All these concepts offer an alternative perspective to the deficit-oriented approach" [11].

Accordingly, resilience means demonstrating a certain capacity for survival despite adverse circumstances and applying necessary and appropriate coping mechanisms and strategies in life, and, if necessary, acquiring new ones. Resilience is not a factor that can be precisely quantified or scaled. Depending on the author, resilience is viewed from one of the following two perspectives [11]:

1. as a fixed ability or trait of a person,
2. as a flexible variable in an ongoing (developmental) process in a person's life.

From my experience, resilience, although it is certainly a personal trait, can be accessible or inaccessible depending on the situation, and can increase or decrease over the course of life.

In my own experience, the ability to set boundaries seems to me to be an important competence in relation to resilience and its personal development. By boundaries, I mean a healthy and conscious distancing from script-bound (behavioral, emotional, and cognitive) patterns, imperatives, and beliefs (see Phase II—The Flood Wave—Illness), but also in interactions within the social environment, when it comes to perceiving, setting, maintaining, openly communicating, and, if necessary, assertively enforcing boundaries for oneself and others. This includes the ability to consciously perceive one's own needs and communicate them externally, as well as allowing oneself to think, feel, act, or decide differently—perhaps differently than is customary in society or practiced within one's circle of friends or family. Living according to one's own needs, regardless of how others would act in the same situation and regardless of what expectations are implicitly or explicitly placed upon oneself, or what expectations of expectations one assumes.

Expectations of expectations, according to Luhmann [12], is an intriguing concept in this context. Luhmann describes the expectations that a person, arising from the social context, mentally establishes for themselves and to which they orient themselves, alongside their own expectations, in terms of their thinking, actions, experiences, and feelings. In social interactions and collaboration, it is helpful to review these respective expectations of expectations together. This leads to greater trust and mutual understanding.

Healthy boundary-setting in private social interactions, but also in professional collaboration, in this sense means consciously perceiving, accepting, and respecting one's own and others' physical and psychological boundaries; expressing or, if necessary, reviewing needs and expectations; and, based on the situation, seeking, jointly finding, and, if needed, negotiating compromises and solutions for a shared and appreciative coexistence, in order to maintain mutual respect and appreciation.

Schulze and Sejkora have comprehensively described, in eighteen dimensions [13], what characterizes a resilient person in today's working world:

1. Intuition: the extremely rapid, predominantly unconscious grasp of situations, combined with matching relevant prior experiences and responding accordingly
2. Problem identification: the rapid, conscious, and cognitive filtering out of what is currently unimportant and the setting of solution-oriented priorities
3. Understanding: the precise intellectual and emotional grasp of backgrounds and motives
4. Setting boundaries: being able to say "no" and make autonomous decisions while remaining capable of compromise
5. Letting go: being able to accept what cannot be changed, consciously process what has happened, and learn from mistakes
6. Communication: the ability to build bridges from my world into the worlds of others, in order to understand and be understood

7. Conflict competence: the willingness to endure and work through internal, interpersonal, and organizational contradictions and ambivalences

8. Relationship competence: being able to establish, engage in, and maintain social contacts, relationships, and bonds of varying closeness

9. Emotional competence: continuous awareness of a wide range of feelings and the willingness to use them for problem identification and problem solving

10. Stress competence: being able to balance, constructively define, and constructively implement high pressure and demands

11. Problem solving: being able to maintain an overview both intellectually and emotionally, and to set priorities

12. Creativity: being able to find new paths, think outside the box, and leave well-trodden tracks

13. Willingness to change: being able to see life as a continuous process of farewells and new beginnings

14. Humor: the ability and willingness for ironic, especially self-ironic, reframing and for inner distancing

15. Personal ethics: reliable, constructive inner positions in dealing with oneself and the world

16. Goals and visions: having rewarding and motivating images and ideas of the future

17. Perseverance: enduring and withstanding frustrations and defeats, and the determination to achieve goals

18. Flexibility: healthy adaptation to changing conditions

These eighteen dimensions provide a meaningful approach to identifying personal resilience factors. In addition, each person has other approaches and opportunities in different areas and phases of life that prove to be sources of strength.

There are thus no limits to the individual definition of resilience factors—this refers to anything that does a person good, brings them joy, takes them away from everyday life and/or rumination, and generates new energy. Resilience factors therefore have a highly individual, situational, empowering, and supportive effect on mental and physical health.

For the individual, it is about discovering entirely new, personal resilience factors, but perhaps also reintegrating and reviving familiar ones, for example from childhood, into life in the here and now. In this sense, the term "resilience factors" refers to all things, activities, images, objects, people, memories that are beneficial to the person as a whole and offer opportunities to recharge, mentally switch off, but also to consciously perceive one's own body, feelings, needs, and personal boundaries. In addition to the eighteen dimensions of Schulze and Sejkora, these can also include, for example, sporting activities, hobbies, inner ideas and images, photos, inner mantras, encouraging beliefs, guided imagery, meditation exercises, spiritual rituals, coaching/counseling, etc.

From my personal experience following my burnout illness, but also from my work as a counselor and coach with people affected by burnout, I have defined four (life) domains for better orientation, which are particularly important for a healthy balance and thus for strengthening resilience and for (self-)reflection, and which enable a holistic perspective, approach, and way of life:

- **Workplace** and conditions (values, meaning, leadership and collaboration culture, etc.)
- **Private life** and social connectedness
- **Personality** and individual characteristics
- **Health-conscious behavior** and integration into everyday life

Where possible, personal resilience factors can be found in all four areas and integrated into everyday life to such an extent that physical and mental balance and equilibrium can be consciously and sustainably enhanced.

At certain stages of life, it can happen that one area falls out of balance or, for specific reasons, does not receive the necessary attention. However, persistent issues over an extended period can drain valuable (life) energy. Therefore, they should be addressed and changed as early as possible—actively, courageously, and with a solution-oriented approach.

If this is postponed or neglected for too long, over time, several areas may fall into imbalance, which further increases the strain and can promote the development of burnout. It is also important to note that circumstances and the behavior of the person concerned can change gradually and be unnoticed in individual areas, so that a potential burnout is not recognized and treated early enough and adequately as such.

In terms of strengthening and maintaining resilience, it therefore makes sense to keep the four areas in focus and to handle the available (energy) resources sustainably and mindfully.

Work as a School Principal

From my perspective, working as a school principal is demanding, as different interest groups come together and the range of expectations and diverse needs is correspondingly broad. The daily routine is often tightly scheduled; unexpected events and seemingly never-ending "to-dos" can at times lead to high pressure and overload. The reputation of the job of school principal is partly negative in society. The estimated rate of resignations and burnout is high, and in some places, the work of a school principal is referred to as a "wear-and-tear job."

For my part, I appreciate the various tasks and activities in the role of school principal, which match my strengths, my broad expertise, and my available resources. Moreover, from the very beginning, I had the impression that I was able to pursue a very meaningful profession. It always brought me joy to work with people and, together with a team, to accomplish important, high-quality, and professional work. During the time of my burnout, I worked in the field of special education. As a leader, I managed four separate classes in three different mainstream school buildings in a decentralized manner and also supported integrative settings in about twelve mainstream schools.

In integration, students with cognitive impairments are taught and supported in individual settings, integrated into a regular class with about twenty mainstream students. In most cases, they are accompanied by a special education teacher and a teaching assistant. In separation, students who had more severe limitations and required a smaller, more closely managed setting were taught and supported. Here, it was possible to respond even more to individual needs. A class usually consisted of seven to nine students, who were often closely supervised and even supported on a one-to-one basis. A team consisted of a special education teacher in the role of class teacher, as well as social educators, care specialists (male or female), and teaching assistants. Here, I was responsible for three classes: one lower, one middle, and one upper grade class. In total, up to forty employees reported directly to me at that time. In addition, I dealt with a wide variety of other interest groups. These included parents and students, as well as teachers from the mainstream school and the mainstream school leadership. There were also various specialist agencies and stakeholders. I worked closely with the school board, with school psychologists, with early childhood special educators, with doctors, residential home directors, daycare center managers, etc. Each had their own needs and concerns depending on the situation, all of which came together with me as the school principal.

Throughout the year, in addition to the day-to-day business of responding to the various needs and expectations of stakeholders and interest groups, I also dealt with many additional administrative tasks. These included, for example, deployment and scheduling, quality assurance and control, assessing and determining personnel resources, planning work assignments and staff workloads, organizing substitutes, monitoring absences, selecting and hiring new staff, conducting crisis and conflict discussions, approving vacation requests, conducting classroom visits, advising and supporting on professional issues, organizing professional development and other events, conducting staff appraisals and target-setting meetings, budget control, leading (team and quality) development processes, organizing planning and quality days for quality development and internal training, and so on.

The range of tasks and responsibilities was truly diverse. Many tasks could be planned, but in everyday school life, urgent matters and events often arose, so that work plans had to be changed and reprioritized at short notice. This, too, was part of the daily work of a school principal.

On top of all this, as an organization, we had also been in a change process for years, which, among other things, depended on structural decisions and a planned leadership transition due to retirement. And so, at that time, it had become completely normal for me to be repeatedly confronted with new circumstances and to have to find new solutions. It somehow never occurred to me to actually doubt the feasibility of these tasks. I loved challenges and was surrounded by people who themselves liked to achieve a lot and showed great commitment every day. A stressful but also exciting professional life was therefore inevitable, and it was always a challenge not to lose balance in all of this. My motto was: Just keep moving, and things will work out!

Despite the many challenges and the high demands of everyday school life, my other employment conditions were very good.

At the beginning of my burnout, I was working at almost one hundred percent capacity. As the change process continued, and due to political changes, personnel resources were significantly increased, which led to a substantial reduction in workload.

Both the overall system and the organization itself thus proved to be capable of learning and change, which personally made me very happy and optimistic. This gave hope that such structural changes towards a more balanced and manageable workload would also be possible in other organizations and (society and work) systems.

Transactional Analysis

Engaging with the approaches of transactional analysis has greatly helped me in identifying and managing stress patterns. For this reason, I will briefly introduce important concepts to which I will return later in the book. Transactional Analysis (TA), developed by Eric Berne, is a model for explaining human personality and interaction. It offers fundamental concepts from psychology that are profound and have a lasting impact, expanding our understanding of ourselves and others. The theory of transactional analysis is divided into four pillars:

- **Structural Analysis (also called Ego State Analysis)**
  helps to explain and understand what is happening within us (intra-psychically in human experience). Berne distinguished three ego states:

  - Parent Ego State: stored memories, experiences, and imprints in thinking, feeling, and behavior that we have adopted unfiltered from our parents or parental figures,
  - Child Ego State: encompassing all experiences made in childhood and the associated thinking, feeling, and behavior,
  - Adult Ego State: the state of reality-based thinking, feeling, and behavior.

- **Analysis of Transactions**
  focuses on interpersonal contact and on how we can communicate with each other in a meaningful, comprehensible, and goal-oriented way.

- **Game Analysis**
  examines interpersonal communication in terms of negative, recurring patterns that can limit our autonomy and effectiveness.

- **Script Analysis**
  draws on our childhood and considers which thoughts, feelings, actions, and experiences still relate to our past today. In this sense, script analysis makes it possible to shed light on the unconscious life plan.

Each of the four pillars contains different concepts that can be considered individually, but are fundamentally interconnected. Our lives can be viewed through the perspectives of transactional analysis concepts, leading to greater awareness and understanding. Human thinking, acting, feeling, and experiencing thus become more tangible, comprehensible, and accessible, and can be meaningfully used for personal development and reflection, thereby sustainably strengthening resilience.

Training and further education in transactional analysis empower people in the areas of personality, communication, and relationships. The concepts of transactional analysis can be usefully and profitably applied in various contexts of professional and private life. There are four fields of application in which one can specialize further during the course of training. These are organizations, psychotherapy, counseling, and education.

Within the scope of this book, various concepts of transactional analysis will be discussed. For the sake of readability and length, these are often deliberately not described in greater detail. For personal in-depth study, additional sources and recommendations for self-study are provided in the bibliography at the very end of this book.

References

1. Hochstrasser, B. (Februar 2023). Burnout und Erschöpfungsdepression. *Zeitschrift für Psychiatrie und Neurologie, 3–4,* 2–7.
2. Bundesinstitut für Arzneimittel und Medizinprodukte. Internationale Klassifikation psychischer Störungen. ICD-11 (deutsche Entwurfsfassung) 2022. https://www.bfarm.de/DE/Kodiersysteme/Klassifikationen/ICD/ICD-11/uebersetzung/_node.html;jsessionid=8F3D339C-9CAC512936E554400BF05785.internet271. Accessed 17 Feb 2023.
3. Freudenberger, H. J. (1947). Staff Burn-out. *Journal of Social Issues 30,* 159–165.

4. Maslach, C. et al. (1981). The measurement of experienced burnout. *Journal of Occupational Behaviour, 2,* 99–113.

5. Maslach, C. et al. (1997). Maslach burnout inventory. In C. P. Zalaquett & R. J. Wood (Hrsg.), *Evaluating stress: A book of resources* (3rd edn., pp. 191–218). Scarecrow Education.

6. Schaufeli, W. et al. (1996). The maslach burnout inventory – General survey. In C. Maslach et al. (Eds.), *MBI manual* (3r edn.). Consulting Psychologist Press, Palo Alto.

7. Hochstrasser, B. (Februar 2023). Burnout und Erschöpfungsdepression. *Zeitschrift für Psychiatrie und Neurologie, 3–4,* 2–7.

8. Buchenau, P., & Nelting, M. (2015). *Burnout – von Betroffenen lernen!* (pp. 302–309). Springer Gabler.

9. Freudenberger, H., & North, G. (1992). *Burn-out bei Frauen* (Vol. 2nd edn., pp. 38–39). Wolfgang Krüger.

10. Welter-Enderlin, R., & Hildenbrand, B. (2006). *Resilienz – Gedeihen trotz widriger Umstände* (Vol. 13, pp. 22–23). Karl-Auer.

11. Luhmann, N. (2013). *Soziale Systeme* (Vol. 53, pp. 103–104). Akademie.

12. Schulze, H., & Sejkora, K. (2015). *Positive Führung – Resilienz statt Burnout* (pp. 102–103). Haufe-Lexware.

13. Weltgesundheitsorganisation, Internationale Klassifikation psychischerStörungen, Kapitel V (F), Klinisch-diagnostische Leitlinien, ed. Dilling, H. et al. (1993), Huber.

Phase I—The Inevitable Approaches—Premonition

Abstract Together with the author, the reader immerses themselves in the experience just before the standstill of burnout, at the point where nothing seems possible anymore and the inevitable is approaching. The extent of the illness only becomes apparent over time. Individual symptoms and challenges emerge. The reader experiences firsthand what it feels like to fall into burnout and gains an initial impression of the various fears, anxieties, and challenges that can arise during this phase. Each chapter repeatedly provides different theoretical concepts. In this chapter, the overarching focus is first on the topic of resilience and on a personal perspective regarding the issues surrounding burnout and resilience.

© The Author(s), under exclusive license to Springer Fachmedien Wiesbaden GmbH, part of Springer Nature 2025
R. Petersen, *Tsunami in the Head – Better Understanding and Coping with Burnout*, https://doi.org/10.1007/978-3-658-49737-8_2

The Inevitable

I run. Try to get away. But I can't. I'm afraid. It's like a bad dream. The evil comes toward me unstoppably. I sense it, but I can't pinpoint exactly from which direction it's coming. I listen inward. Try to calm my breathing. My body is stressed. Ready to defend itself in an emergency. To fend off the attack as best as possible. I run. Desperately try to get to safety. But I can't move. I've lost my sense of direction. It's dark and damp. I'm freezing. I'm alone. Calling for help is pointless. No one can hear me. There is no way out anymore. I have to face my fear. Look the unstoppable in the eye. Muster my last reserves of strength. Hope that things will turn out well. I'm ready to let go. My body still wants to fight. Giving up is the last thing I will do. Only when there is truly no other way out. Only when my back is against the wall and I can't move anymore. Only then will I let go and surrender to my fate. Until then, I fight. If I stop fighting, it's all over anyway. My heart pounds. I listen intently to the silence. Only my rapid breathing gives me orientation and makes it clear that I'm still alive. My eyes strain to make out something in the darkness. A shadow flits by, breaking through the dark night. Then it's quiet again. I'm alone. I long for the coolness and clarity of dawn. How long has it been since then.

My Story—How It All Began

I remember that as a school principal starting my new position, I began with great joy and motivation. I wanted to do things right, get up to speed quickly, and perform well. As a leader in the school system, I felt I could use all my skills and strengths for other people and learn a lot of new things. That was exactly what I wanted from my new job. Even as a teacher and special education teacher, I was always passionate about my work. Working for and with people inspired me. In recent years, however, I noticed that working in various class teams challenged me even more, and it unsettled me internally when very different values and ideas about school and special education clashed. But I always felt that this was simply part of my job as a special education teacher and just came with the territory. To balance things out, I did a lot of sports in my free time. I also enjoyed taking part in various further training courses and delving into the field of counseling and development, especially transactional analysis. Immersing myself in a world outside of school was an important resilience factor for me, which at the same time always motivated me to contribute and get involved in the school context with high commitment, new perspectives, and expertise.

The work as a school principal offered me a new challenge. If I did something, I absolutely wanted to do it right. However, as a principal, I quickly realized that no matter how much effort I put in, the work never really got less. I even had the impression that, although I had become well acquainted with the job over the years, the lists of pending tasks and to-dos never got shorter, and the temporary workloads throughout the year kept increasing and fluctuated unpredictably. I felt more and more controlled from the outside.

Secretly, I was already aware that I was demanding a lot from my body over a long period. But that's just how I knew it, and I thought it was normal. After all, who isn't constantly stressed and overworked these days? In all the hustle and bustle, I simply had no time to think about it or consider an alternative. I never took the time to reflect deeply on it. I had already heard from colleagues that the shelf life of a school principal was only a few years, but I was firmly convinced that I would manage. Failure was definitely not going to happen to me.

A few years later, the time had come: I was sitting there with burnout and incredibly little energy, completely devastated. It was as if someone had pulled the plug on me, although until then I hadn't even realized I had a plug. I was already looking back on some of the first exhausting months of the healing process. Or at least I suspected that, in the long run, this was the direction things would go.

Luckily, I was able to save myself just in time for the winter break. It had already been an extremely exhausting school year. On the one hand, a little over a year ago, I had gotten a new boss. From my perspective, this wasn't particularly noteworthy. However, I was already experiencing increasing fatigue regarding the internal change management process that had been ongoing for over three years. I could even understand my discontent, since I was a trained organizational consultant myself. Signs of fatigue in such a process were completely normal and thus a classic symptom under the circumstances. Added to this were the new additional tasks due to the Covid-19 situation. We had what felt like endless paperwork to deal with, the overall mood was tense, and there was a lot of uncertainty. That, too, seemed understandable to me under the circumstances. If I could make logical sense of something, I often tended to simply "file away" the emotions that came up as well. Anything I could make logical sense of put me in a "You can't change it, so accept it!" state. I took my role as a leader very seriously and was very aware of my responsibility during this crisis. I saw my job as providing my staff with a sense of security and taking good care of their health. That gave me orientation, support, and stability myself. I wanted to maintain composure. In the hectic school day, I still often simply had no time to think much about it. There was always more than enough to do. Challenging and demanding situations were part of my daily business. However, I noticed that I was reacting more and more stressed to problems and expectations from outside. I became more thin-skinned. I usually managed to keep up appearances in social interactions, but inside I was excessively and persistently stressed. Increasingly, I was annoyed with everyone and everything. I simply had no energy or motivation left to engage with others and their experiences. I had so much to deal with myself, with my workload and my leadership tasks. Even the occasional exchange with team colleagues did little to help me gain some distance. I also noticed that the "venting" and shared discussions, which often brought out feelings of frustration, fatigue, and anger in everyone, burdened me more than they helped. I realized that these conversations hardly brought me closer to workable solutions, but often led to more fatigue, anger, and frustration. So at some point, I stopped the collegial exchange altogether. After all, I could use the time more productively for my work. Annoyance and frustration in contact with others then only occurred regularly once a week, namely when we had our weekly management meeting. In between, the many emails and to-dos kept me on my toes. Even here, I found it increasingly difficult to set boundaries. I would quickly fly into a rage, as I was confronted daily with things that didn't work and that I, as principal, had to "fix." The topics of school development and change management were really getting on my nerves. After the two-hour meetings, I regularly had to go for a brisk walk to consciously calm down and become able to work again. Realistically, though, after the meetings, I felt I was good for nothing for the rest of the day—so caught up was I in my own world of (self-)critical and negative thoughts and feelings. A real vicious cycle!

At home, things weren't exactly easier because of the lockdown. I was single at the time and was surprised at how well I could handle the social isolation. I actually didn't find it that bad, because I needed a lot of space to recover from work stress. I had no energy left to engage with friends or family members. I was glad to be left alone. Since the Covid situation created additional turmoil, I often watched series in my free time. I didn't primarily doubt that everything would turn out well again. I had inherited this trust in the world from my Christian grandparents. That was very helpful and encouraging in this uncertain time. By nature, I was a very optimistic person. So I never felt that the whole Covid situation could really harm me. But still, the series gave me a good excuse to rest and distract myself. Often, weekends were little more than that! Those were difficult times, and I had apparently found my way of dealing with them sensibly.

However, over time I noticed some changes. Today I would say that these were like a veil in my subconscious. I felt increasingly stressed and demotivated. I used to always enjoy going to work. Now, on Sunday evenings, I really had to force myself and often had trouble falling asleep because my mind was already back at work. At some point, this wasn't just the case on Sunday evenings, but also on weekdays. In addition, I was making more and more mistakes at work without realizing it. I became careless, forgot appointments, and, in my view, worked imprecisely. I'm not sure whether I was just being driven much more by my high standards or whether I was actually performing worse. I think it was probably both.

One morning, for example, I found myself standing in front of a closed classroom door in a regular school building as early as six o'clock. I wondered why the class teachers were not yet on site for the upcoming meeting. I saw that there was already light in another classroom. When

I asked the teacher about it, it suddenly dawned on me that I must have misjudged the time. How embarrassing! Still completely confused, I went to the staff room and sat down alone for another coffee break. What had happened? I had woken up before my alarm and, at the same time, thought I had overslept. I had then rushed frantically to the school because I assumed I would be late for the meeting. Oh dear! What confusion! I really had too much on my plate! Well, I wanted to make the best of it and not get upset about my own incompetence. I hadn't had time to answer my emails yesterday. Actually, this was ideal! I immediately started reading and responding to the latest emails on my phone. I had already gotten used to dealing with them whenever I had a free moment, because the daily flood of emails was often overwhelming, even though I had already learned to sort them by priority and urgency.

Falling asleep became increasingly difficult for me. I felt as though I had never really had a deep sleep, so I attributed this to a variety of causes. With the Covid measures and working from home, I was able to further optimize my daily rhythm. I noticed that I worked particularly well in the morning, able to work efficiently and with a clear head. In addition, my internal clock woke me up earlier and earlier, even before the alarm. Regularly, from five o'clock in the morning, sometimes even as early as four thirty, I simply could not fall back asleep. So why not use the time and tackle the flood of emails from the previous evening? This gave me the opportunity to go to the gym around eleven o'clock without feeling guilty and to take a short "power nap" after lunch. Because of my sleep problems, I was hardly productive at that time of day anyway. Over time, I made a virtue out of necessity. Covid had put social life on hold for the time being anyway. So why should I even bother staying up late in the evenings?

By six o'clock I was usually so tired and exhausted that I could have collapsed. To help myself fall asleep, I would turn off my phone early, watch some TV series, and try to push the issues and problems of the workday out of my mind. By eight o'clock I was so worn out that I fell into bed dead tired and drifted into a restless sleep. By midnight at the latest, I would wake up for the first time. My subconscious was on full alert. I often woke up several times during the night in a state of shock and confusion. I didn't know what had happened. Usually, I woke up four to five times a night and each time found it hard to get back to sleep. But at the time, I honestly wouldn't have classified this as a severe sleep disorder. I had somehow gradually gotten used to it.

During the day, I felt increasingly exhausted and drained. I completely lost my motivation for work and for personal conversations with my staff or professional colleagues. I withdrew more and more without really noticing, saying I had so many appointments and therefore wasn't in the office and couldn't be there in person for a meeting. I only answered phone calls reluctantly, and sometimes I even ignored calls when I felt particularly depleted. I simply didn't have the nerves to face all the demands, questions, and issues. But even here, everything felt muffled, as if wrapped in cotton wool. I observed my behavior and experience as if in a trance and was unable to realistically assess the situation, let alone bring about any change.

As every year, the situation came to a head just before the holidays. The stress was paralyzing, as everyone wanted something from me and, subjectively, every issue seemed extremely important. Because of my dwindling energy, I tried to focus more and more deliberately on the core business of "students, parents, and team." I also expressed this wish in my performance review with my new boss.

She reacted completely calmly and said I could easily give up my additional roles, such as my work in the association, as long as I found someone to take over for me. Fortunately, I managed to do this quite quickly. Within a few weeks, I had organized everything so that at least these extra tasks would no longer steal more of my time and energy. However, I also felt somewhat underappreciated, as I had carried out all these roles and additional tasks for years with passion and high commitment. Now, hearing that they didn't necessarily need to be continued and could easily be handed over to someone else, hurt me. In addition, I increasingly had the impression that my boss was monitoring my work behind the scenes or weighing my comments during meetings very carefully or reacting critically. I don't know if this was true or if I was simply becoming more self-critical and my self-perception was clouded. My interactions with my boss unsettled me more and more, and I began to increasingly doubt my own performance. I lacked appreciation and trust. In return, the well-being of my team became ever more important to me. I reacted noticeably irritably when I couldn't get their concerns addressed with my boss or in the staff meeting. This preoccupied me mentally and emotionally for days and kept me on high alert day and night. By this time, I was no longer even aware of these personal changes in my character. The cocktail of hormones in my blood was already clouding my perception and making it impossible to see the situation realistically.

Shortly before the next holidays, the announcement came that a professional colleague would be staying home for an extended period due to exhaustion. I felt incredibly sorry! I was personally very affected, because I knew exactly what it must feel like to be that exhausted. On the other hand, the news also made me sad and angry, because I myself didn't have the courage to give myself the desperately needed break. I admired my colleague for the courage to seemingly step away for a few weeks and stay at home with ease. For me, the hurdle of getting a doctor's note for sick leave was enormous. I didn't want to give up! I wanted and had to make it work somehow! I didn't want anyone to get wind of my weakness and self-doubt.

Finally, vacation! I had made it. Unfortunately, I soon realized that even during the holidays, I couldn't really unwind from the stress. The first week, I paced around the house like a caged tiger. Traveling wasn't possible for anyone during Covid times. But even going to the gym, visiting the sauna, or having coffee around the corner was no longer possible. These had been my islands in everyday life. Now, they were off-limits for an indefinite period. On top of that, I had been experiencing severe back pain again for weeks. It was almost unbearable! Strangely, the pain was especially pronounced when I went into my office to work. So the recommendation and requirement to work from home suited me just fine. The social isolation also actually came at the right time for me. Even in the past year and a half, I had less and less desire to meet friends on weekends. If I did, my energy was usually only enough for a coffee on a Saturday or Sunday. The rest of the time, I holed up in my four walls to give myself rest, get enough sleep, and recover from all the expectations and stress of the workweek.

My good fortune was that I was already in therapy at that time. A few months earlier, I had already felt that I could use psychological support. With my background as a psychological counselor, it was not a big hurdle for me to seek professional help in the form of psychotherapy. However, burnout was never mentioned. Several times, my therapist offered during our sessions to write me a sick note for relief. But at that point, I absolutely refused to accept it and instead summoned up new, unexpected strength week after week, which enabled me to keep working at this high level of performance and stress until the next school holidays and simply keep functioning. For the vacation days, I set myself the goal of recovering as well as possible. I just had to give myself enough rest, and then everything would be fine again. I was a master at convincing myself of this in various ways.

However, I was absolutely unable to recover during the vacation days. In the second week of vacation, I already noticed that something was wrong. I felt irritable, tired, and stressed, without any reason I could explain. I simply couldn't return to my relaxed, normal self. I consciously avoided any social contact so I wouldn't have to explain myself. I barely had any energy left for everyday things like showering or shopping. On top of that, there was an annoying eye twitch, which had occurred a few weeks earlier. This seriously worried me, as I feared that the high stress level might be causing neurological damage. By the end of the winter break, I had managed to get a grip on myself enough to downplay the situation again. I had stabilized my thoughts, internally motivated myself anew, and was determined to actively tackle my problems and find solutions. What exactly the problems were, however, was still unclear to me—or rather, I only dealt with them superficially. For me, it was simply clear: You can't give up now! It'll be fine! So I made an appointment with my family doctor because of the twitching in my eyelid and forced myself to meet up with a good friend. I told her about my eye problem and said that I was probably close to severe exhaustion, but that I wanted to go back to work next week because I couldn't postpone an extremely important meeting. My friend was, of course, skeptical and tried to talk sense into me. I somehow dodged her objections and replied that I probably knew best myself how to proceed and that I was already seeing a psychologist. So, for me, the matter was settled.

In the first days after the winter break, I consciously made sure to have as few additional external appointments as possible. I wanted to give myself a relaxed fresh start. It was probably my own fault that I wasn't able to set boundaries sufficiently. After all, many other school principals faced the same challenges and managed as well. So I was determined to keep going, to push through no matter what, as the saying goes. I had a strong will to persevere. I just barely managed to attend the incredibly important planning meeting that I absolutely wanted to be at on Thursday. I succeeded in maintaining a façade in social situations and showing adequate performance and presence, but afterwards I went home completely exhausted. At that point, it suddenly became clear to me: This can't go on! I can't do this anymore! I was on the verge of an internal breakdown, but still couldn't cry.

Now the time had come: At the end of the week, my family doctor put me on sick leave for two weeks due to exhaustion and severe back pain. He assessed my eye problem as a stress symptom and prescribed physiotherapy again for the back pain. Apparently, I had developed a severe inflammation. Inside, I felt dissolved, weak, but also relieved and guilty. I was worried about my team. I wanted and needed to go back to work after two weeks, no matter what! Everything that was left undone, I would have to catch up on later anyway. I absolutely wanted to avoid that. I told my boss the same thing. In two weeks, I would be back on my feet! I was convinced of that.

The following weeks continued in exactly the same way. Just like during the winter break, I was barely able to reduce my stress level, even with a break. My sleep disturbances were now even worse than before, and at the same time I felt a leaden, inner fatigue and restlessness.

My thoughts raced day and night. At times, it was enough to drive me crazy. I clung to the idea that I would be able to return to work in two weeks. I continued to read my emails and thus remained mentally in constant contact with my staff. I wrote to my boss that I would certainly be back on my feet soon. I clung to this idea with all my might.

The thought that my team or others might find out or think that I had burnout worried me immensely. Two weeks after my sick leave, I went to the doctor again. I had constant muscle and limb pain. Together with the fatigue and exhaustion, these were almost unbearable. However, I had had similar symptoms for years and attributed them to histamine intolerance. But maybe these pains were also related to exhaustion or a serious illness? I definitely wanted to get this clarified now. Fortunately, my family doctor took me and my symptoms very seriously. He ordered several blood tests and referred me to a rheumatologist. I told him that my psychologist approved another two weeks of sick leave. I myself had such severe back pain, limb and muscle pain, as well as sleep disturbances and persistent fatigue and exhaustion, that I allowed myself to extend the sick leave for another two weeks, just this once. Pathologically, I still stuck to the initially stated symptoms of "exhaustion and severe back pain" as my justification.

At the beginning of the week, I wrote to my friend via WhatsApp that I would be going back to work and that the twitching in my eyelid was already getting better. I was so ashamed of my inability and weakness! Mentally, I was still clinging to the idea that I would soon be back on my feet, even though deep down I felt that I wouldn't be able to muster the necessary energy in the coming days either. Up to that point, I still didn't feel like I was really experiencing burnout. From my perspective, it was primarily the back pain, the sleep disturbances, and the enormous work-load that were the main reasons for my absence from work and, understandably, were just temporarily draining all my strength and knocking me out of commission. I would get it under control again—somehow.

At this stage, I would have only partially admitted to having sleep disturbances. I couldn't really sleep through the night, okay. That meant concretely that I woke up every two hours, sometimes even startled awake, but didn't really know why. I also had trouble falling asleep in the evenings, yes. But how many people have these problems too?! That wasn't really anything special, was it?! The fact that I regularly woke up as early as four thirty in the morning and couldn't fall back asleep, I didn't accept as an excuse. In my misery, I simply tried to go to bed even earlier in the evening, since I was actually just dead tired throughout the day. From this, I concluded that I was more of an early riser and that this would probably become more pronounced with age. And besides, I had a lot on my plate at work. Everything could be explained quite logically. My body was just reacting to all these chal-lenges. Actually, from my point of view, everything was still perfectly fine. Once the exhaustion was finally over, I would soon be back on my feet. I just needed a short break. That was all!

Burnout Diary—Snapshots

"Burnout is like a widespread forest fire. You don't really know where the fire started or what caused it. But when you look at the flames up close, it becomes unmistakably clear that the situation is, quite literally, 'critical' and the consequences are akin to an ecological disaster."
Rebecca Petersen

I am tired. Finally, it's vacation time. I just barely made it. Luckily, no one noticed how I was really doing. Now I have some time to recover. It will be fine. Just like it always worked out before. My job is demanding. But I love being challenged and being able to use my skills in a meaningful way. I just need some peace now. A lot of peace!

I am restless. The first week of vacation is already over and I feel anything but refreshed. I pace around my four walls. I can hardly concentrate on anything during the day. I try to distract myself. I try to consciously wind down. But it just doesn't work. I'm still tired. So tired. And in the evening, despite all the exhaustion, I can't fall asleep. What is wrong with me? Maybe I just need to give myself a little more time? Just wait it out? Allow myself to rest? Yes, that's how it will work.

The vacation is coming to an end. I have to go back to work. I have to go back, there's still so much to do. And the meeting next week is really important. If I'm not there, I block further planning. That's not possible. That's my job and responsibility. I have to go. I absolutely have to be there in person.

My psychologist would sign me off sick. But I don't want that. Actually, it's not much different from the other times. My job has always been demanding. I've always been very tired at this time of year. What's new is that I can't wind down anymore. I'm like a tiger in a cage. I feel trapped. But I am the problem. My colleagues have been doing this job for years. I just have to learn to set better boundaries. On the other hand, I am truly endlessly tired. So tired. That scares me. I've never had it like this before. I don't know what to do. I really don't know what to do. Maybe it's best if I just keep going as before.

I got through the meeting successfully. I hope no one noticed how empty I felt. A shell that somehow still functioned. Smiling comes naturally to me. I'm a master at playing my professional role at work. Keeping up appearances. But I can't do it anymore. I really can't do it anymore. Now it's different. Different from the last times when I started back after vacation. My body feels empty and numb. Everything in me is resisting collapse with the last of its strength. I don't feel myself anymore and yet inside I feel like crying. This is no longer me. I actually don't even know who I really am anymore.

I have to keep fighting. The doctor has now signed me off sick because of my back pain and exhaustion. For now, for two weeks. That has to be enough! What will my professional colleagues think? At least I can say that the back pain was the reason for my absence. It wouldn't be the first time. Being out longer is not an option. Otherwise, I'll have to explain myself! I want to avoid that. So I have to keep fighting. I won't give up! What other choice do I have? No one can help me.

Now I've been at home for over a month. I barely feel any better. I still don't feel myself. I can hardly fall asleep and wake up four or five times a night. For no reason. Sometimes I dream and wake up crying. I'm glad I can go to my therapist weekly. That's my only fixed point, but I desperately need it. I consciously avoid other social contacts. I have no energy for it. Why should I? No one can help me anyway.

I pace around. My whole nervous system is still on high alert. At the same time, I am completely exhausted and totally tired. I sleep a lot, but not well. I usually go to bed as early as seven in the evening because I wake up around four thirty in the morning. What kind of sleep rhythm have I gotten myself into? But I can't think logically anyway, let alone be part of normal society and perform. At the moment, I'm good for nothing. I feel guilty. I'm ashamed. That's also why no one around me knows that

I'm not working right now. I don't say the word burnout because it immediately brings me to tears. I want to avoid that. I don't have the strength to endure all these emotions. I have to set boundaries and, ideally, suppress what's happening to me right now.

I still read my emails. I still want to know what's going on at school. I can't let go yet. When I hear from my boss that she has already found a replacement, I'm shocked. I really am just replaceable. But what about my team? And the upcoming tasks that need to be done? I can hardly imagine how someone can just "take over" like that. But I have to let go. Somehow. I'm still thinking about school, my boss, my colleagues, and my team day and night. How will I ever explain that I couldn't work for so long? What will people think of me?

I'm slowly realizing that I really do have a problem and that it won't just disappear in the next few weeks. Now, the doctor's notes are issued directly in four-week intervals. This is a relief for me, because every time, days before the decision to extend the sick leave, I am under great stress. Then I can hardly suppress it anymore, and the uncertainty and guilt rise up in me, take over, and dominate my everyday life. Therapy is going well, even though I actually have no idea or concept of what the long-term goal is, let alone how I will get there. I am overwhelmed by what is coming up inside me. I have no access to myself or my feelings. So much is inaccessible at the moment. I live a very withdrawn, isolated life. I know that's not "normal," but honestly, I hardly know anything else anymore. And I don't have any energy or strength right now anyway. It's just enough for the everyday things, even though I still sometimes struggle just to get out of bed in the morning. Showering or stepping outside is sometimes already too much. And so there are days when I'm just by myself, in my small apartment. And that's okay, as long as I don't run into anyone or anyone asks me how I'm doing. And luckily, I can consciously control that by withdrawing.

Again and again, I get stressed out in my thoughts. I just hardly notice any improvement. What if my condition never gets better? What if I never become truly able to work again? I can hardly cope with this uncertainty. All I know is that right now I still need rest and don't want to talk to anyone in my circle about it. It's best if everyone just leaves me alone! I just want to sleep and finally, finally find some peace and feel at least a little bit better.

Figuratively Speaking—The Inevitable—Not Wanting to See

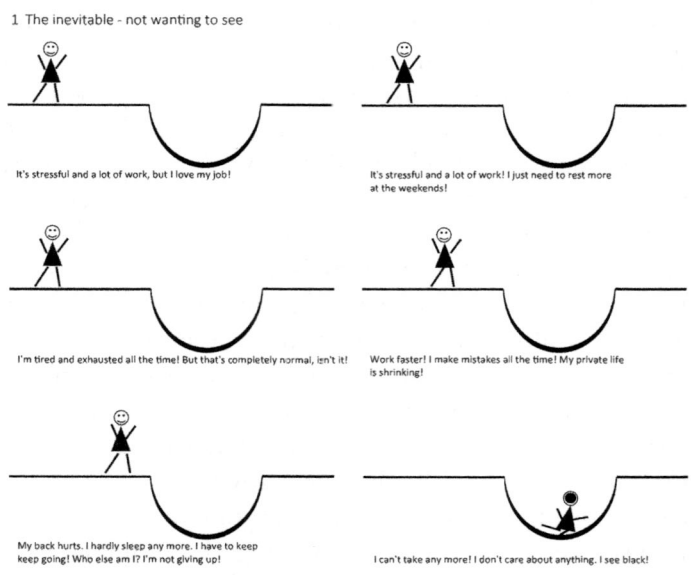

1 The inevitable - not wanting to see

It's stressful and a lot of work, but I love my job!

It's stressful and a lot of work! I just need to rest more at the weekends!

I'm tired and exhausted all the time! But that's completely normal, isn't it!

Work faster! I make mistakes all the time! My private life is shrinking!

My back hurts. I hardly sleep any more. I have to keep keep going! Who else am I? I'm not giving up!

I can't take any more! I don't care about anything. I see black!

For (Potential) Affected Individuals— Learning Self-Reflection and Resilience

In this initial phase of my burnout illness, I was so stressed for months that I couldn't really feel or perceive myself. For a long time, I was not aware of the actual situation or the severe (health) condition I was in. Every two weeks, I wanted to return to work, even though my back pain was almost unbearable and I suffered from severe sleep disturbances, which I did not recognize as such. Added to this were motivational problems, dejection, anxiety, intense restlessness and exhaustion, as well as joint and muscle pain. Despite all these symptoms, nothing stopped me from wanting to return to my stressful work routine and putting myself under immense pressure in this regard. My old patterns, the drive for high achievement, and the desire to "not appear weak" still had a strong hold on me. I am grateful that my body ultimately sent me such clear signals that I simply could not return. I believe I would not have allowed it otherwise. I was so trapped in my thinking and routine of "constantly pushing past my own limits." My stubbornness and relentless drive for achievement would probably have pushed me to keep working and functioning until I had a heart attack.

> Please, do not do this to yourself! Take time for self-reflection! Take a closer look! Tune in to yourself! Be honest with yourself! Do not wait too long until the hormonal cocktail distances you even further from yourself. Listen when a friend or acquaintance brings it up! Seek professional support early enough! Nothing else is worth it!

Looking back, what I lacked most in this situation was simply the courage and perspective to see possible alternatives and the bigger picture. What else could I have done? What could I have changed? Quit my job? I actually loved my job, and working with my team was a lot of fun. I did not want to change positions, even though I occasionally considered it. Towards the end, just before I could not go on at all, I no longer had the strength to engage in job searching or actively pursue another position. Internally, I had already given up and was only focused on working through my to-do list! I just kept functioning as best I could. In that situation, it seemed to me the simplest and most efficient way, even though the actual goal was completely out of sight and I lost myself in the process.

In retrospect, this was by far the most efficient and easiest way to systematically deplete myself and my body and to push past my physical and mental limits. And at what cost? I had become an emotional and energetic wreck, a machine that only functioned. For months, I suffered from intense feelings of guilt and shame. I avoided people as much as possible because I was afraid of confrontation. I could no longer set emotional boundaries, had become almost porous, and consequently experienced great anxiety. I also had existential fears. The thought that I might never recover and regain my original strength and capacity was almost unbearable. Who would I be if I could no longer work? I had severe physical complaints, many of which were somatic in nature, making treatment neither simple nor linear. For some symptoms, I simply had no explanation. For a long time, I struggled with intense self-doubt, motivational problems, and severe exhaustion. Everyday tasks like showering, motivating myself for a walk, or preparing dinner were a real effort. Stronger and weaker depressive phases alternated. Although I would not have classified myself as depressed, I was very exhausted and had severe physical complaints. In between, there were a few hours or days of hope, when I could go with the moment and accept the current situation and my limitations without devaluing myself. Those were the good moments I wanted to orient myself by.

The period of acute illness and recovery was a major personal challenge for me, requiring a great deal of patience, self-acceptance, and self-reflection. This phase lasted several months and was both physically and psychologically very intense.

In this first phase, I had no energy left to make decisions or expose myself to contact with other people. For this reason, I decided not to tell anyone about my health condition and inability to work. Not even my family! One might assume from this that my relationship with my family was not good enough. But I can honestly refute that! The decision to focus entirely on myself during this phase and not to expose myself to external judgments, advice, or discussions was solely a decision to protect and strengthen my autonomy. During this time, certainly also due to the intense feelings of shame and guilt, I had a strong need to set boundaries. From transactional analysis, I knew that this was reasonable and acceptable in terms of autonomy. I consciously resisted the inner urge to involve others in my experience and illness. Of course, I thought a lot about what my family would think of this decision, and that again triggered feelings of guilt in me, because I was denying them the opportunity to be there for me. And yet, looking back, I can say it was the right path for me and an important decision. Because in this phase, I had no choice but to remain 100% true to myself, my needs, and my health. The wake-up call had come with the burnout. I had to change something, and that was the first step I took and felt from within. I accepted that my fear was in control and that I needed to set boundaries, and that was OK!

From this, I would like to emphasize: No one can tell you what is right or wrong. No one can tell you how long the recovery period will last. No one can say whether things will ever be as they once were. I had to learn to deal with this tension and fear. And honestly: Even though, in retrospect, the burnout made me a new, better person, I would not wish this experience on anyone! So be wiser than I was! Take a closer look and be honest with yourself!

If you need support yourself or suspect that you may be affected by burnout, seek advice and a professional assessment from a specialist, even if you are unsure. There are many counseling centers that can refer you to an appropriate professional if needed. You can fill out an initial questionnaire that may provide you with some clues. Take the challenging situation and your worries, concerns, and fears seriously, and do not wait too long until the hormonal cocktail clouds your perception.

> If you are still unsure about what next steps to take or whether you are actually at risk of burnout, the idea of a "Letter to Those Affected" might help. You can find the description and letter templates (Parts 1 and 2) in the appendix.

The strong person is the one who can allow and admit weakness and, if necessary, actually seeks support independently and proactively! Even if it does not always feel that way, I can say this with conviction and from experience in retrospect!

The fear that you will never get up again once you have given up did not come true in my case. This fear accompanied me for a particularly long time and kept me from admitting to myself that I might have burnout. The phase of weakness and recovery was indeed exhausting, unpleasant, and personally challenging, but I had to allow it in order to regain my original strength and power. Now I know: It is possible for the body and soul to recover after a period of healing, and new strength and clarity can emerge from it. After the burnout and a sufficiently long period of recovery and reintegration, I feel stronger, wiser, and more competent than before, even though I never thought that would be possible at the beginning.

It is therefore possible that after a period of weakness, improvement can occur. It is worthwhile to honestly assess your own situation and to allow yourself to be weak, even if the situation seems inescapable and no solutions are yet visible! Seek support if necessary and trust yourself! You do not have to change your entire life at once. The first next steps can already make a big difference, bringing more clarity and confidence. However, it is important to take your own situation seriously and not to underestimate the effects of prolonged stress.
I sincerely wish you all the best!

For Relatives, Friends, and Colleagues—Systems Thinking

My friend had brought up the topic several times and tried to raise my awareness about burnout. At that time, I reacted defensively. I didn't want to admit it to myself. I also believed that I knew best what was good for me and where my limits were. In retrospect, I can clearly deny that.

As relatives and friends, it is still extremely important to grant the affected person their autonomy and self-determination. Honestly: I don't think my friend could have done more for me! At that point, I simply was not (any longer) open to any input or advice, especially not in direct confrontation.

From other affected individuals, I have learned that their partner intervened and that, due to external pressure, it became possible to seek therapeutic help. Someone from the support group reported that it was actually a relief for her when she was approached about a possible burnout. As you can see, the range of possible reactions here is also very diverse. Unfortunately, it is often the case that those affected cannot (or will not) accept help because they feel trapped in a dead end between internal and external expectations. In particular, accepting one's own limits and recognizing the problem represent an insurmountable hurdle.

Perhaps I would have listened if someone who had been directly affected themselves had spoken to me about it. Maybe then I would have tried harder to look at my situation more honestly and compare it with the current state of knowledge. For this reason, I have written a letter to potential affected individuals, which is printed in the appendix and is intended to help you facilitate access to people who may be affected.

In this sense, I want to encourage you to trust your gut feeling and your assessment and to share it with the (potentially) affected person. Everything else is then the responsibility of that individual! You are not inherently responsible for their well-being or insight, and that's a good thing!

Accordingly, behave in a caring yet well-boundaried manner. Only in this way can you strengthen the autonomy and personal responsibility of the person who may be affected, which in turn will have a positive influence on their recovery and willingness to recover.

Overview

If you are still unsure about what next steps to take and whether it is a good idea to address someone about a possible burnout, the appendix "Letter to Those Affected" may help you. You will find the description and letter templates (Parts 1 and 2) in the appendix.

I sincerely wish you good judgment, mindfulness, and understanding!

For Managers—Corporate/Social Responsibility

Perhaps the news that one of your employees is suffering from burnout comes as a complete surprise. Or perhaps you saw it coming and it has become apparent over the past weeks and months.

The symptoms and circumstances of burnout are as varied as people themselves. And yet there are clear signs and conditions that favor burnout. You can read more about this in Background/Burnout.

As a manager, you play a pivotal role in your organization in various ways, even if only indirectly regarding the health of your employees. However, you have a direct influence on the atmosphere, culture, and working climate in your organization. Are these characterized by mindfulness? Is the topic of health and resilience something that is openly discussed in your organization? How closely do the individual teams work together? How much and how consistently is teamwork developed? How open, appreciative, and direct is communication among colleagues? How are workplace conflicts handled? Is there a collegial working environment? How can you tell? How much do competition and performance take center stage? Are there opportunities for informal, honest, and open exchange? What is the general attitude toward diversity? How are differences—i.e., different attitudes, values, and norms—exchanged and meaningfully integrated? Are these encouraged, overlooked, or even devalued? To what extent are individuality and individual strengths and resources promoted and purposefully utilized within the team? What kind of feedback culture is practiced? Is it characterized by appreciation and mindfulness? In what ways are boundaries and individuality lived and valued?

These and other questions help create a work culture and atmosphere that minimizes burnout and fosters resilience! Unfortunately, burnout is often recognized too late and leads to a longer absence of the affected person. This is costly for both the individual and the organization—not only financially, because health insurance and case management services must be used, but also because the extended absence affects team collaboration and performance. Usually, it is unclear how long the person will be unable to work, so you repeatedly have to find and train a replacement at short notice. This is very exhausting and time-consuming for you and the team. In addition, you lose valuable know-how and a highly committed employee, who ideally returns to your organization after recovery or, depending on the situation, leaves the organization entirely. As you can see, the organizational impact of burnout is significant.

For this reason, it is worthwhile for organizations to take active steps and assume responsibility for early detection and prevention. As a manager, you can make an important contribution. You can be mindful yourself, get to know your team with genuine interest, so you have a better sense of their strengths and weaknesses. You can model open and appreciative communication and address potential workplace conflicts directly and early, or seek support from an external expert, coach, or consultant.

By reading this book and informing yourself thoroughly and holistically, you have already taken a first step in the right direction.

If you have someone on your team who may be experiencing burnout, I recommend addressing this in a protected setting. You will also find information on this in the section Facts and Questions in Phase VI—The Lighthouse—Making Sense of Uncertainty. If you are still unsure about what next steps to take and whether it is a good idea to address someone about a possible burnout, the idea of a "Letter to Those Affected" can provide important guidance. You will find the description and letter templates (Parts 1 and 2) in the appendix of this book.

But the usual leadership topics of communication, attitude, creating a functioning team culture, structure, and leadership, etc., are also important. In terms of burnout prevention, it is important to create a supportive, appreciative, open, and mindful working environment, where, for example, workplace conflicts can be addressed and resolved in a solution-oriented manner. A positive error culture is needed, where individual strengths are utilized and weaknesses are seen as opportunities for development. As a manager, you are both a role model and a driving force in all of this! Have the courage to place topics such as health, resilience, and burnout, as well as communication, appreciation, respect, attitude, values, diversity, etc., responsibly and consistently at the center, to address them directly, and to shape them sustainably. You will make a decisive difference! Your employees will thank you for it!

This type of leadership can be challenging. Nevertheless, it is worthwhile to initiate the necessary changes and build a climate of appreciation and trust. I sincerely wish you much success and all the best!

(Self-)Reflection—Steps Toward Self-Awareness

In the chapter (Self-)Reflection, I repeatedly provide you with suggestions and questions for your own practice and personal (work)day. I recommend that you record your thoughts and reflections in writing, including the date. This allows you to look back throughout the process and notice possible changes, and, if necessary, initiate next steps. At the beginning, we will look at the topic of resilience and the risk of burnout from a general perspective. Starting from Phase II - The Tidal Wave—Illness you will gradually learn about concepts from transactional analysis, which have an impact and effect in all areas of life. I wish you much joy and exciting discoveries as you work through this!

For (Potential) Affected Individuals—For Personal Self-Reflection

You have now learned quite a bit about burnout disorder and have probably already reflected on your own history in dealing with stress and performance pressure while reading, although burnout disorder actually involves many more triggers and contributing influences. The challenge in self-assessment is to view yourself and your current situation honestly, without judgment, and realistically. Burnout develops gradually and increases in intensity and severity through different phases. Therefore, it is important to take this into account in your assessment.

Depending on how much time you have available, you can use different resources for self-assessment. A good option is Bernd Schmid's Three Worlds Model. It depicts the private world, the organizational world, and the professional world. At the center is the core of your personality, which influences all three worlds. Schmid aptly writes: "You have to know who you are—even without a specific role in a specific organization" [1]. When an imbalance or stressful situation arises, it usually manifests at the interfaces of the three worlds. Each world is defined by experiences, culture, values, meaning, attitudes, unconscious beliefs, (mutual) expectations, competencies, tasks, responsibilities, etc., associated with the respective role. Schmid makes it clear: "Focusing on only one or two worlds may be appropriate for certain phases of life. But in the long run, you need to consider how you want to find your place in all three worlds" [1].

This could be one of your first (self-)reflection tasks.

- Examine in which of the three worlds, and through what, you encounter internal or external (value) conflicts or bottlenecks.
- Tune in to yourself and notice what triggers internal or external tensions and what unnecessarily drains your energy.
- Also consider in which areas you experience a particular sense of fulfillment or perhaps miss it.
- Where could certain expectations perhaps be shifted to another area of the Three Worlds, or be increased or decreased, so that tension and pressure are reduced?
- Where might there be new opportunities for development that you could review as the next step in terms of feasibility?

I also recommend that you take an online self-assessment test regarding burnout. These are usually available free of charge and serve their purpose. Complete the test without overthinking and select the answer that feels right to you on first impulse.

In addition, I recommend a critical self-reflection with regard to the following four areas, focusing on resilience and existing stress factors, which in my experience also play an important role in maintaining a healthy balance in life, especially in relation to possible burnout:

- **Workplace** and working conditions (routines, values, meaning, leadership and collaboration culture, etc.)
- **Private life** and social connectedness
- **Personality** and individual characteristics
- **Health-conscious behavior** and integration into everyday life

1. Reflect for yourself on how intact these four areas are in your life and how well they function alongside each other, or how great the strain is in each area and what triggers these strains. It is also helpful to rate the specific stressors, for example, on a scale from 1 to 10. Again, follow your first impulse and be honest with yourself!
2. Alternatively, you can document for yourself how much energy each area gives you or takes away. Depending on where you place your focus, you may gain different insights or draw different conclusions. If you feel an area could be improved, give yourself some time and consider small steps for change, which are usually easier to implement but have been shown to positively affect mood and experience. With a little patience, you will gradually achieve your goals with greater ease and can make adjustments along the way as needed.
3. If you are still unsure where you stand regarding a possible burnout disorder, plan to repeat the assessment described above in two to four weeks. The progression will show you whether the situation is deteriorating or

whether a strain was, for example, "only" temporary in nature.

4. If things worsen or your uncertainty increases, be sure to seek professional help and an external assessment. Do not wait too long! Once the downward spiral of burnout has started, it becomes increasingly difficult to recognize and break out of it.

5. If you are still unsure about your next steps, the appendix "Letter to Those Affected" may help you. You will find the description and materials (Parts 1 and 2) in the appendix, and you could, for example, use Part 2 of the letter to obtain an external assessment!

Questions for Self-Reflection

- What drives you in your everyday life and professional work? What inspires you?
- Which values and beliefs do you embody in the different areas of your life? Where do conflicts, contradictions, ambiguities, or misunderstandings arise, either internally or externally?
- Which area of Schmid's Three Worlds Model currently fills you with the most energy? How do you achieve this?
- Which area of Schmid's Three Worlds Model is currently particularly draining for you? What triggers this?
- What changes or next steps could you take in one of the three areas to initiate a noticeable improvement in your (energy) balance?
- How do you manage to regularly integrate mindfulness into your daily life in order to consciously perceive your body, needs, and feelings?
- How would you rate your current resilience (on a scale from 1 to 10)? What do you base this assessment on?

- How do you manage to allow yourself to feel weakness, fear, and uncertainty? To what extent might a strong masculine or feminine role model play a part in this?
- How important is it to you to appear strong and confident and to show this outwardly?
- As a man/woman, how do you take care of your health and resilience? To what extent might a strong masculine or feminine role model play a part here?
- How would your best friend likely answer this question when assessing your resilience?
- What competencies do you see in yourself regarding resilience?
- Which of the 18 dimensions of resilience do you already possess? Which could you still develop or strengthen (see Background/Resilience)?
- Which of the 18 dimensions of resilience are evident in your family or relationship? Which could still be integrated or developed together (see Background/Resilience)? In which areas would improvement or adjustment be beneficial for your health? What could the next concrete steps look like in this regard?
- What is currently preventing you from treating your health mindfully and appreciatively?
- Who in your family might have served as a role model in this respect? Did they model a more exploitative or a more caring approach?
- What would your gut feeling advise you if you let it speak honestly and directly?
- Imagine that a miracle has happened overnight. The change is positive and does not concern your environment, but your inner world. What would this change be, and how would you recognize that the miracle has actually happened?

For Leaders—With a Focus on the Organization

The four areas I have defined can also be used in your school or organization, with a focus on resilience and existing stress factors, for (self-)reflection. How do you assess the resilience capacity of your employees in the following four areas? What could lead to experiences of stress and pressure?

1. Workplace and framework conditions (routines, values, meaning, leadership and collaboration culture, etc.)
2. Private life and social connectedness
3. Personality and individual characteristics
4. Health-conscious behavior and integration into everyday life

Although you cannot read your employees' minds, as a leader you do have a certain sense for assessing the current situation and can use this as a perspective. Here are some possible questions:

- What is the current mood on site? Rate it from 1–10.
- Are there unspoken (value) conflicts that are causing strain?
- How is the work-life balance among your employees?
- How is your own work-life balance?
- How do you, as a leader, manage to regularly integrate mindfulness into your daily routine in order to consciously perceive your body, your needs, and your feelings?
- Who or what currently requires the most nerves and energy in your professional life?

- Are there people you know who are additionally burdened in their private lives?
- Are there employees who particularly focus on their profession because family life is not a priority?
- Are there people who tend to strongly identify with their role and tasks, or who are already showing signs of overwork?
- Are there people who, for example, tend to skip lunch breaks or always seem stressed?
- What work attitude and value (culture) predominates in your organization? Do you perhaps even recognize a pattern?
- What is the personality structure of your employees like? Are there perfectionists? Are there particularly value-driven individuals? Are there workaholics who work even on weekends or late at night? Are there alpha personalities with especially high and clear value standards who strongly drive quality or organizational development?
- Is there sufficient space in your organization for boundaries and individuality? When and how does this become apparent? How is this expressed and appreciated?
- How "healthy" do you consider your team to be?
- Is the topic of health and resilience even an issue in your organization? If so, where and how does this become apparent?
- Is conscious attention paid to physical and mental health? Are employees encouraged to take care of their health? If so, how?
- Is there an open culture regarding individual mental hygiene?
- How do you assess collegial exchange within the team?
- When is particularly strong motivation and willingness to perform noticeable among your employees?

- Do your employees seem stressed? What triggers this feeling of stress?
- How would you describe and externally assess the level and type of strain?

It is important to remember that these assessments are subjective. They are purely hypotheses that must be verified in exchange and conversation with those affected. This requires a great deal of sensitivity and mindfulness, and absolutely a protected, safe environment! This can take place, for example, as part of team development focusing on resilience, burnout, and employee health, or during annual employee reviews. It is important that you respect each individual's personal boundaries and strengthen their autonomy. It can be helpful to share your thoughts and/or concerns with the other person. However, only do so if the other person wishes it and there is openness to reflection and a trust-based relationship.

At the same time, it is also important that you take your subjective assessment seriously and use it mindfully and effectively as a valuable resource and a kind of GPS.

Questions for Self-Reflection

- What consciously or unconsciously drives you at work?
- Which values are particularly important to you? How do you live these out in your daily life?
- Are there perhaps contradictions, bottlenecks, or (value) conflicts?
- How do you assess your current resilience capacity? What do you base this assessment on?
- How do you assess the resilience capacity of your employees?
- What is the prevailing attitude in your company regarding "taking sufficient care of oneself and one's health"?

- What attitude do you personally model regarding "taking sufficient care of oneself and one's health"?
- Which of the 18 dimensions of resilience do you already possess? Which could you still develop or expand (see Background/Resilience)?
- Which of the 18 dimensions of resilience are evident in your team? Which could still be integrated or developed together (see Background/Resilience)?
- In what ways could the topic of resilience receive more attention in your company?
- How would you recognize that the topic of resilience is receiving more attention in your company?
- What positive changes would result from this? What would noticeably change in attitudes, in employee behavior? In leadership? In customers?
- Overnight, a miracle happens. However, it does not concern you personally, but your company, your employees, and the management level. What would this change be, and how would you recognize that the miracle has actually happened?

Reference

1. Schmid, B. (2008). *Systemisches Coaching – Konzept und Vorgehensweisen in der Persönlichkeitsberatung* (pp. 65–68). EHP.

Phase II—The Tidal Wave—Illness

Abstract In the stage of the tidal wave, there is no holding back. The author describes how exactly this manifests in relation to burnout in this second phase. You will delve into script theory and learn how experiences from childhood can still unconsciously and restrictively influence your current life, as well as what possibilities exist to increasingly leave these behind.

The Flood Wave

It comes inevitably, with such force and impact that you cannot even comprehend what is actually happening. Your entire organism is in a state of shock paralysis. Escape is pointless. You sense that something momentous is about to happen. Your subconscious is ready to face the unstoppable. Your consciousness is incapable of grasping the catastrophe in its entirety and wholeness. It is this silence,

R. Petersen, *Tsunami in the Head – Better Understanding and Coping with Burnout*, https://doi.org/10.1007/978-3-658-49737-8_3

this deathly silence, until it finally overwhelms you. You are about to go under. Your body is swept along with such force that it takes your breath away. You surrender yourself. You accept whatever comes your way. You let yourself drift, ready to shatter on the jagged, hard edges and stare your end in the face. At some point, what feels like an eternity later, it becomes quiet. You look around. Is this the end? You are still breathing. It is quiet. Deathly quiet. You cannot move. You are wedged in all the trash, dirt, and debris. It doesn't matter. You have no strength left. You are ready for whatever comes. Whether you survive doesn't matter at the moment. You are glad that it is finally quiet. That this premonition no longer paralyzes you. You enjoy the silence, without grasping the extent of the catastrophe. Your body is calm. Feels heavy. But you are not in pain. Probably the state of shock. Whatever. You won't get out of here on your own anyway. Maybe someone will find you. Maybe it will start to rain soon, so the ground softens a bit and you can free yourself. Who knows. It doesn't matter. You surrender to your fate. Your strength ebbs away. You become calm. It's over. Finally.

My Story—Learning to Understand and Classify

This phase of denial from the first sign and the refusal to see clear symptoms dragged on for the next weeks and months. With my psychologist, the same topics kept coming up: feelings of guilt towards my team, correspondence with my boss, sleep disturbances, shame and guilt over the prolonged absence, grief over the lack of energy, anger at my inadequacy and at not being able to work or function as I used to. My body had always played along before. I was used to pushing myself to my limits and saw that, in a way, as an important skill and strength. Even now, I still wanted to push through with sheer willpower. Every time another extension of my sick leave was due, I worried a lot and slept even more restlessly than usual for four or five days beforehand. I was in a constant emotional stress marathon. My psychologist remained steady, calm, and always left it up to me to decide how to proceed with the absences and sick leave. After about two months, I realized that it might be sensible and necessary to break off all correspondence with my boss, as even email exchanges still triggered a heightened stress level in me. I was truly on edge and did not feel any more recovered than before.

Symptomatically, it was a real horror run. I was constantly tired and at the same time totally stressed. At night I woke up several times and often couldn't get back to sleep after four in the morning. At night I woke up four to six times and of course was completely exhausted the next day. But not just because of the poor quality and quantity of sleep. I simply couldn't find any peace, still had severe back, muscle, and joint pain. Sometimes my migraines would return as well. My body was probably completely thrown off by the whole cocktail of hormones. I was completely beside myself and avoided normal everyday life as much as possible. I spent most of my time at home in my bed, where I either tried to sleep, brooded over my thoughts, or worried intensely. When I couldn't stop the rumination, I tried to distract myself with TV series. I had no energy for anything more.

A particularly hard blow during this initial period was when my boss told me after about five weeks that she had found a replacement and that no handover meeting was necessary. I should just focus on myself and my health now. That completely threw me off! I felt misunderstood and that my work and commitment were not sufficiently appreciated. How could she just hand over my tasks to someone new and actually believe that was possible without a handover meeting?! Was she not aware of how demanding and important my job was?! Completely beside myself, I called my psychologist and asked for a short-notice crisis session. I felt totally lost. What was I now? Or rather, who did I think I was?

In this session, we worked intensively on filling the "new" identity and the resulting gap, or at least piecing together the remaining fragments of my identity. I felt miserable, lost, and completely overwhelmed by the new situation. I now truly had no work and no assigned tasks anymore. Unrealistic existential fears like possible job loss, emerging resentment from my professional colleagues, rumors about a possible burnout in my team, were now part of my mental reality. It was still very important to me that the term "burnout" was not made public. I was terribly afraid that rumors about my absence would start circulating.

After I informed my boss that I would no longer be reading my emails, the situation calmed down a bit. Although it took another two weeks or so to adjust to the new circumstances, over time I gradually managed to become calmer. The general stress level subsided. I noticed that I was constantly afraid in my neighborhood of running into someone from my professional life and thus facing difficult questions. How would I react? What questions would I have to answer? This led me to avoid being out in the city during break or lunch times whenever possible and to generally avoid crowded places. I was already doing that anyway, as a walk in the woods simply brought me much more peace and mental distance. Over Ascension and Pentecost, I treated myself to a break in the mountains. I planned a change of scenery and booked a cozy holiday apartment in the Alps for longer hikes. This distance from my "home reality" did me a world of good. Even though at first the back pain increased due to the extra strain from hiking, I felt a little better each day. Overall, I could breathe more freely here and my thoughts became lighter. Over time, I managed to push my negative feelings like grief, anger, shame, and guilt a bit into the background. I became increasingly relaxed. However, the tension immediately shot up again as soon as I arrived back home in the city. It was as if someone had flipped a switch. The recovery and the mental and emotional distance simply evaporated within a few hours. The environment thus had a significant impact on my well-being.

After about three months and weekly therapy sessions, I decided on my own to take a burnout online test. The result nearly knocked me off my feet. I answered about 95% of the questions with "strongly pronounced," which indicated a clear "burnout tendency." Afterwards, I asked my psychologist if she could give me materials and information on the topic of burnout. I wanted to read up in more detail and better understand the phenomenon. I received two brochures. Reading them required a lot of strength. I was emotionally very affected and therefore worked through them step by step. A few pages each day. One brochure per week. After that, it was clear to me as well: I was actually suffering from "burnout"! It was a revelation. I simply hadn't recognized the symptoms or didn't want to see them. Admitting to myself that I was now actually suffering from a "real" and serious burnout made me infinitely sad and further intensified the feelings of guilt. I felt so small, shabby, and weak. I was a trained psychological counselor and actually had enough know-how on this topic. What had gone wrong here? How could I have deceived myself about myself and my abilities for so long?

Gradually, I managed more and more often to use the word "burnout" in therapy sessions, even though it often still brought me to tears. Over time, it was a relief to have a label for it. I was obviously ill. I had burnout. I had a serious illness. And it was curable.

Despite the definition, I still found it very difficult to talk to others about this issue. I was still very socially isolated, avoided any contact with friends, as these encounters drained me of energy and left me completely exhausted afterwards. I think a big part of the effort was that I still wanted to keep up appearances. I didn't want to talk about myself or my condition and at the same time saw no way to avoid the topic when asked, "How are you doing?" So I didn't engage in meetings with friends or family members at all. With the situation around Covid, this didn't stand out. People in my social circle still knew that I was working as a school principal, and everyone could imagine how much work and extra effort that must have meant in recent months under the influence of Covid.

In talk therapy, I dealt with issues of identity, illness, self-care, and my still very strong feelings of guilt. From my training as a transactional analyst, I knew that many script issues could resurface more strongly during times of stress and crisis. Script issues refer to beliefs, patterns of thinking, feeling, and behavior, etc., that originated in childhood and are no longer helpful—or can even be inhibiting and restrictive—in the here and now. This was also the case for me. I put a lot of pressure on myself, wanted to be strong, and to recover as soon and as quickly as possible. For me, feeling weakness and admitting it to myself was a personal defeat, which for a long time I could not recognize as a strength. I still often wanted to push through with sheer willpower and would have preferred to force my body and soul to be productive again. But that was not possible, and so I kept running up against my personal limits again and again. On top of that, I also had to somehow cope with the physical symptoms. These were still very pronounced: weakness, muscle and joint pain, back pain, migraines, sleep disturbances, anxiety, existential fears, social isolation. During this challenging time, I was competently and well supported by my general practitioner. He helped me by remaining calm, listening attentively, and at the same time not overinterpreting the sometimes diffuse symptoms. I felt heard, understood, and taken seriously. He also managed to convey to me that it was okay to rest and to give myself and my body enough time to recover.

An important milestone for me was the realization that I am not my illness. It did not define my identity. And as mentioned, it was treatable. I had to keep reminding myself of this, especially in moments when I intensely felt my limits, the fatigue, and exhaustion. It would get better eventually, even if it didn't feel that way at the moment. This almost became a mantra for me, something I reminded myself of daily.

Throughout this time, I continued to avoid telling those around me about my illness. I deliberately avoided social contact with friends. On the one hand, because it cost me a lot of energy and I usually preferred to be alone. In addition, I wanted to avoid having to give evasive answers or even lie if asked questions. I could hardly reconcile that with my conscience. On the other hand, I sensed that I needed to grant myself enough protection at the moment. Social withdrawal seemed to me the best and only solution. I had the right to withdraw and protect myself. Even if others missed the contact. At the moment, I absolutely had to focus on myself and my health. I had no other choice!

After about three months, I finally managed to meet a friend for coffee again. What could possibly happen? Actually, nothing. I had probably just convinced myself otherwise over time. I would notice in the moment whether it felt right to tell the truth. I gave myself this pep talk so I could actually go through with the meeting. By now, I was a master at consciously steering conversations back to the other person and giving evasive answers. This had become a new survival strategy. The afternoon with my friend flew by and we had a lovely time. Towards the end, however, my friend started to ask more specifically about my work situation. I would have had to lie, so I decided to tell the truth. My friend responded with understanding, but was so busy with childcare and a visit from neighbors that, apart from a few well-meaning, generic pieces of advice, the conversation remained quite superficial overall. On the way home, a wave of emotions overwhelmed me. What was I thinking? I broke out in a sweat and suddenly tears welled up in my eyes. How could I so easily cross my own boundaries and confide in an outsider that I had burnout? How could I be so careless? Once again, I was overcome by intense feelings of guilt and a paralyzing sense of shame. Rationally, I knew this was exaggerated. Emotionally, however, I was completely at my wit's end. My thoughts kept circling. I tensed up completely and could not see the point or purpose in ever confiding in anyone again in the future. It just wasn't worth the risk of being hurt. Of course, this experience was a topic in my next therapy session. It was always about the same issues—boundaries and protection, and how I could manage to take sufficient care of myself. As a result of this encounter, I decided, for self-protection, not to tell anyone else about my situation or my illness for the time being. I simply didn't have the strength!

During this time, I engaged intensively with the topic of intuition. I simply had no answers to so many questions. When I searched for them in my thoughts, I tended to get stuck in a mental carousel and couldn't get off. This made me totally stressed and tired, and I realized that in many cases it was completely counterproductive. Accessing my intuition was therefore much easier, and I noticed how this topic inspired me and, in many moments, gave me new perspectives, hope, and confidence. And I needed that more than ever in my current state.

Several weeks later, I met another friend for coffee. At first, I was very nervous again, had a lot on my mind, and kept telling myself that if I didn't want to, I didn't have to share anything about myself. It was my right to protect myself sufficiently. We strolled through a small town and I relaxed. For a moment, I could even forget the situation I was in. And then, unexpectedly and spontaneously, I found the courage to talk about my illness after all. My friend reacted completely differently. She simply listened quietly. I told her about the persistent sleep disturbances, the exhaustion, the self-doubt, and the feelings of guilt. She didn't give me any well-meaning advice. She just listened! I felt understood, without being judged or categorized. What a relief!

At that time, I was still toying with the idea of returning to work before the end of the school year. The constant inactivity, combined with the ongoing feelings of guilt, was getting to me, and the only way out seemed to be to face the challenges again. My friend said about this idea that, from her own experience as a school principal, she knew that a well-managed school team could get by without the boss for a while. She also said that, given my current state, this was complete "nonsense." The team would certainly manage without me for a bit longer, and I should now "gopf nomol" (Swiss dialect for "for heaven's sake") finally focus on myself and my health. She hugged me tightly. That gave me courage! I felt taken seriously! Once again, I was moved to tears. How much I had needed such encouraging support from outside! In addition, her reminder that my team would certainly manage without me for a while longer helped me. That was certainly true, because I really did have a great team!

Now I had an encouraging experience regarding opening up to a friend. The experience of being able to offer myself both openness and protection gave me courage and a good foundation on which my self-confidence could continue to build. Up to that point, I had not yet spoken to my then-partner about my condition. We had met shortly before I went on sick leave, and because I thought it would only be a short break, I initially didn't tell him about my problems. Over time, it became increasingly difficult to bring up the subject at all. Since we didn't live together and were only in the early stages of a possible relationship, I also decided to remain silent here. By now, it was almost normal for me to successfully avoid the topic of my well-being and health in social interactions and conversations with him. This conscious suppression gave me, on weekends when we met, a kind of island that provided me with mental relief and a break from reality. That did me a lot of good. Of course, he noticed how exhausted I often was. But even here, I tried to come up with good and plausible explanations to keep up appearances as best I could. I invented plausible excuses and tried during the week to rest up sufficiently and as quickly as possible after our often intense time together as a couple.

At some point, I wanted to tell him the truth. I could feel it. It was important to me to let him in and see how he would react. But even for this, I first had to work up the courage over several weeks. After my positive experience with my friend, I finally managed, after a few weeks, to let him in on the topic of my illness. Fortunately, he also responded with understanding, without judgment, lovingly, and with good boundaries. He had already noticed a certain incongruence between my statements and actions. However, he had never really been able to make sense of it or put it into context. In retrospect, many of my statements and actions made more sense to him this way. This had a clarifying, relaxing, and overall positive effect on our relationship. Another hurdle was overcome, and I became increasingly relaxed.

Now, three people in my immediate circle were already aware of my burnout illness. However, I continued to consciously keep silent with my family. I did not want my mother and siblings to worry about me unnecessarily. I was afraid that the topic of burnout would then be discussed everywhere and all the time, making it even harder for me to gain some mental distance. Moreover, it was much easier for me this way to set sufficient boundaries, both in terms of time and emotions. Keeping silent made it easier for me to fully focus on myself and my recovery in the coming weeks. At the beginning of June, in consultation with my psychologist, I decided that it would only make sense to return to work after the summer holidays. This gave me another good two months for the healing process. Hopefully, that would be enough.

Burnout Diary—Snapshots

"Burnout is like a free fall into the abyss. You only realize in midair that both the ripcord and the parachute were left behind at takeoff."
Rebecca Petersen

I still sleep very poorly. Throughout the day, I have to lie down several times. In the evenings, I always go to bed very early; on the one hand, I see no reason to stay up any longer, and on the other hand, I am usually so tired from 6 p.m. onwards that I could drop dead.

The back pain has slowly gotten a bit better. The physiotherapy is contributing to that. Luckily! However, I am still too exhausted to exercise or do strength training again. That will have to wait! Through self-reflection, I notice how the back pain comes and goes, depending on the situation and my agitated thoughts. By now, I can even gauge how much I am worrying or how much a situation is weighing on me by the pain. The pain seems to be connected to my feelings of guilt and shame. At this point, I probably have to admit to myself that there is a psychosomatic connection here.

Nevertheless: Time passes quickly. The days seem to just fly by. I feel like I hardly accomplish anything meaningful. That gnaws at my self-worth. Who am I if I can't achieve anything? What meaning does my life have then? Can it really be that my work has taken on such a high value that it ultimately defines my entire identity? What did I actually used to enjoy? It's been so long since I can remember doing something for myself that truly brought me joy. Not that it wasn't important to me. I was just always too tired or too busy and probably missed the moment to admit it to myself early enough and make a lasting change.

Once again, it's about deciding when I will return to work. The holidays are almost over, and I am getting nervous and restless again. Am I ready yet? I don't think so. What will my colleagues and my boss say? How will they react to me when I come back? Am I even able to work and perform again? In conversation with my therapist, I realize that even just thinking about it is too much for me. The fear blocks me and puts me under great pressure. Even just a conversation with the case manager means additional stress for me, which I have to process and digest for days before and after. On top of that, my psychotherapist will soon stop working. That's a setback! How am I supposed to build enough trust with someone new again? That will take time and set back my recovery process. I am afraid of changing therapists and feel cornered. But I have no choice but to continue where I left off and make do with what is and what will come.

Fear dominates my world. I find it hard to remain optimistic. I have so many worries. I seem to have lost trust in my body and my ability to perform. I have a lot of self-doubt. The memory of the last weeks before I left work saddens me. Realizing now how rushed I was and how much I denied my condition and misinterpreted my situation deeply unsettles and frightens me. What if it happens again? I have already experienced it once, and after "dropping out," it took months before I noticed the "alienation" from myself and could fully recognize it.

There are also good days. These are the days when I can overcome myself and try to see the good. Days when I focus on what is happening around me in the here and now. When I don't make my well-being dependent on my work or my achievements. When I "trick" myself into being optimistic, even if I sometimes feel guilty about it, because suppressing things doesn't really fit into my "perfect" world. I have learned to tackle problems and take action. That's how I have overcome every hurdle so far. Step by step, always moving forward toward the goal. This strategy no longer works for recovering from burnout. I am condemned to patience; I cannot force my recovery to progress faster. It does not proceed linearly, and I feel like I contribute little to it. My task is to go with the moment and to repeatedly find trust in myself and in life, to tell myself that everything will be okay. To allow myself to be weak sometimes and to see and acknowledge this as a "newly discovered" strength.

During the week, I always live the same daily routine. Get up, read, meditate, shower, write or go for a walk, eat, rest, read, rest, go to bed. I do not maintain any social contacts. Usually, I have one additional appointment per day, whether it's physiotherapy, psychotherapy, a doctor's consultation, etc. That is already stressful enough for me, and I enjoy every day when I don't have such an appointment. If possible, I schedule such appointments for the afternoon, because it takes me a while in the morning to get going. And if I have to be somewhere at a certain time, it is very stressful and puts a lot of pressure on me. I am definitely no longer as productive and organized as I used to be. And I have developed an aversion to "having to." I want to be able to want, out of inner joy and meaning, with a focus on my well-being and my health.

When I go for a walk, I make sure not to be out at times when I might run into colleagues or employees. I avoid being in my office neighborhood. Feelings of guilt and shame quickly arise, making me infinitely sad. I consciously avoid that. In any case, I prefer to go to places where there are hardly any people. A walk in the woods or in the park does me good and lets me forget for a few hours the difficult situation I am currently in.

Still, only small improvements are visible and noticeable. That is increasingly discouraging. My sleep is very restless, and I can hardly fall asleep without medication. By now, I see my daily task as keeping myself in good spirits and doing my best not to lose my courage and self-respect completely. My mood fluctuates. There are days when I feel extremely miserable and just want to crawl into bed and cry. And that without any apparent reason. And there are days when hope rekindles in me. The only thing I can do is learn to deal well with these highs and lows and not measure myself, my self-confidence, or my self-worth by them. That often takes a lot of strength. I still do not have enough energy and see no point in discussing my illness with other people. Life is hard enough as it is, even without having to integrate more perspectives or advice into my world or consciously focus on what is not working in my life. I want to be positive, and at the moment, I manage that best when I am alone and can look after my own needs.

Time passes. I am still not working. The feelings of guilt and shame are strongly present. But they do not help me move forward. I keep searching for possible reasons and explanations for my condition. I try to figure out how it could have come to this. I try to somehow find meaning in it. At the moment, I cannot yet name it. I hope so much that this will never, ever happen to me again! On the other hand, I just want to make the best of it, leave the past behind, and look ahead. But in any case, all I can do is look forward and endure and be present in the moment. I realize that it is not very helpful to make any plans already. It is what it is, and I must slowly but surely accept that nothing in my private or professional life will ever be the same as it was before my burnout illness.

Figuratively Speaking—The Flood Wave—The Fall into the Depths—Crisis of Meaning

2 The tidal wave - the fall into the depths - crisis of meaning

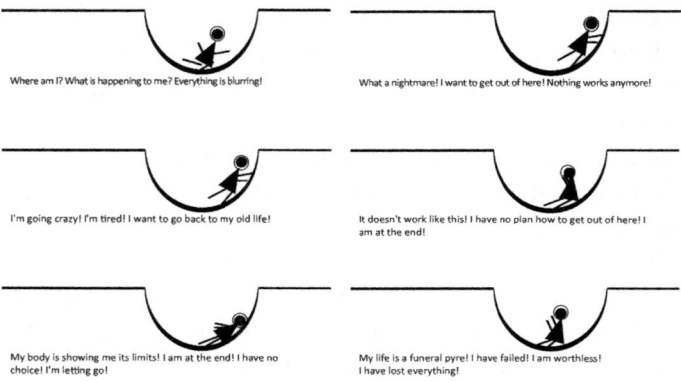

Where am I? What is happening to me? Everything is blurring!

What a nightmare! I want to get out of here! Nothing works anymore!

I'm going crazy! I'm tired! I want to go back to my old life!

It doesn't work like this! I have no plan how to get out of here! I am at the end!

My body is showing me its limits! I am at the end! I have no choice! I'm letting go!

My life is a funeral pyre! I have failed! I am worthless! I have lost everything!

For (Potential) Affected Individuals— Strengthening Self-Reflection and Resilience

In the acute phase of burnout, you may find that alongside total exhaustion and fatigue, you also feel sad, irritable, angry, or aggressive. Any emotion is possible and okay, even if you can't always attribute it to the situation. Emotions such as sadness, shame, or guilt are not uncommon. It seems that the hormone balance, completely thrown off by stress, thoroughly shakes up emotional perception. It is possible that at first you may not really feel anything at all or are unable to perceive yourself and your body! That was the case for me for a long time, and the frightening part was that I could no longer even recognize it as a change from before! It seems that, in my stress and survival mode, a disconnection from my own perception and feelings occurred as a form of self-protection. Looking back, I often think that my body and soul actually reacted cleverly all that time—a breakdown as self-protection. I simply didn't want to listen and overlooked or consciously ignored the countless physical and emotional warning signs.

In this second phase, I experienced the symptoms as even worse than before the actual withdrawal. This may be because, after much time, sleep, and rest, I slowly returned to my thoughts and realized what was actually happening. I became much more aware of the pain and exhaustion and interpreted them as clear signs of weakness and failure. In this phase, entirely new and different symptoms can emerge, affecting both the body and the psyche, the inner life. From my experience, it has become clear that the physical symptoms are found at the end of the perception scale, and that an inner discomfort, deluge, boundary violations, injuries, etc., had already occurred unnoticed beforehand. At the beginning of the acute phase, I was simply not aware of this. From my perspective, the back pain was the real problem! I would never have thought that the prolonged stress and its resulting physical effects were the actual cause of all my complaints and symptoms. I was not aware that I had allowed far too much stress and pressure for a long time without responding appropriately or changing anything about the situation.

Shortly before the burnout, I simply had almost no strength or energy left to think about such things. After a few months of recovery, I was gradually able to perceive my body and thoughts better and better, and to classify events (external or internal) for myself and associate them with a bodily sensation. However, this "self-training" took a long time, and I repeatedly caught myself falling into the trap and realizing too late what had originally triggered the physical pain.

Added to this was my impatience regarding recovery, which repeatedly mixed with feelings of fear, hopelessness, and despair. Regaining trust in your own body and yourself is a lengthy process! It is hard work, to be honest! But it does get better, and it is worth it! Even if there are setbacks from time to time or no noticeable improvements for a long period. It will get better! Hormonally and psychologically, you will make progress that will gradually help you find your way back to yourself! Hang in there, stay on track, and whenever possible, orient yourself toward your needs and what feels good to you in the moment and gives you the necessary strength and confidence.

> It is worth sticking with it and not giving up! Improvement will come, even if it feels otherwise and setbacks can happen! That, too, is part of the recovery process! Take the opportunity to get to know yourself and your body anew! I sincerely wish you all the best and continued confidence!

For Relatives, Friends, and Colleagues— Systems Thinking

The acute phase of burnout is a difficult period that manifests very differently depending on the person. In addition, well-being can fluctuate throughout the day without any clear trigger. It is therefore important to provide plenty of space, calm, and protection in daily life and, if possible, to go with the moment. The affected person already has enough to deal with themselves, and that is usually effort enough. Simply functioning is no longer possible at this point and, in my view, is also counterproductive. It takes trust in the affected person and the situation, trusting that their body and psyche will recover over time and improvement will occur.

Even small everyday tasks can already be a challenge, even if no depression has been diagnosed. People with burnout are also masters at keeping up appearances. Often, you cannot see from the outside how the person is really feeling inside. And talking about the burnout may not necessarily be helpful. Sometimes it is good just to switch off and be in an environment where you can pretend everything is fine and you don't have to explain yourself.

This phase requires a lot of sensitivity and understanding from others and is a major challenge for family life. The acute phase is characterized by the need for a great deal of patience, hope, and confidence from everyone involved, without really being able to predict when or if well-being will actually improve. Often, positive changes happen imperceptibly and are only recognized in retrospect "as a bigger picture." Sometimes improvements are first noticed by those around the person, long before the affected individual can perceive them themselves. For this reason, personal exchange from time to time can be helpful. Of course, only if the affected person also feels the need. Here, it helps if you simply communicate openly and honestly, sharing how you are feeling and what uncertainties or questions you may have. This alone can significantly ease a situation and contribute to mutual understanding.

As family and colleagues, you have an important role in the recovery phase. Active assistance is not always necessary.

However, your presence, appreciation, and support are important. It is not always easy to recognize what is helpful at any given moment. But you do not have to figure this out on your own. If in doubt, just ask! The road to recovery can be long and exhausting—for those involved as well! I sincerely wish you strength and perseverance in the face of uncertainty!

For Managers—Corporate/Social Responsibility

The acute phase of burnout and what the affected individual will go through during this time will likely remain largely hidden from you as a manager. There are so many ideas and prejudices about burnout that can circulate within the team. Therefore, as mentioned, it makes sense to address the risk of burnout early and preventively in your organization, or ideally, to regularly integrate the topic of resilience into team development and sustainable health management.

The diagnosis of burnout does not always have to be clear from the outset or communicated externally. If the affected person is on sick leave due to exhaustion and physical symptoms, it may be a case of burnout, but it does not have to be. The exact extent will probably only become apparent over the course of the sick leave. Often, those affected by burnout do not recognize the symptoms themselves during the acute phase, or only recognize them in isolation, and have lost sight of the bigger picture.

Often, they sense that something "central" in their life is no longer right. They may notice that they are constantly under stress, can no longer perform at their usual level, and that their motivation has completely bottomed out. However, some affected individuals are adept at keeping up appearances and deceiving both themselves and those around them. They simply do not want to see what is really going on and have no real idea of what could improve their situation. Towards the end, they lack the strength to actively change the stressful situation. Many affected individuals would prefer to return to work, but at a certain point, their body and mind simply will not allow it. At this stage, it is not only the usual overload from stress at play, but possibly already the hormonal cocktail of the progressing burnout, which sustainably clouds self-perception.

Addressing burnout in this situation is a balancing act, because the person affected may reject or not take the hints seriously. However, I believe that the more sensitized a team is in their interactions and regarding burnout, the easier it becomes to communicate one's own perceptions to another person in an appropriate and well-defined manner, and thus to share impressions and assessments in a respectful and effective way.

Managers and team members often feel uncertain about addressing the issue because they themselves know too little about burnout and therefore do not want to presume to make a judgment or offer a subjective assessment from the outside. However, it is also often the case that the affected person is very conscious and skillful in hiding their condition. Sometimes, it even affects those who outwardly appear especially supportive and motivating to others, even though things have been "boiling" inside them for some time, so that the burnout remains undetected until the body and mind collapse. This means that, in the worst case, you may not actually recognize the burnout at all, and therefore should trust your gut feeling while still maintaining clear boundaries. Some affected individuals later say that they were extremely relieved when someone in the team or the manager finally addressed the issue with them. Only through this external perspective were they able to admit to themselves that they were suffering from burnout and seek help.

The fact is that in some cases, burnout cannot actually be prevented. In my view, however, it still makes sense to take the issue seriously, to consciously incorporate it into the team development process, and to regularly focus on and discuss the resilience and health of employees. This is closely linked to successful, appreciative communication within the team, clarification regarding attitudes, values, and goals within the organization, and the opportunity for self-reflection regarding personal orientation, strengths, and resources, all of which contribute to the overall success of the company. If an organization manages to consciously and purposefully address and promote these different levels, and to create a "healthy" team culture, much has already been achieved in terms of preventing burnout.

> As a manager, you play a key role during the illness phase. The area of tension between the questions "What does the employee need?" and "What does the team and/or the organization need?" is often challenging. It may also remain unclear for a long time how things will proceed for the person within the company. Both sides must endure this uncertainty! I sincerely wish you strength and perseverance during this challenging phase!

(Self-)Reflection—Steps Toward Self-Knowledge

An important concept from transactional analysis in this context is the script [1]. It describes emotional, cognitive, and behavioral patterns developed in childhood, which can resurface more strongly under stress and crisis. The script contains values, norms, beliefs, experiences, limitations, expectations, etc., which we have consciously or unconsciously adopted from childhood and which still shape our experience, thinking, feeling, and behavior as adults in the here and now. According to Eric Berne, the founder of transactional analysis, the script is formed as an unconscious life plan in the first seven years of life and from then on influences our further life. According to more recent views, other authors have postulated that the script can be subsequently adapted and supplemented. Nevertheless, experiences and insights from early childhood can have a particularly formative effect and influence our experience in a limiting way, either unconsciously or consciously. Becoming aware of possible (thought, feeling, and behavior) patterns, limitations, script beliefs, and imprints can therefore mean a kind of liberation and relaxation, leading to greater autonomy and freedom of action. Depending on the personal situation and the presence of (burnout) symptoms, it may make sense in certain situations to seek psychotherapeutic sessions in order to address emerging script issues and possible crises, as well as to process them and, in the sense of strengthening autonomy according to Eric Berne (see Phase III—The Sea—Recovery and Setbacks), to anchor new insights and behaviors as sustainably and life-changingly as possible. The type of treatment in each case, however, always ultimately lies in the responsible self-assessment of the affected individual, in consultation with the treating therapist.

For (Potential) Affected Individuals

With regard to the topic of burnout and resilience, examining one's own script and script beliefs (Schlegel, 2002) can be particularly helpful. Below, I have listed some questions for your reflection:

* What was the time during pregnancy like, before you were born? How relaxed/stressed did your mother/father experience the pregnancy? How stressful was your birth?
* What motto or guiding principle accompanies you in your professional life?
* What was your parents' attitude toward work effort and fulfilling duties?
* How did your parents experience stress? What triggered stress? How were stressful situations handled?
* How were emotions expressed in your family? Which emotions were allowed? Which were predominant? Which were not tolerated or even devalued?
* Are there events that you particularly remember in relation to exhaustion and overload? How did you feel at the time? What did you think? How did you behave? What did you conclude from it?
* Which beliefs particularly shaped you in your childhood?
* What drives you in your professional or private everyday life? How does this manifest in your thinking, feeling, acting, and decision-making?
* What next steps could provide you with relief regarding your work attitude?
* How easy is it for you to delegate tasks or hand over responsibility to others?
* How do you deal with setbacks or uncertainties? How do you explain them to yourself? Who do you consider responsible?

- How would you describe yourself as a person? Who are you? What defines you as a person? What is your reason for being? How important is your work to you?
- What brings you joy besides work? What brought you joy as a child? How much does this "inner child" still find expression today?
- What long-held wish or dream has been dormant within you for years? What could be the next, first steps toward realizing it?
- How and for what were you praised in the past? For what did you receive attention and appreciation from your parents? How was this expressed? For what were you especially praised or encouraged? How was it for your siblings?

For Leaders—With a View to the Organization

In relation to the organization, the field of organizational development in transactional analysis also speaks of a script. This refers to a kind of "organizational memory or organizational history." There are some interesting questions for reflection on this:

- Are there topics that keep recurring in your organization? Which ones? What possible benefit arises from this?
- Is there a story/event/person that has particularly shaped your organization? If so, which one? How and in what way is this influence still noticeable today?
- Are there emotions that are particularly strong in your organization or that are not allowed to be experienced/expressed at all?
- Which beliefs/mottos/phrases, etc., shape your organization?

- Are there unspoken rules, rituals, or behaviors?
- How would you describe the style of leadership? How does it compare to your predecessor's?
- Which leadership culture is particularly valued by your team? What do you base this assessment on?
- What roles do you take on in your organization? How important are you as a leader to your team? Which values are especially important to you? How do these manifest in everyday life?
- Where could more be achieved with less? Where, on the other hand, is more commitment needed?
- Where does your team draw energy and motivation from? Where, in your view, is the most energy and motivation lost? How could improvement be sought here?
- How do you show your team/your employees your appreciation?
- How much room does each individual have for their own creative ideas and implementations?
- Are there topics/areas you would like to change? What is the benefit of leaving them exactly as they are? What of this could/should even be preserved? Where would a redesign make sense and for what purpose?
- How would you describe your organization in an image?
- How would an outsider describe your organization in an image? Are there striking differences? If so, what are they? Do they mean anything?

References

1. Schlegel, L. (2002). *Handwörterbuch der Transaktionsanalyse* (2nd edn., pp. 272–277). Herder Verlag.

Phase III—The Sea—Recovery and Setbacks

Abstract The sea, with its endless expanses and gently swaying, calming waves, provides the perfect entry point into the next phase of burnout. Various challenges emerge, and the symptomatology remains complex. New challenges and obstacles continually arise. The concept of autonomy, which in transactional analysis is more far-reaching than what is commonly understood as independence, offers a holistic, healing approach. It opens up a new perspective and approach for a fulfilling, conscious life with one's own sphere of influence and responsibility—in harmony with the nature of being human.

The Sea

I drift aimlessly. Water splashes into my face. I wake up. Where am I? Nothing but water everywhere. No land in sight. I am drifting in the open sea. Good thing I am an

© The Author(s), under exclusive license to Springer Fachmedien Wiesbaden GmbH, part of Springer Nature 2025
R. Petersen, *Tsunami in the Head – Better Understanding and Coping with Burnout*, https://doi.org/10.1007/978-3-658-49737-8_4

excellent swimmer. But how long will my strength last? In which direction should I move? How can I orient myself? What should I use as a guide? I keep swallowing water. The waves are quite high. I am alone. Fear rises within me. How did I get myself into such a predicament? How did I even let myself drift out this far? Will I ever feel solid ground beneath my feet again? Will I ever find myself safe again? Where is my path leading me? Where will the current take me? Is there any point in choosing a particular direction? Does it make sense to try to stay in control? Or should I just let myself drift and save my strength? Again, I swallow water. I must have swallowed quite a lot of saltwater by now. I am getting restless, almost hysterical. Just thinking about what creatures could attack me out here in the open sea?! What if a storm really does come up and the waves drag me down into the depths? In that case, the saltwater is probably the least of my problems. I have to stay calm. Trust that things will turn out well. That I will be rescued. That I can rescue myself. I have to find a middle ground between active effort and simply letting myself drift. I must keep my composure. I have to stay awake and not lose hope. Just keep my head above water as best I can. Survive! That is the goal. It will turn out all right. Somehow. It has to. I am not ready to let go yet.

My Story—Light at the End of the Tunnel

In the initial phase, I could hardly perceive myself, my needs, or my body, or only poorly. Severe exhaustion, physical complaints such as muscle, joint, and back pain, heart rhythm disturbances, and sleep disorders dominated my daily life. Now, there were more and more phases in which I felt physically better, at least regarding the pain. However, my condition changed daily, sometimes hourly, without my being able to identify any specific trigger.

Over time, I noticed that I had a little more energy available throughout the day. And we are talking about approximately thirty minutes that I could invest in something specific. I had energy again to think about things for the future or to spend a little longer reading a book. It also became easier for me to go for walks or to take a shower in the morning. My whole daily routine began to take shape again, even though usually just one appointment, like physiotherapy, where I had to be on time at a specific place, would completely throw me off and noticeably stress me out. I realized it was advantageous to move these appointments to the afternoon so that I had enough time in the morning to start the day at my own pace.

I still had no desire for social contact at all. The motto was still withdrawal and keeping a safe distance. I also continued to hide my illness from my family members and friends. I simply had no energy to deal with other people's reactions in addition to my own thoughts, or to engage with questions about burnout on that level. So if I did manage to force myself to meet a friend, I would simply give evasive answers and consciously set boundaries. At first, I reacted to planned meetings with intense anxiety. I noticed that even the time before the meeting, often several days in advance, caused me great mental stress. To protect myself, I would inform my friends in advance via WhatsApp that I wasn't feeling well but didn't want to talk about it. If the person responded with understanding, I felt relieved and could approach the planned meeting a bit more calmly.

I also noticed that strong feelings of anger and frustration kept creeping into my everyday life. The sense of meaninglessness I felt at the beginning of my illness had lessened. In its place, anger and frustration—toward myself and others—were now sometimes so intense that I didn't really know what to do with them. It was often difficult for me to pinpoint where these feelings came from. However, I had plenty of time for mental reflection. I realized how much my burnout was not just dependent on myself, but had a strongly systemic character. Of course, I couldn't simply shift the responsibility. Many of my personal issues were the trigger for the problems that ultimately manifested. But over time, I also saw my own powerlessness and helplessness in the face of workplace events and circumstances. In my case, it was a new boss with a completely different leadership style, difficult communication, little understanding, trust, and appreciation, and a very high workload, an incredibly wide span of control, in addition to the "normal" everyday life of a school principal with complex issues, unpredictable events, and many different expectations and demands from numerous stakeholders. Even before my illness, as a trained organizational consultant, I had already recognized and reflected on the systemic challenges within our organization to some extent. But admitting to myself that these accumulated challenges may have contributed to my burnout, and that I ultimately did not have the courage and strength, as others did, to leave the system and resign, was hard for me to accept. Fortunately, since my back pain had almost completely disappeared, I was able to start strength training again. This helped me to deal with the emotions I was experiencing in a meaningful way and to challenge and feel my body in a positive way. My fitness had declined significantly in recent months, as I simply had no energy to move enough. I had always been very athletic, even as a teenager. For me, sports had always been a good way to keep myself in balance and recover from the stresses of everyday life. I was therefore very happy when I was able to attend short strength training sessions again.

In contrast, I had developed a new sensation. I felt a strong resistance as soon as I got the feeling that I had to do something. My therapist explained to me that this was common among people with burnout. There is a certain point at which the "not wanting to have to anymore" becomes very pronounced, because in the past, someone with burnout was a master at putting themselves under pressure and pushing the "must" beyond their personal limits. This made sense to me, but the intensity of this need to "not have to anymore" was often overwhelming for me. I felt like a rebel who, in my estimation, would no longer find a place in society. I often wondered whether I would ever find a place in today's performance-oriented world when it came to work. I loved my job as a school principal. At the same time, I felt that I never wanted to return to that state of overload and deprivation, and never again exploit my body physically and emotionally in that way.

It took a great deal of effort for me to attend the first examination with the company doctor. Here, too, I felt strong feelings of guilt and shame. I already found it difficult to talk about my current state and my shortcomings with my psychotherapist. Now I was supposed to go through this with a stranger. The back pain became so severe again the day before that I could hardly walk. The examination lasted a good three and a half hours. For me, it was an ordeal from which I needed the next two days to recover. Since, in my case, it was no longer just exhaustion and severe back pain as I had initially stated in writing, the company doctor decided that the next step should be another examination by a psychologist. That made sense to me. However, it meant another hurdle to overcome. Nothing was spared me! However, I appreciated the doctor's thorough approach and the additional support from case management. In my view, this increased the chances that I would succeed in making a fresh start after the summer holidays. Even though this goal still seemed far off at the moment, I was already thinking about how to implement it concretely.

I was increasingly able to accept my illness and find my way in my "new" everyday life. It was still the case that one appointment per day, such as talk therapy, physiotherapy, a visit to the family doctor, etc., was a challenge for me, and the fact that I had to be at a certain place at a certain time often overwhelmed and stressed me out. There were still days when even taking a shower in the morning felt like an almost insurmountable task, and I would drag myself, already exhausted, from the mailbox up to the third floor. But I tried to maintain these small routines in order to experience at least a somewhat "normal" daily life. Fortunately, my stress level had decreased somewhat. I lived in a kind of bubble and avoided getting worked up about things that, at the moment, were not as I would have liked them to be. Of course, I didn't always succeed. My body and soul needed a lot of time to heal, and I was still constantly thinking about my work and my team.

I repeatedly had very bad days, when I struggled with feelings of meaninglessness and heavy thoughts. The fear of not being able to return to a "normal" life, of no longer being able to perform, paralyzed me and robbed me of all confidence. I often had the impression that my recovery was progressing only sluggishly, if at all, in a positive direction. There were repeated setbacks. Days when, seemingly for no reason, I felt physically and/or emotionally worse again. Days when I woke up already tired and dejected. Days when I had muscle and limb pain or my back pain returned with renewed intensity. Days when I thought about my team and my boss, and the intense feelings of shame and guilt resurfaced. I hated those days and yet I couldn't prevent them from catching up with me uninvited.

At some point, I decided for myself that things couldn't go on like this! I felt like I was just vegetating and not making any progress regarding my health. I felt angry and helpless. I had no strength to fight these feelings, let alone to drive and accelerate my healing. I felt as if I had completely lost control over my life. I simply couldn't get out of my own skin or escape the situation. I felt cornered, completely with my back against the wall. The urge to be able to do something actively and not just "wait it out" put me under pressure. Overall, this was of course counterproductive for my development. On those days, my brain searched through all possible options for positive change. I had consciously decided against a stay in a clinic. I sensed that this would mean more stress than support for me. I liked being in my own four walls. At the same time, I strongly doubted myself and the path I had taken so far. Was I really capable of managing the healing process on my own with just weekly talk therapy? Or had I overestimated and overburdened myself? I felt my sense of responsibility towards my employer and the feelings of guilt taking over again. I owed it to myself and my employer to get well again! I simply had to do everything to become fit for work again as quickly as possible! However, I didn't really have a plan for how I could achieve that.

One evening, I remembered a complementary medicine practitioner whom a friend had recommended to me years ago for my back pain. Maybe she could help me and advance my healing? A few weeks later, I was on my way to Ticino. In addition to the treatment, I also planned a few days of "vacation" and distance from everyday life. Even though I almost had to force myself to pack and leave as planned, I still had the impression that I was doing the right thing. At least this way, I had left no stone unturned. My exhaustion and back pain were still predominant. I literally dragged myself to the train station and just barely made it through the journey to Ticino. After arriving, I was very tired and emotionally exhausted. I had the appointment with the complementary medicine practitioner that same day in the evening. I don't know if it was the new environment, the sun and/or the wonderful view and the distance from everyday life, but after the first treatment I already felt noticeably better after a short time. Fortunately, I had followed my gut feeling. I regained some hope and spent very restorative days in Ticino.

This positive mood was only dampened by my boyfriend's visit over the weekend. I could hardly bear someone getting so close to me again and focusing on me. I was ashamed of these feelings because I cared deeply for my boyfriend. But somehow I had no other choice and at the same time sensed that I probably wasn't really ready for a relationship again. That may sound a bit harsh now. But the need to simply be able to focus on myself and to experience the days without obligations, appointments, or pressure had become my primary survival strategy. I never knew myself what state I would be in the next day or what kind of emotions, and with what intensity, would overwhelm me. So when I spent the whole day with someone, I had many expectations and ideas about how I would feel, and also a certain sense of responsibility towards the other person. Trying to meet all of these demands was at times very overwhelming for me. Of course, I couldn't actively control my condition and experience. My boyfriend never actually had these expectations or expressed them in this way. That was just my own perception. This situation and the feeling of powerlessness triggered strong anger at myself and deep sadness. A vicious cycle that increasingly strained my relationship with my boyfriend, even though he showed a great deal of understanding for me and what I was going through.

Back in my everyday life, after those few days in Ticino, I had regained some physical strength, but I soon noticed how heavy my heart felt after my return. Work—or rather, the "not being able to work and function"—weighed heavily on my mind again. And at the same time, the very fact that my work and my team meant so much to me, and that I derived part of my identity and sense of purpose from them, was one of the reasons why I was so committed as a leader. I realized I still had a lot of work to do on myself.

Overall, I was not often away from home during my sick leave. The weeks passed incredibly quickly anyway, and I usually had just a few appointments that already filled up my entire weekly schedule. It was still the case that just one appointment a day was enough to challenge me, and I quickly became stressed and overwhelmed. During the official school holidays, I had planned another week in the mountains. In consultation with the case manager, it was discussed that I would return to work as a school principal after the summer holidays. A therapeutic work trial was planned as a first step. However, the following incident showed me that I was still far from ready to return to working life.

It was about planning the journey for the vacation. My then-boyfriend and I had failed to coordinate in advance. My boyfriend confronted me with the fact that, due to a work appointment, he couldn't travel with me on the same train for the vacation, but would join me later. That hit me right in the heart. Not that I couldn't handle it. It just came so unexpectedly and was contrary to my expectations. I stumbled along, completely distraught, my heart racing and unable to think clearly. My whole body went into a state of alarm. I could feel it throughout my body and felt totally helpless and at the mercy of it. I had such severe chest pain and suddenly became afraid that I was having a heart attack. On the way home, I tried everything to calm myself down mentally. I sat on a bench and meditated. I put my feet up and tried to focus on my body and my breathing. Nothing helped! I was completely done. And all that just because of a minor disagreement? There was no way I could return to working life like this. How often had I, as a school principal, had to deal with stressful, unforeseen incidents or unpleasant phone calls? If such small things were to throw me into a state of stress every time, my body would quickly be back at an excessively high, unhealthy stress level, and I absolutely did not want to risk that. So, a return to work was out of the question for the time being. It was simply still too soon!

In general, I increasingly noticed how quickly I was overwhelmed by external stimuli and reacted hypersensitively. Noise, smells, hustle and bustle, colors, and patterns quickly became too much for me and triggered intense stress. Shopping in the city was a horror for me. I couldn't relax while shopping like other people. I tried to avoid crowds altogether. I preferred to go to a quiet café. I avoided exposed places as much as possible. I also deliberately dressed inconspicuously. Internally, I usually had the urge to simply disappear into the crowd and thereby forget my own world (and the burnout illness). It was still so painful to be aware of my own limits and ongoing overwhelm.

This continued to have a major impact on my social contacts. I absolutely did not want to talk about myself and therefore continued to withdraw. I couldn't stand hearing the question of how I was doing anymore. So it was easier to deliberately avoid my friends so I wouldn't have to explain myself. It was a constant dilemma between feeling like I had to lie to someone or respond evasively, or alternatively act beyond my own inner, emotional boundaries. The latter was something I could hardly tolerate at the moment! I constantly felt like I had to deny my true feelings and thus was not being true to myself. The experiences of the past few months had shown me that I was very bad at dealing with the different reactions of others. If I had a bad experience, it was all the worse. But even the good ones could, depending on the situation, stir me up a lot. I quickly felt overwhelmed, became anxious and insecure, and then angry at myself. It was a constant emotional rollercoaster that cost a lot of energy, and I simply didn't have that energy available at the moment.

The more I found peace within myself and was able to feel and perceive myself again, the more I became aware of how much I had changed and become estranged from myself due to the burnout. It also became clear to me how much I was being controlled and limited by stress, physical exhaustion, and emotional overwhelm in everyday life. That often made me so sad and at the same time angry at myself. Why couldn't I just function like everyone else? Why couldn't I just get well again?

At some point, I had the idea to seek support from a self-help group. I searched online for an option and found one. I had no prior experience with such a group. The meetings took place every two weeks. Of course, I was a bit uncertain at first, but I had the impression that it could help me to talk about my experiences with like-minded people in a safe environment. I hoped that I would encounter a lot of understanding and that, through sharing, I would be better able to make sense of my feelings. Fortunately, I was very well received. The exchange felt encouraging and enriching to me, even though confronting the topic was at times challenging. This was an important step for me toward having regular social contacts.

In dealing with the many emotions, which I could now feel more clearly and intensely again and which at times threatened to overwhelm me, I tried to calm and center myself with daily mindfulness meditations. Sometimes this worked quite well. Letting go and giving healing time—this was the goal I set for myself. Going with whatever was most present at the moment. Not overthinking things. Of course, this was a long journey. On certain days, the past would catch up with me again. I simply could not turn off my thoughts. My mind was racing. Unimportant things that I tried to organize in order to regain some sense of control over my life. Even though I knew this helped me very little, I simply was not able to turn off my thoughts or let go.

Despite the relaxed daily routine, life often seemed excessively exhausting to me. I wanted more, wanted to achieve and accomplish something, wanted finally to be happy and carefree again. I especially missed that feeling from earlier, when I was younger. I wanted to reclaim it. Since my youth, I had been used to my body simply doing what I wanted. It was completely normal for me to occasionally push past my emotional and physical limits. Why shouldn't I? At that time, I had no idea what I would be doing to myself in the long run with this attitude and the constant overstepping of boundaries. Now, of course, this was different!

Grief was a constant companion during this phase. Sometimes, out of the blue, I would feel a heaviness in my heart and not even know exactly why. It was similar with anger. Suddenly, it would well up inside me and I often didn't know what to do with this negative energy within me. Actually, these emotions were a clear sign of my progress. Because at the beginning of my burnout, I didn't feel anything at all and had no access to my bodily sensations or my emotional world.

In one therapy session, I once described my perception as follows: It's as if I started a few months ago with a small hole (full of problems). Over time, the hole got bigger and I fell into a kind of pit. Today, I look ahead and am shocked to discover that I am standing in front of a huge crater after a massive explosion. My psychologist then said to me: "You know, Ms. Petersen, it's not the hole that has changed. It's your perspective on it!"

Yes, the crater was really big and often paralyzed me in my existence and confidence. I felt powerless and at the mercy of the burnout. Social contacts continued to be a particular problem for me. I simply could hardly motivate myself to expose myself to another person and engage in a relationship, even if they were very dear to me. This feeling and the need for distance made me strongly doubt myself. How was I ever supposed to be well integrated into social and working life again?

A colleague, one of the few who knew about my burnout and with whom I felt reasonably safe in contact, once asked me what I did all day and whether I didn't get bored or feel cooped up. "No, that's not the case," I replied. I usually had enough to do with myself, tried to distract myself or motivate myself with an activity and get my mind on other things. In addition, there were the various appointments that gave me structure, but were often also stressful. I also still slept a lot and often restlessly, so on many days I still went to bed very early. Either from tiredness from the previous night, when I hadn't slept well, or from exhaustion due to the events and physical or emotional exertions of the day.

There were days when I felt like I was really stuck in a depression. Before, I would never have spoken of depression. The frequency, intensity, and unpredictability of my emotions and sensations were a new challenge for me. It was as if my feelings had settled over me like a veil. I could physically feel the heaviness of grief and anger as pain, and they were more intense than ever before. This was a new situation for me, since in the first phase of the burnout I hadn't felt anything at all. Now the emotions had returned with full force, and it was up to me to learn how to deal with them. This was another important developmental step for me, one that cost me a lot of energy and strength.

From the theory of transactional analysis, I knew that there were both authentic feelings and substitute feelings. According to Eric Berne, there are four authentic feelings—anger, fear, sadness, joy—which can occur in the here and now, are appropriate to the situation, and serve a purpose. Substitute feelings (also called racket feelings), such as powerlessness, greed, guilt, shame, envy, etc., on the other hand, essentially cover up an original, authentic feeling, because this feeling was not acknowledged, tolerated, or was devalued by caregivers in early childhood. Authentic feelings can also manifest as substitute feelings, i.e., anger can be experienced as an authentic feeling or as a substitute feeling. Concepts and theories like these helped me in many hours of my recovery with self-reflection. Transactional analysis had been an important companion for me for years and, in many moments, a support for making sense of things. When dealing with feelings, it is primarily about consciously perceiving them in the body, observing them nonjudgmentally, differentiating, categorizing, and being able to express them appropriately. The range of my emotional perception during the acute phase of burnout and after about six months, when my hormonal balance slowly normalized, was enormous! It was as if I had become a new person who could suddenly perceive life in many vibrant colors again. I realized that, during the burnout, I had actually become completely and totally estranged from myself without even noticing. This realization shocked and deeply hurt me. On the other hand, the fact that I could feel again made me infinitely grateful. Nevertheless, I still kept coming up against my personal limits. Moments when I felt lost, helpless, and useless. But apparently, that too was part of the healing process.

On my way back to a healthy, normal life, repeatedly reflecting on childhood experiences helped me. Being able to understand and make sense of why I felt or reacted a certain way in certain situations gave me orientation and security. At least sometimes, I felt that I didn't just have to wait patiently, but could actively do something for my healing.

This stood in stark contrast to my inner drivers: "Be strong! Try harder! Be perfect!" (cf. Phase V—Drivers). I increasingly managed to recognize my restrictive patterns (in thinking, feeling, and acting) in more and more areas of life and to make new, autonomous decisions for my life in the here and now. Of course, there were setbacks. Especially in stressful situations and in social contexts, we humans tend to fall back into our old (behavioral, emotional, and thought) patterns. That was the case for me, too. And yet, the peace and time of recovery helped me to get to the bottom of my negative thought and behavior patterns and schemas more and more, and to gain new insights from them. This self-awareness often required courage and strength, and I was glad that my family doctor, my psychologist, and my case manager showed me a great deal of understanding during the long period of recovery. In this way, I was increasingly able to allow myself this space and enough time for healing, both internally and externally.

The way back was rocky. Every time I had to submit another doctor's note, intense feelings of guilt and shame would resurface. This unsettled me, and each time it took me several days before my thoughts could shift away from

my workplace, my team, and my boss, and return to the
here and now. I consciously used methods from positive
psychology to speed up this process. I focused on what
was going well and changed my perspective in challenging situations. I worked with encouraging affirmations
and shifted my evaluations to the positive. When I had
the energy, walks helped me to feel myself and my body.
When I was once again paralyzed in a terrible low and
spent days in a depressive, sad mood, I had a personal
insight that gave me new courage. I imagined my recovery
as a kind of "roller coaster," and although I couldn't predict the ups and downs, I knew that after every low there
would also be a high. The moment of stillness, of being
suspended, might simply be a sign that the ride would
continue, even if I couldn't notice it at the time, and that
the highs and lows were just part of the roller coaster ride.
Could it really be that my life was picking up speed again
and that I could trust I would eventually reach my des-
tination? This thought stayed with me for several weeks,
and I was often afraid that I was "celebrating too soon." At
the same time, I drew new hope. In many moments, I still
felt very vulnerable and unstable, and yet the first positive
changes were noticeable.

After more than six months, my general condition
noticeably stabilized. Falling asleep and staying asleep
became somewhat easier again. My energy lasted longer
throughout the day and regulated itself without my
active intervention. I had more nerves and patience, and
sometimes even enjoyed engaging in social contacts. In
addition, I suddenly found myself thinking about a possible return to work! Not long ago, this topic had been
absolutely taboo in conversations with my psychologist,
because I would immediately feel an inner block. And
now, from one day to the next, I sensed on my own that
I was ready and wanted to actively engage with the idea of

returning to work. That was new and an absolutely wonderful feeling!

Burnout Diary—Snapshots

"Burnout is like your reflection shattering into a thousand pieces, and as you pick up the shards, you realize it wasn't just the reflection that broke. Only then does it really make sense to start gluing the fragments back together."
Rebecca Petersen

I feel like a little worm—shabby and insignificant. I would most like to just disappear into the ground and never come back up.

It's probably not for nothing that burnout is called an exhaustion depression. First the exhaustion, then the depression. I feel this deep emptiness inside me, a sadness I can't explain or categorize. It visits me even in my dreams. Sometimes I wake up crying or sobbing and can barely remember the content of the dream.

I keep going as before. What else can I do? All I can do is be patient with my recovery curve and not lose my balance when there are bad days and noticeable setbacks. The back pain is steadily improving. I notice that my energy level stays more constant throughout the day. I experience more consecutive days when I can successfully bring confidence and hope into my presence and awareness.

When it comes to social contacts, I've taken a step forward. Specifically, I've learned to protect myself preventively: I inform my friends that I'm not doing well health-wise and therefore don't want to be asked how I'm doing or what the reasons are. This allows me to protect myself sufficiently and still stay in contact with others. That's exactly what I need. I know I have to relearn how to feel safe and carefree in social interactions. But I can't do that overnight. So this is a first intermediate step that lets me sleep a little more peacefully. I'm still nervous before meetings and I carefully consider whom I really want to see. I question my friendships more and am more mindful of which people in my environment are good for me and under what circumstances I can truly enjoy a meeting.

I ask myself what reasons there are for people to seek social contact. In the past, we were much more directly dependent on each other, even for survival (hunting, defense, etc.). How is it today? I feel that we also use social contacts to distract ourselves from problems, feelings, and thoughts—and sometimes to excess. Many people can hardly stand to be alone with themselves for a few hours, and I wonder why that is. For my part, during my illness, I have come to appreciate "me-time" even more and realized that the truly important answers come from within myself. I usually find the helpful clues when I am alone, endure the silence, listen mindfully, and patiently tune in to myself. This (encounter) space is exactly what I enjoy and need most right now. It gives me strength and creates clarity and focus for the next steps I need to take. Then I have a strong feeling and certainty that I am not alone and am connected to something greater. That feels good. I will find my way somehow.

My recovery status is unexpectedly poor. I regularly forget appointments, even though I have written them in my calendar and only have one appointment per day. Appointments at a specific time overwhelm me as a matter of course. Multiple appointments in one day are an even greater overload, and I still have to be very careful to build in enough time for recovery and not let my thoughts, feelings, and a sense of inadequacy and weakness completely overwhelm me. Even the social contacts I sometimes force myself to have are difficult for me and make me nervous and insecure days in advance. I don't even know exactly why that is and can only partially describe what I'm afraid of.

My mood is at rock bottom. I feel like I'm just not making any progress. Recovery is sluggish. I hardly notice any improvement, physically or mentally. I'm about to lose hope and my mind. On top of that, for several weeks now, I've been experiencing a really strong memory loss. I forget that I wanted to get a bottle of mineral water from the cupboard. I forget to pay at the self-checkout and only just realize, before leaving the store, that I skipped that step. What is going on with me? Am I slowly going crazy? Is this the beginning of early dementia? I'm getting scared. What kind of damage is this stress-induced hormone cocktail actually doing to my body? I urgently need to talk to my family doctor and find out what's happening to me.

At the same time, I start reading up on burnout in professional journals and books on my own initiative. Actually, it's a bit late, but before now I simply didn't have the strength to face it. I need to know more about the illness. Only now, as I go through the facts, do I realize how clear my symptoms actually were. I take another self-test. The result is clear: "You are in burnout! Seek support from a doctor or therapist." Great! I've already been there. It's like scales falling from my eyes. Why didn't I recognize it earlier? I read and read. There are countless guides and books on stress and burnout. But only a few report from the perspective of those affected. Yet it is precisely these books that give me courage and calm me a little. Others have gone through the same thing, even though everyone's life story is completely different. And burnout really does seem to occur in all phases of life and in all kinds of social classes and professions. And it is possible to recover from it! This realization does me good. I'm not an isolated case. There is hope! And yet I still find it hard to see my inadequacy and weakness as strength and opportunity. How could I have been so blind? How could I have so completely misinterpreted the facts and, unnoticed, over-stepped my physical and emotional limits for so long? I never want to experience that again! I want to learn from it and reshape my life so that I don't fall back into old patterns. I owe that to myself.

Because of the depressive mood, I've recently started drinking St. John's wort tea, as recommended by my doctor. If that doesn't help, I'll probably have to resort to psychotropic medication after all. At the moment, I can't imagine starting work in this state. The problem is that both the tea and the antidepressants require a certain period of use before their effects set in. I therefore feel a bit under time pressure, since my return to work—post-poned for what feels like the thousandth time—is planned in two months. So I have to decide soon whether the tea is really the right strategy. In addition, the literature often recommends antidepressants, as they also help with sleep disorders and help normalize hormone balance and related brain activity, which have been severely affected by the burnout. I probably have to come to terms with the idea that this might be a sensible next step.

Social gatherings and events are still a challenge for me. I feel cornered because I never know what sensations and emotions will overwhelm me. I depend on people not getting too close, because I still have difficulty setting emotional boundaries. And I definitely don't want to break down in tears, because then I would have to explain myself to others. I absolutely want to avoid that.

In addition to my sleep disturbances, I have been experiencing heart arrhythmias for about a week and a half. My heart suddenly beats fast and irregularly, so that I feel as if it is about to jump out of my body. I can't identify a specific trigger. The doctor says I should try to calm down.

The arrhythmias could indeed be related to the burnout. Recovery may simply take longer than expected. But I shouldn't worry too much.

I feel like I'm on the verge of an emotional breakdown. It's as if I could watch myself from the outside. Inside me is this deep sadness and sorrow, which I rarely let show. But it's there, and it feels as if I'm about to burst from the pain. This is roughly how I imagine a depressive mood. I'm afraid. I think I need to get going soon. But my body is reacting the wrong way. I notice various symptoms. In addition to the sadness, I immediately become anxious and nervous just thinking about an event where I have to "function." And in everyday life, I am noticeably absent-minded. Not only do I constantly forget appointments, but things I actually wanted to do, like writing down an important to-do, suddenly and unnoticed slip from my mind and I forget them. It feels like a blackout, which I only become aware of minutes later, in retrospect. In between, I do something else, a bit as if in a trance or wrapped in cotton wool. Only when I see the email again do I remember that I wanted to write the appointment in my calendar. How is this supposed to go on?

My life is really a rollercoaster. There are days when I am hopeful and feel confident about returning to work. Although I have to honestly admit that I am still success-fully avoiding the thought. The memory of my own inad-equacy and inability is too painful. On other days, I feel demotivated and lost. Then I lack any perspective on how my life could become "normal" again. I become insecure and doubt my abilities. I know it's unrealistic to assume that I can't get anything done anymore. But the fear I feel in those moments seems very real and terrifying.

I decide to go to my family doctor again to discuss the situation and perhaps start taking antidepressants after all. This sadness and dejection frighten me. I can't get rid of it. This heavy feeling around my heart remains, and I'm afraid it might get even worse. I want to prevent that.

Maybe it's really as described in the professional articles. Maybe it takes the use of antidepressants over a certain period so that my body can recover and my hormonal balance can normalize again. Maybe that's the next sensible step?

Since my physical symptoms and emotional state have actually worsened again and I seem increasingly nervous, I have decided, in consultation with my psychologist, to give myself another almost two months of distance and a break from work. These constant emotional "ups and downs" that arise for me with a possible return to work are counterproductive. I need rest and distance, and that over a longer period. I will feel when I am ready again, and until then, I need to be patient and maintain my confidence.

I actually feel calmer since deciding that I definitely won't be going back to work for another month and a half. The thought of being able to give my recovery enough time is healing. I'm glad I have this option and am not constantly confronted with having to make a decision. My whole being longs to finally come to rest.

The time has come. My therapist is gone, earlier than expected. The change of my responsible psychologist is challenging for me. I think a lot about who the new person will be and how quickly it will be possible to actively continue working on my issues in a familiar setting. I am aware that this will take some time. I find it difficult to build trust with someone. Now I feel like I have to start all over again. But I can't change it. And somehow, I will manage.

My nephew's confirmation is coming up. I'm looking forward to it, and yet I've been nervous for about a week and a half. It's a big event where I will meet many people

I care about, who know nothing about my illness. This thought almost tears me apart inside, and yet I know that for now, "keeping it secret" is still the right thing for me. I would be even less able to cope if they knew about my burnout. Well, I try to calm myself with positive thoughts. I want to be able to enjoy the family event. Fortunately, I was able to arrange that I don't have to make an active contribution to the celebration. I probably wouldn't have managed that. Just being present will already be a big challenge for me. I'm curious to see how I will cope in this situation.

The family celebration actually went quite well, even though my back acted up again from sitting so long in church, and I had to stand up in between because I could hardly bear the pain. I haven't had back pain this intense in a long time. I keep thinking how absurd it seems that all these people assume I'm fine and don't know that I'm suffering from burnout. You just can't see it, and by now I've become a master at giving evasive answers, pretending, or escaping the situation if I feel uncomfortable or my emotions get the better of me. The questions about school were especially difficult for me, because I had to refer to the past. It felt like lying. It seems as if I have definitely missed the right moment to confide in my loved ones. Although I'm still sure that it wouldn't have been any better the other way around. I just have to hold on a little longer. Maybe when I've gotten through the worst of the burnout, it will be easier for me to admit my weakness and failure. Of course, my intellect tells me that this isn't really a weakness. But deep down, I still feel differently. I still have a lot of work to do on myself in that regard.

Writing does me good. It's as if I can confide all my thoughts and worries to a good friend, without her saying anything or giving me advice. Even now, when I read past notes, I am amazed at what I've experienced, and I feel a great sadness, but also humility, that I have already recovered so well from the burnout. That is truly a gift, even though I am still far from my goal. There are so many things I am consciously suppressing at the moment because they would overwhelm me emotionally. And that's okay. That's what I've learned in recent months. It will be time when it's time, and I will notice when I am ready for the next steps and insights.

In therapy, I have now successfully managed the change of therapist. There was indeed a need for clarification in the first few weeks, but sticking it out was worth it. Regaining trust, taking time to get to know each other, being patient, even though I already feel like I don't have enough time for all my issues again—that was exhausting. The return to working life is getting closer and closer. It's incredible how time flies. Even though, overall, I see great progress, at the moment it still feels as if I haven't gotten anywhere. My emotional stability is fluctuating, even though by now I can usually hide it very well in social contact. I still only rarely and selectively meet with good friends. And that's okay for now. I have developed more calm and acceptance for myself and my condition. I have learned a lot. For that, I am infinitely grateful.

For the first time in a long while, I am attending a larger professional event again. Two hours of informational session followed by a reception. For anyone else in the world, this would probably be a great experience. For me, it is a huge challenge, not only because it takes place in the evening. I have been extremely nervous about it for several days. I keep wondering what it will be like and whether I will be able to endure it emotionally and physically. But I want to consciously and gradually expose myself to such moments to see what is possible in terms of energy and emotions. A kind of trial run for my social skills and resilience. In the moment, when I am present among so many people, I actually feel quite okay. It helps me to be able to take on a sort of professional role on site. Again and again, I am reminded that I actually have burnout. The fact that these people do not know this triggers feelings of guilt in me. Rationally, this makes no sense at all, because I am sure that many of the participants would not be interested in my health status. And yet it stirs up so many emotions in me. After the event, I first feel euphoric, and then the tidal wave of fatigue, shame, insecurity, fear, and self-doubt returns. This experience is further intensified by the tiredness and the late bedtime. I know that I should not listen to my thoughts, doubts, and nagging self-judgments right now, and yet they penetrate even deeper into my innermost being and drain me. I have to go to bed, and hopefully tomorrow the world will look different again.

I am more nervous again than I was a few weeks ago. I notice this in my feelings, in my thought patterns, but also in the dreams that rob me of sleep at night. I bravely tried the sleep-inducing antidepressants. But the severe migraine attacks I experienced the next day quickly put me off them. Now I only take St. John's wort drops. These seem to have sustainably stabilized my emotional balance. I have more energy again and overall stronger nerves. I am less easily unsettled in everyday life. Falling asleep now works better with enough valerian drops and calming tea, especially since I have more energy in the evenings again and can stay up a bit longer and read.

I continue to attend the self-help group, even if I am not always motivated to do so. The exchange is only somewhat beneficial for me, as the topics are sometimes unsettling. I am also alarmed by how many participants experience burnout multiple times. But the meetings are a distraction and a good opportunity to talk about my burnout illness with people in a protected setting, to gain new insights, and to share valuable experiences.

I keep asking myself why I actually want to write this book. The fact that I find it so difficult to inform my environment about my illness seems to be in stark contrast to my plan to publish a book. What is the difference?

I believe it has to do with wanting to overcome myself and my fears. I want to be free from the thoughts and worries about what others might think of me. I want to be free and to dispel the many prejudices against mental illness. Surely it must be possible to suffer from burnout and then become fully capable again. Of course, I am aware that adjustments are needed in everyday life and in self-perception. But I definitely do not want to be one of those people who relapse. Not me! It must be possible somehow!

I notice that I am feeling better day by day. I am gaining confidence and can increasingly imagine returning to my workplace and being strong enough to withstand the challenging situations that will come at me at first. That is a wonderful feeling, one I first have to get used to again.

I am working a lot on myself and my issues. The therapy sessions are an important part of this. With my knowledge and experience as a psychosocial counselor, I can also take many small steps toward self-awareness and personal development in my remaining time. At the moment, I have the impression that I am getting to the "heart of the matter." That is, it is no longer a thousand overwhelming and paralyzing issues, but only two or three that I can address in a targeted and in-depth way. I now have the strength again to perceive and endure the emotions that arise. That is a huge step forward! At the beginning of the burnout illness, I was not able to consciously perceive feelings in the here and now or to make sense of them for myself. I unconsciously suppressed them because

I could not withstand their intensity and power. The stress had silently eaten me up from the inside and turned me into a shadow of myself. Only now do I recognize the extent of my burnout illness. Because I have the comparison and can perceive myself better again. It is a new quality of life, as I am more in touch with myself again, can feel myself, and am no longer at immediate risk of collapsing from exhaustion or being overwhelmed. What a gift that I have found myself again and my life is regaining shape and color. The hoping, enduring, and persevering has apparently paid off.

Figuratively Speaking—The Sense of Hopelessness

3 The sea - hopelessness

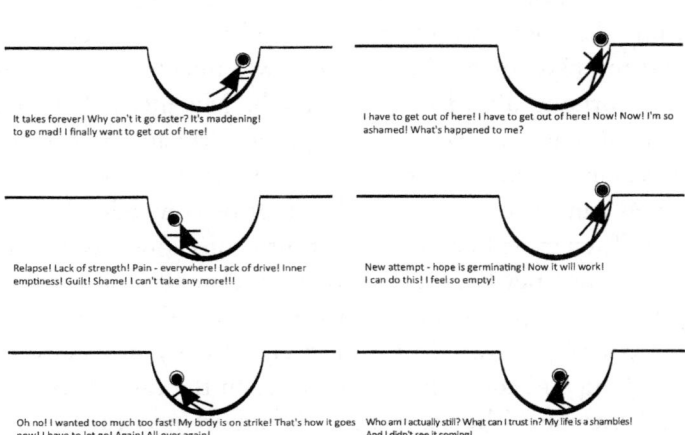

It takes forever! Why can't it go faster? It's maddening! to go mad! I finally want to get out of here!

I have to get out of here! I have to get out of here! Now! Now! I'm so ashamed! What's happened to me?

Relapse! Lack of strength! Pain - everywhere! Lack of drive! Inner emptiness! Guilt! Shame! I can't take any more!!!

New attempt - hope is germinating! Now it will work! I can do this! I feel so empty!

Oh no! I wanted too much too fast! My body is on strike! That's how it goes now! I have to let go! Again! All over again!

Who am I actually still? What can I trust in? My life is a shambles! And I didn't see it coming!

For (Potential) Affected Individuals— Learning Self-Reflection and Resilience

At some point, after the acute phase, seemingly suddenly and then increasingly over time, small changes become visible. These are often so minimal that you might hardly notice them individually. However, taken together, they do spark a glimmer of hope. It also becomes increasingly clear that a longer break from work is a meaningful step for recovery and that there is no way around it.

When considering a burnout disorder, there are various levels at play, which act as a whole but also individually influence personal life in different ways. For example, there is the intrapsychic process and one's own personality structure. This includes evaluations, internal drivers (see Phase VI—The Lighthouse—Making Sense of Uncertainty), beliefs, feelings, thoughts, fears, experiences from the past, etc. Despite my ability for self-reflection and my psychological expertise, I was unable to recognize the burnout disorder early enough. My internal drivers were also at work, as these are particularly activated when a person is under stress. Moreover, most intrapsychic processes run unconsciously and cannot be controlled by reason. They must first be brought into consciousness and, in a next step, newly experienced and internalized. It is therefore about experiencing, empathizing, and developing new behavioral patterns. This is precisely why psychotherapy or coaching and counseling make sense in the case of (potential) burnout. The exact type of support needed depends on the extent of the disorder and the stage of mental health the person is in. It is about understanding, feeling, and experiencing new situations and circumstances together with the professional. It is also important that new experiences can be made in a protected environment. This often requires courage and overcoming personal barriers. But only in this way can healing occur both internally and externally!

In addition to the inner experience, areas such as private life or one's own physical health also play an important role. Are you mindful of your fitness? Do you get enough exercise in the fresh air? Do you pay attention to healthy nutrition? How do you maintain social contacts? Body and mind form a unity. They have a direct influence on each other—both positive and negative. If your thoughts keep spinning in circles and you constantly worry about the future or the past, this inevitably affects your physical well-being. If you manage, for example, to go for a long walk every day, it not only benefits your circulation and physical well-being, but also brightens your mental state. It therefore makes sense to incorporate such helpful routines into your daily life and, whenever possible, to stick to them and implement them regularly.

At a certain point, I was able, for example, to decide to return to strength training. This seemed sensible to me because I knew that it would release endorphins, which in turn increased my motivation and lifted my mood. So if the burnout hormone cocktail was still at work in my case—and this can still be the case for several months after "dropping out"—I at least wanted to do everything I could to restore this imbalance. However, this was only possible again towards the end of Phase III, and only very slowly and step by step. There were weeks when I set myself just one goal each day: to go to the gym. Everything else could wait! I was determined to retrain myself in a meaningful habit that would improve my health and resilience. At the beginning of Phase III, this was not possible at all, because my back pain kept interfering. So it was important to wait for the right moment and to find the inner balance for a new start.

It is important that you continue to give yourself time to recover in this third phase, despite noticeable improvements! Sufficient mindfulness regarding personal stability is needed. It is possible that you already feel very good on the surface and your environment hardly notices from the outside that you are still burdened by the burnout disorder. Internally, however, there can still be ups and downs that only you notice. Just as the small improvements at the beginning are only sporadically noticeable, the stumbling blocks are also only partially visible at first glance. And this can be a challenge if you expose yourself to stressful situations again too soon and too quickly.

It often happens that people recovering from burnout are confronted with strong emotions during the course of recovery, which do not necessarily have to be related to the current situation. Here, it is about perceiving and accepting what is, without judging or trying to understand the origin. Of course, it makes sense to discuss this issue with the professional you have chosen and to find a meaningful way to deal with it. In addition, it is also about accepting what is. For me, the professional explanation "that my body had triggered a hormone cocktail", which can still be present in the blood during this phase and can lead to emotional ups and downs—which cannot be logically explained—often helped me to better accept my internal limits and to allow myself to be weak. The expert knowledge and understanding of the physical processes and connections thus helped me to make some sense of the lack of knowledge and uncertainty.

For me, for example, social contact was always very challenging. Even when I was already feeling much better "on my own," because I was increasingly able to listen to myself and my body and learned to perceive myself, I lost myself all the more quickly in social contact. This drained so much energy from me in a short time that after a meeting or a small emotional disagreement or argument, I sometimes needed days to recover energetically and emotionally, and felt an even stronger urge to be alone and left in peace. I then became even more thin-skinned and sensitive. Unforeseen incidents and disagreements were particularly difficult for me and occupied my mind for days afterwards.

In this phase, it was also important not to put pressure on myself. As so often, I slipped into this pattern, wanted to achieve more, and then had to realize again that it just didn't work that way. The well-known saying "The grass doesn't grow faster if you pull on it" fit very well here. Most of the time, my body's reactions were so clearly noticeable that I had no choice but to let go of my ideas and expectations of myself. Then I would simply carry the unfulfilled wish or planned project with me in my thoughts and try to bring the positive aspects of the moment into my awareness. And suddenly, seemingly out of the blue, I was able to implement it with ease a few weeks later. It almost happened by itself, and I was able to observe my actions from a higher perspective. These moments were extremely empowering and filled me with hope. I desperately needed these small successes and glimmers of hope, because recovery kept dragging on. At the same time, this was exactly my next important learning step. Healing from a burnout disorder simply required a great deal of time and patience and could not be forced by effort, expectations, or pressure on my part. "Trying to break through the wall with your head" was definitely the wrong approach in this phase.

Restrictive patterns can be changed, even if it sometimes takes longer and setbacks occur. Wanting to achieve more than your body and mind can currently handle is often a challenge. But it is precisely here that the strength and space for new insights lie! I wish you much wisdom on your journey and the strength to keep focusing on the positive!

For Relatives, Friends, and Colleagues— Systems Thinking

Unfortunately, this phase is no less demanding for the affected person than the acute phase, because the highs and lows repeatedly lead to euphoria and overexertion. The recovery curve does not progress linearly upward, and often setbacks cannot be logically explained and are therefore also unpredictable. All those involved need a great deal of sensitivity.

In addition, this phase can trigger a lot of uncertainty for everyone involved. How will things continue? When will a return to work be possible? Will the affected person regain their original strength, stamina, joy, and vitality?

Yes and no. I see burnout as an intense phase of transformation that touches and changes a person at their core. It is essential that the affected person learns during this phase to perceive themselves better and thus to set and protect boundaries both externally and internally. Depending on one's personality structure, this is a major challenge and a longer learning process. After all, the person affected by burnout did not, live far beyond their mental and physical resources and overstep their own limits for an extended period without reason. The causes for this are manifold and run deep.

In addition, the burnout illness has probably led to the family life, circle of friends, and one's own healthy lifestyle being massively neglected and suffering for a long time. Here, depending on the person, gradual changes and a creative redesign of meaningful, new habits are needed.

Everyday life, especially at work, will continue to be a challenge in the future and can tempt one to fall back into old patterns. To ensure stability in the various areas of life, it therefore makes sense for calm to first return to the private and inner life of the affected person, and for new habits, if necessary, to be established, adjusted, and gradually stabilized. This provides security and self-confidence, which are urgently needed for the further course of recovery.

The affected person will certainly be grateful for any support. However, only if there is actually a need and if contact is made with great sensitivity. It is important not to undermine the autonomy and self-efficacy of the affected person and to respect personal boundaries. An overactive helper syndrome would be completely out of place here. Therefore, if you have doubts or feel uncertain yourself, it is sensible to name these, ask questions, and make statements from your own perspective. The affected person knows this uncertainty from their own experience. The courage to allow and address it can have a positive and connecting effect. Statements from the "I" perspective are also usually less judgmental and hurtful and can therefore be better received by the other person. If you can stay with yourself and your own feelings and express these outwardly, the other person can respond and contribute their own needs, ideas, or perspectives. This is the best foundation for an understanding exchange and for jointly finding consensus as well as cooperative and feasible solutions and intermediate steps. Incidentally, this is useful in any challenging conversation and in dialogue at eye level. It is also helpful not to put the person under (time) pressure. Being able to make decisions can sometimes be a major challenge. It helps to allow some time for reflection and, for example, to let what was heard in a conversation sink in calmly before considering what next steps, a good conclusion, continuation, or deepening might be needed. Depending on the situation, this approach may also be helpful for you and your family and may even lead to a new, positive culture of conversation and interaction.

> Perhaps this very phase is an unexpected opportunity to get to know yourself and the other person in a new way! Mastering difficult situations together, allowing each other insight into one's experiences, and adopting different perspectives without judging them can strengthen the relationship and lead to new understanding and mutual trust. I sincerely wish you much confidence and every success!

For Managers—Cooperate/Social Responsibility

In this phase, it is possible that there is repeated talk of the affected person returning to work, but the reintegration then has to be postponed again. This is probably because the affected person wishes to return but then realizes that their body or psyche is not yet ready. In addition, there is no clearly marked road or ready-made guide for the way back into working life. Here, each affected person must find their own way, and that is an achievement in itself. I had to learn that it is difficult to plan the return to work several weeks in advance. Most of the time, I could only really assess shortly beforehand how I was doing and whether I was ready for reintegration. Understandably, this was very exhausting and time-consuming for my supervisor in planning a possible replacement and, overall, led to a lot of misunderstanding and negative expectations.

Reintegration can be a real test of patience for the employer. Especially if contact with the affected person during the illness and recovery phase is sluggish or cannot be established at all. This uncertainty must be handled with understanding, because it is highly likely that the affected person is in an equally empty and unclear space. He or she probably cannot foresee how things will continue in the future, as this is part of a burnout illness.

This requires a lot of patience from you as a manager and from the team. There is little point in filling this waiting period with speculation, hypotheses, or expectations. Every recovery process from burnout is individual and not linear, and you can really only see step by step what is needed at the moment, without wanting to plan too far ahead.

Enduring this emotional and recovery rollercoaster is already very exhausting for the affected person. It is helpful if you can send hopeful signs of appreciation during this phase while still respecting boundaries. As is well known, a card with flowers says more than a thousand words. Ask beforehand if you wish to contact the affected person. Depending on which phase the person is in, contact is not always sensible or desired. Do not take this personally under any circumstances!

Ideally, human resources is already involved for case management, providing a neutral (buffer) point of contact and facilitating communication. It is possible that a clear break from the workplace is necessary for the person affected by burnout, and it may therefore be counterproductive if he or she is confronted again with the same issues and/or people from the work environment. This may sound a bit harsh, but it is important to mention at this point. This need for boundaries has nothing to do with you or the team! It is simply that the person affected by burnout already has enough to deal with themselves during the recovery phase, and the necessary mental distancing is often difficult. After all, the person is not in this situation for nothing if they have precisely these difficulties with self-perception, lack of boundaries, protection, and a strong drive to perform as personal issues. Many people affected by burnout are very committed, motivated, and performance-oriented employees. They want to do their work particularly well. This high level of commitment, combined with a strong drive to perform and perfectionism, can become an obstacle for the affected person during the recovery phase, which must be addressed individually in therapy and counseling.

Of course, it may be that such distancing is not necessary at all and the affected person even wishes to have contact with their team and you as their supervisor. As mentioned, the needs of those affected are very individual. In case of doubt, it is best to simply ask. It can also help to address your own helplessness and uncertainty directly in conversation in the presence of case management. This gives the person affected by burnout the opportunity to take your perspective. In addition, it encourages them to consider for themselves what support might be helpful and to learn to stand up for themselves. By your example, you encourage them to communicate this openly as well. This is an important step towards a successful return to work and builds trust in mutual contact. Moreover, an open, honest, and appreciative approach to one another also makes the work of case management easier, which, especially in the case of workplace conflict, does not always have an easy role in conflict resolution.

> Remember that people affected by burnout are very committed and performance-oriented. If you succeed in reclaiming this resource, your organization can benefit greatly and learn from the situation. I sincerely wish you much confidence and every success!

(Self-)Reflection—Steps Toward Self-Insight

For (Potential) Affected Individuals

When I work as a psychological counselor and coach, the overarching goal in every collaboration is to strengthen the client's autonomy [1]. In my own experience with burnout, it was precisely this autonomy that diminished more and more, without me truly realizing it, because with ongoing stress and overwhelm, I increasingly lost touch with myself. Transactional analysis offers an intriguing definition here, which goes beyond the concept of autonomy as mere independence. According to Eric Berne, autonomy comprises three factors: awareness (mindfulness of one's own experience), spontaneity (flexibility in thinking, feeling, and acting), and intimacy (capacity for relationships). Leonhard Schlegel clarifies: "According to Berne, a person is autonomous if they do not blindly adopt the values imparted by their parents, if they have freed themselves from their script, if as an 'adult person' they judge, decide, and act without distortion, and thus can freely access their ego states" [1].

These three areas—awareness, spontaneity, and intimacy—as components of autonomy in the sense of transactional analysis, can be considered both in general and especially in relation to the topics of burnout and resilience.

Awareness refers to mindfulness of one's own experience, thinking, feeling, and behavior. The more I become aware of my script-bound behavior [2], which originates in early childhood, the more I can reflect through this awareness and actively initiate change. In this way, it becomes increasingly possible to live a fulfilling life in autonomy, no longer subject to limiting rules, fears, and expectations.

Spontaneity describes flexibility in one's own experience, thinking, feeling, and behavior. The more I free myself from my own script, the more I create genuine access to the here and now. I can increasingly experience authentic feelings that relate to what I am experiencing, and I am able to enjoy time with others from within, in full awareness and presence, thus appearing authentic and free from expectations.

In the area of intimacy, I create an honest, attentive, and trusting space with people I love and who are close to me. I allow myself to engage in encounters because I can truly be with myself and do not lose myself in interactions with others. I am not afraid of relationships; instead, I experience them as valuable, enriching, and empowering.

Autonomy in this sense is not a completed process or a final state. However, in the sense of transactional analysis, steps toward autonomy [1] can increase joy in life, strengthen the relationship with oneself and others, and enrich and intensify experience by expanding one's awareness of unconscious, script-bound processes [2] and by strengthening autonomy and self-determination in various areas of life.

I have compiled some questions for your self-reflection:

Awareness

- How would you rate your current stress level? Rate it on a scale from 1–10. Describe your current situation.
- What stressors do you encounter in your daily life? Rate each stressor on a scale from 1–10. Justify your assessment!
- What exactly triggers this perceived stress? Are there perhaps recurring patterns or processes?

- How has your perception of stress changed in recent months? For example, has it become noticeably more pronounced or has it focused on a particular stressor?
- Have you already tried to minimize stress or to avoid or reduce individual stressors? If so, what approach did you take? What experiences did you have? What positive changes resulted? Where is further adjustment needed?

Spontaneity

- How would you rate your flexibility and spontaneity in experience at the moment? Rate it on a scale from 1–10.
- How flexible and spontaneous are you in your daily life? Do you struggle with last-minute changes? If so, which ones? Where and when do you find it easier to respond flexibly and spontaneously? Where do you also need routine and structured processes that provide you with security in everyday life?
- Has your ability to be flexible in your behavior noticeably changed in recent months? If so, in what way? How would you describe this change in relation to your energy reserves?

Intimacy

- How would you rate your current contact with other people? Rate the frequency on a scale from 1–10. Has the frequency noticeably changed in recent months? Has your experience regarding social contacts changed in recent months? If so, in what way?
- How satisfied are you with your social contacts at the moment? Rate it on a scale from 1–10. How does your

satisfaction manifest itself? What do you particularly appreciate about successful social contacts?

- How easy is it for you to be alone with yourself? Can you enjoy this time alone? If so, how do you shape this relationship time with yourself?
- Which social contacts do you particularly enjoy? Which friendships give you energy? Which contacts tend to drain your energy? How do you recognize this? What triggers this change in your perception regarding your current energy level?
- Do you enjoy being around people? If yes/no, please explain! Has this need noticeably changed in recent months? What reasons do you see for this?
- How comfortable do you feel in large crowds? In what setting do you prefer social contact? Why do you feel particularly comfortable in the setting you mentioned? Has your perception in this regard noticeably changed in recent months?
- How would your closest friends describe you as a friend? Might they have noticed any significant changes in your behavior or personality? If so, what changes?

Autonomy and Self-Determination

- Where and how do you already express your need for autonomy and self-determination? Describe!
- How could you possibly expand your space for autonomy and thus gain more room for self-determination? Where could you currently use more external support? Describe and justify.
- How much space for autonomy do you naturally need? In which areas is this freedom particularly important to you? Where are you currently experiencing limitations in this regard? How does that make you feel? Describe!

- Where/when do you possibly feel stressed if you cannot exercise this freedom? Where/when do you possibly feel stressed if you have too much freedom? Justify your answer!
- How much autonomy and self-determination were you granted or modeled in your childhood? Where would you have wished for more freedom? Where might more boundaries and rules have been needed? What would have changed for you as a result? How could you consciously redesign this for yourself in the here and now?
- How could you, as an adult, catch up on aspects of autonomy and self-determination, make them newly accessible to yourself, and actively shape them? How would this manifest? How could an outsider recognize that you have taken important next steps toward change in this area? What advantages and changes would result for you and/or your environment?

For Leaders—With a Focus on the Organization

The theory of autonomy can also be applied to organizations. Below you will find some questions for reflection.

- How important is the topic of autonomy and self-determination to you in your team? Rate on a scale from 1–10. How does this manifest in your thinking, feeling, and behavior?
- How does this show up in your leadership style? Where do you grant your employees particularly high or low levels of autonomy and self-determination? Justify the degree of freedom you provide in each case!
- Are there employees in your team for whom you would wish for more (or less) autonomy and personal

responsibility? How would this be reflected in their behavior? How would you recognize a change? What advantages would result from this? How could you address this proactively and appreciatively in an employee discussion?

- How could you more actively shape and promote the three areas (spontaneity, intimacy, and awareness), which are considered essential for autonomy in transactional analysis, in your daily work or organization? What changes would be needed for this? What benefits would arise?

- How would you describe the social contact within the team? How supportive would you rate it? Rate on a scale from 1–10.

- How aware is your team of the impact of team dynamics and successful, appreciative communication? Would you wish for changes in this regard? If so, which ones and why?

- Are there team members who are more on the sidelines when it comes to social contact? Are there group formations? If so, which ones? Where do you see opportunities, but also risks? What changes in group dynamics would benefit your team? Please justify! How do you think your team would answer this question? What differences would there be compared to your assessment?

- Are there team members who particularly shape social contact (positively or negatively)? Who are the individuals who significantly influence team dynamics? How does this manifest? Where do you see a need for change? Where are there opportunities or dynamics that you could perhaps leverage more deliberately?

- How would you rate the social competence in your team? Rate the quality on a scale from 1–10.

- What characterizes the social competence in your team? Which factors do you consider important? How do you recognize their impact? Where is there still potential for development? How do you actively manage this as a leader? Where might a change be needed?
- How flexible and spontaneous would you rate your team? Rate on a scale from 1–10. What advantages do you see in spontaneous behavior? When would this be beneficial in your organization? Where could a shift more toward movement and change be beneficial for you and your team?
- How would you describe the atmosphere in the team? To what extent do you see particular strengths regarding autonomy (spontaneity, intimacy, and awareness)? Has there been a noticeable change in this respect in recent months? If so, what kind? Do you have any ideas about possible reasons?

References

1. Schlegel, L. (2002). *Handwörterbuch der Transaktionsanalyse* (2nd edn., p. 15). Herder Verlag.
2. Schlegel, L. (2002). *Handwörterbuch der Transaktionsanalyse* (2nd edn., pp. 272–277). Herder Verlag.

Phase IV—The Driftwood—Being Supported and Allowing the Good

Abstract This chapter primarily addresses the process of reintegration and the potential stumbling blocks and obstacles that may arise during this phase. There are also important considerations at this stage to ensure that the next steps are successful and that a new, supportive way of interacting as a family and work team can be established effectively and beneficially. The concept of the integrating adult self offers an understanding of one's own humanity and a holistic perspective. An initial idea emerges as to how one's own (experience of) life could be made simpler and more pleasant. The integration into a more meaningful, greater whole offers new hope and confidence.

© The Author(s), under exclusive license to Springer Fachmedien
Wiesbaden GmbH, part of Springer Nature 2025
R. Petersen, *Tsunami in the Head – Better Understanding and Coping
with Burnout*, https://doi.org/10.1007/978-3-658-49737-8_5

The Driftwood

I am still very afraid. The waves rock me up and down. Sometimes I choke on them. If I weren't in this unfortunate situation, I might even be able to enjoy the rocking. But this fear, it keeps rising up inside me. It floods me from within, paralyzes me, and robs me of my last reserves of strength. What if I don't survive? What if I can't muster enough strength to keep myself afloat long enough? Then it will all be over! Then I will have certainty! Then it will be clear: I just wasn't strong enough!

But I don't want to give up! I have to find a way to survive! Maybe I can make it? Maybe I am stronger than I think? I have to have faith—in myself and in the world!

Suddenly, I see something right in front of me in the water. What is that? A piece of driftwood! What luck! With my last bit of strength, I swim toward it and cling to it. How lucky that I was able to react immediately and hold on. How lucky that I am still alive!

I love my life! I want to remain hopeful. I am still exhausted and tired. The cold has taken over my body. The danger is not yet over. But what if I somehow managed to survive this disaster?

I begin to remember the good times in my life. I begin to remember how strong I really am. Hope sprouts within me once again. I feel warmth rising up from inside, spreading everywhere. Survival is possible, even if it doesn't always feel that way. My confidence is growing. If I manage to focus myself and my thoughts on the good, then maybe more is possible than I dare to hope. I will survive! Somehow!

My Story—Developing Self-Confidence & Reclaiming (Self-)Assurance

I was slowly and noticeably getting better. I was moving through everyday life with more strength and stamina again. My body seemed to have recovered somewhat. I was able to exercise regularly again, no longer constantly needing to take breaks to shut myself off from the outside world. I could think more clearly again, was less forgetful or scattered. I still forgot appointments and struggled to keep fixed dates, but when I had to, I could successfully complete these to-dos with moderate effort. I was also able to concentrate on one thing for longer periods and proceed step by step, logically and in a planned way in my thinking. I still needed a lot of time in the morning to start the day calmly and with structure. Such rituals were important and gave me support and orientation. I was also able to work on small writing projects for my blog again, both in the mornings and in the afternoons. In between, however, I needed many breaks. In addition, I found it very difficult to accept that I was suffering from burnout. I was afraid to share this with those around me and to talk about it. I couldn't figure out what I could gain for myself from exchanging with others about the illness, and confronting the topic of burnout was very stressful for me. This was in strong contradiction to my desire to finally move forward, get healthy, and leave the topic of burnout behind me. Because once again, I had to be patient with myself and my (recovery) process. But I knew there was no way around it, and that I could learn something from all the irritations and hurdles that life presented me. Changing therapists challenged me once again to maintain my own balance and to keep securing myself. The biggest hurdles in moving forward were (self-)

doubt and uncertainty in my own thinking. I was very afraid of returning to working life, because I didn't know if I would manage to reintegrate and if I would be up to all the demands again. At some point, in all my deliberations, I realized that a return in the true sense probably wouldn't be possible. After such a long time, it would have to be a gradual new beginning. The organization had changed in the meantime due to internal changes, and I had been absent for more than half a year. First, I had to find out what the situation was like on site. That meant an initial, clarifying conversation with my boss and case management.

I had so many questions and fears. How would my colleagues react? What would my employees think? Should I come out about my burnout or would it be better to stay vague and not go into the reasons for my absence? Was that even possible? Or would that lead to awkward situations? How would my boss react? What expectations would she have of me and my return? What expectations could I have of myself and of a new beginning? What was realistic? All these questions occupied me long in advance, and I realized that I wouldn't find answers unless I was willing to embrace the unknown. But first, I had to figure out for myself what I could imagine regarding my return and what boundaries and protection I would need in this phase.

In all this uncertainty, I realized how important it was in this next phase of recovery to develop my personal resilience factors and to consciously integrate them into my daily life. I was able to do this quite well now, since I could plan and manage my day myself. But how would that be possible when I returned to working life and my calendar suddenly filled up? How could I prepare for that? Was it even possible to build this up gradually? Or would I eventually just have to take the plunge? And how could

I, in the meantime, learn to deal constructively with the fears and uncertainties that kept coming up? They were already paralyzing me again, and I realized that for a while, things would remain at the level of mental games and ruminations.

At some point, the desire to return to work grew on its own. I wanted to face the challenges on my own initiative, but I was still unsure. The closer the planned return came, the more nervous I became and the more I felt external pressure. My psychologist was undeterred by this. She kept bringing me back to myself and my own assessment, encouraging me to listen to my gut feeling. There simply was no right or wrong here! No one could tell me exactly how such a return could be successfully managed. No one could tell me what was right for me. I realized that I couldn't force the necessary insights here either. I would know when the time was right. Enduring this uncertainty was infinitely difficult for me in so many moments. Again and again, feelings of guilt and shame returned. I imagined scenarios of how I would meet my boss, my employees, or my team members for the first time. I tried to picture what it would really be like, in order to clarify for myself what protection I would need in these situations. I really had no plan! And it seemed as if no one around me could give me the answers to my questions.

Somehow, out of this not-knowing, I managed to develop a new inner strength. In the past, I had almost always drawn my clarity and orientation from expertise or the experiences of others. That was now only of limited help in my case. There simply was no guide for my recovery path and for returning to work that I could have implemented based on others' experiences. Or at least I realized that advice from outside wouldn't really help me move forward. I was thrown back on myself and had to accept that I was my own (life and recovery) expert and had to make the decisions that were right for me.

"You are stronger than you think!"—this sentence accompanied me especially during this phase. Again and again, I noticed how I suddenly became insecure and doubted myself deeply. In good moments, I felt my former strength and enthusiasm. In bad moments, my plans for a successful return were thwarted by mental horror scenarios and self-doubt. I had to somehow learn to endure this back and forth between feelings of insecurity and fear, alternating with hope and strength. There simply wasn't one right way! And there probably wasn't a perfect time for a successful return either.

Much was still unclear! I was not out of the woods yet. But the signs were good. It was now up to me again to take the next steps and to assess for myself how things should continue. The answers lay ahead of me, even if I couldn't see and grasp them all yet. I just had to look for them and take the next steps patiently and courageously. Everything else would reveal and resolve itself at the right time. That is what I had learned in recent months: to trust the moment. To trust myself! There was no point in trying to force a decision! I also realized that it didn't help to be afraid of everything and everyone. I could protect myself! I was well on my way to becoming completely healthy again! If I managed to overcome my self-doubt more and more and to stay grounded in reality in my assessments, to check things mentally and objectively, and to listen to my gut feeling instead of falling into my mental merry-go-round, then much would be possible! I was now ready to find out what was inside me and how it would feel and take shape in reality and in concrete implementation. I was finally ready to swim to shore and discover what I would find there and what was left of my previous world.

Burnout Diary—Snapshots

> "Burnout is like thick, suffocating smoke that slowly spreads over your life, imperceptibly but continuously enveloping you, eventually robbing you of breath and sight, so that at some point you fall to the ground, lonely, disoriented, and exhausted, and collapse."
>
> Rebecca Petersen

I have what feels like ten thousand doubts swirling inside me. I am already nervous again because the school holidays are approaching and my return to work is planned for after the break. Am I ready yet? What will await me? I am afraid. I am nervous because I feel like I can't prepare for it. Whatever comes, will come. I don't know if or how I will be able to handle the emotions that will arise. What will my colleagues say? What will my employees think? How will my boss react? How will those around me respond to my return?

One question in particular has been occupying my mind: how much of my illness should I make public? Is it better not to address it and to clearly distance myself from any questions about the reasons for my long absence? What makes sense for me/for the other person? What is needed for a successful new start? What do I need for a successful new start? Do I even want to go back? Can I even go back, that is, am I capable of performing at that level again? What adjustments need to be made? I simply (still) don't know. And that is wearing me down at the moment. It takes so much energy to think about all this. Energy that I don't have right now. I am getting more and more nervous, and the closer the planned date for my return comes, the more my anxiety increases.

I have a private, important appointment that stirs me emotionally and challenges me personally. For about two hours, I am focused and attentive, my senses are sharpened. I am now doing well enough that I can assume people no longer notice my burnout. That gives me confidence. The conversation goes well. I am happy. However, in the evening I find it very difficult to fall asleep. My thoughts are racing. It is a positive tension, but it still keeps me from finding rest. The next morning, I wake up at four o'clock. I am wide awake. I am sweating. My senses are sharpened. I can't fall back asleep, even though I try with the window open and fresh air. So I get up at four thirty. I read, and quickly become tired again. But my second attempt to fall asleep also fails. My parasympathetic nervous system still seems to be playing tricks on me. I assume that my cortisol release was triggered again by yesterday's tension and is now keeping me unexpectedly awake. Will this ever change? Will I ever be as capable again as I wish to be?

I'm ready. In therapy, I am now bringing up the topic of returning to work more and more often. It preoccupies me. I notice that it's time for me to face my fears. More and more, I feel my energy and motivation returning. Sometimes it even startles me, because I don't yet fully trust myself or my body. But I notice that I am increasingly tempted to push my limits again, whether emotionally or physically. It's a wonderful feeling. Still, I know that it's crucial to find a good balance here and to create a gentle transition. That will be a challenge for me. I tend to be the impatient, passionate type. And I am increasingly looking forward to what lies ahead. That's a good sign!

Now it's about planning wise and mindful next steps. I have already written a list of topics I want to discuss with my boss at our first meeting. It's a new beginning, not just a return. I have to rediscover the (work) world for myself and rebuild my confidence and trust in myself and my abilities. That will be another demanding process. But I am looking forward to it. I can do it. I feel that now.

The second visit to the company doctor is coming up. I am curious about it. The conversation is both unsettling and clarifying. I remember well how, a few months ago at the beginning of my burnout, I was doing much worse emotionally and physically. The thought of it still hurts. Even now, I have many self-doubts and a great fear of reaching my limits again and failing. At the same time, I feel that it is time to face returning to work. The company doctor suggests that, as planned, I should gradually return to work in a few weeks and then increase my workload by twenty percent each month. This way, a gradual return with enough time for adaptation should be possible. This concrete approach seems sensible and realistic. I can handle this idea much better now than I could a few months ago. If I take my time, I will manage the return! I will find answers to my questions.

Even though this phase seems very turbulent and often feels uncertain to me, I have to admit to myself that I am in a completely different place than I was a few months ago. I have reached a point where I have to—and want to—accept that the uncertainty exists only in my mind. I am ready! I feel it! I can trust my body again! I can, with a clear conscience, leave all doubts behind and simply enjoy the good feeling. I am worthy of being happy and healthy. There is no longer any obvious reason why I shouldn't succeed. I am deciding here and now to look forward with courage and not let any more doubts arise. I want to keep riding this positive, optimistic wave of thoughts. Let it carry me to shore. Feel the wind and the power of the tides, without letting them confine or unbalance me. And even if I occasionally swallow some seawater, I will eventually reach the coast. I will not allow myself to go under again. I can hold on to my driftwood. I have developed so many new resources. I have already come so far. I owe nothing to anyone. I am allowed to follow my good feelings. I am allowed to change things if they don't feel right. I am allowed to see things in a new light so that they feel better than before. I am allowed to be open to new things. I am curious about what is to come. It is worthwhile to focus on the things that are going well and those I have already achieved. From this, I will draw my strength and confidence in the future. I will no longer feel guilty. I will no longer be ashamed of my experiences, my health, or my happiness. I will no longer look for explanations to justify myself to others. I will take care of myself and my needs. I will set boundaries as needed and communicate and defend them to the outside world. I am strong! I can perceive and feel myself again. I can trust my perception and my gut feeling. I already have everything within me that I need for a happy life! Now it's time to build on that with courage and take the next steps.

Honestly, I have no idea where this confidence is coming from right now. It's a sunny Sunday and I have deliberately spent time on many beautiful things. I took time just to be, without thinking about the to-dos for next week or what I want to achieve for myself in the coming days. For once, I let go, lost myself for hours in a book, longed for a love story with a happy ending, just let myself drift and arrived directly in the moment and in happiness. I feel connected to myself, I am moving and feel my body. I breathe in the fresh air, see the colorful nature before me, am among people and can simply lose myself in the hub-bub and bustle of everyday life—that is something I am especially enjoying right now. What a wonderful day today is! And I am simply allowing myself to be happy. No negative thoughts about my burnout. Not today. Today I am letting all the good flow into my life. I am open and receptive to the good. I am leaving all doubts behind, without feeling guilty or out of place for it. This is the turning point, the most important turning point in the course of my recovery. I am gaining trust in myself and my intuition. I am myself, with my story and my past. And yet I do not let them define, limit, or negatively shape me. Anything is possible. I have a choice. And I choose victory over burnout. Here and now. As of today, the back and forth is over. I will win and emerge stronger from this battle. I feel that very clearly in this moment. I am blessed and don't even have to earn the good. I don't have to be special or achieve anything special. This strength and power lies within each of us, if only we allow it and are brave enough to seek and discover this strength and wisdom within ourselves. I don't have to save anyone! I don't have to please anyone. I am allowed to simply be myself. That is more than enough! I am infinitely grateful and look forward to what is to come!

I present exactly this statement, in short form, in my next therapy session. I am amazed. The good feeling has now lasted for days. And I have decided for myself that I will not let it be taken away from me. I can decide whether I want to allow my environment to cloud my thoughts. They are my thoughts. So I can just as well decide to give priority to the beautiful, encouraging thoughts. That is possible. Now and when I start working again. I want to make it possible. Not just in my imagination, but also in reality. I am looking forward to what is to come.

The holidays are over. Now the return to work is inevitably drawing closer. I feel uncertain. It's as if I have to jump back into a shark tank, even though I can confidently say that the social work environment is anything but a shark tank. But for me, it is still an environment that made me ill, or in which I allowed myself to become ill. Will I manage to find my footing here again? Will I manage to learn to swim again here and, as a fish in my familiar environment, enjoy life healthily and happily and follow my calling? Maybe I have particularly high expectations of my environment, that could be. But for me, my work was and is a place where I want to connect with meaningful activity. I don't want a job that doesn't make me happy and that lacks a sense of purpose.

I notice that my need for friendships is increasing again. I can laugh freely again, and the thought of working life and my incapacity and burnout are gradually receding into the background. That means they no longer overshadow my thoughts and my daily life, even though I am aware that there is still a lot to do before I can say that I have completely overcome the burnout. Small, humble steps and constant checking in with how I'm feeling are necessary. Perhaps it also requires a realistic expectation that there will be setbacks and conflicts. At the same time, I am still free, perhaps even freer than ever before, to make necessary decisions if I realize that the new environment no longer meets my expectations, needs, and wishes. And I am allowed to make mistakes. I am allowed to notice and admit along the way that I want to take a different path. Because I have changed. And that's a good thing! Life really is too short to hang up your dreams. We only have this one life. This one chance to make our dreams come true. I want to remain hopeful so that I can hold on to my dreams and convictions. I want to take care of my health to such an extent that I never again lose this hope, confidence, and strength. I never want to stray so far from myself, my confidence, and my courage again. I want to be brave enough for necessary decisions and actions, especially when I realize that a change is needed. Especially when I don't yet have a concrete plan and it's not yet clear to me what the alternative should look like. Critics would say that I am a dreamer. Now I know that it is precisely

this that keeps me alive and has, in the past, kept me alive
in incredible ways. Sometimes hope is the only thing that
gives you support. And even if it doesn't always feel like
it, it is more than enough for positive changes to happen.
I now have this certainty. I hold on to it, no matter what
comes.

I now have the energy again to contact case management and discuss my return to work. Just a few weeks ago,
that would not have been possible at all, because I would
have felt immediately overwhelmed. Now I can deal better
with the uncertainty and the idea of simply taking it step
by step to see how it goes. However, I am a bit perplexed
when I hear that the case manager suggests I start with a
therapeutic work trial. What am I supposed to do on site
if I don't really have a goal or a concrete task? At first,
the idea of "just being" in the work context seems pretty
pointless to me. But I am glad for this professional assessment and can well understand the considerations and reasons behind the case manager's suggestion. This seems to
be a helpful support to avoid any pressure on me and my
employer. I myself tend to want to start directly with difficult things like a professional meeting, because on the one
hand I feel much better and the euphoria of "being able to
perform again" drives me, and on the other hand, because
I want to test myself and see how far I can go before I
reach my limits. That is probably a really unfavorable strategy, and I am becoming more and more comfortable with
the idea of doing a therapeutic work trial. In addition,
our organization is currently implementing a long-standing change process, which will bring some changes for me
and my professional future. I could now react anxiously
or uncertainly. But I want to remain flexible, open, and
curious, because I believe that only with this attitude will
a successful return to work be possible. That is what I am
holding on to unwaveringly at the moment.

For several weeks now, I have actually been sleeping much better again. Still with the help of valerian and calming tea, but I only wake up once a night and most mornings I can sleep until about seven o'clock. That is an incredible improvement, and I never thought it would be possible again. After all, it's now been a full eight months since I stopped working. Apparently, my body really needed this time to recover.

I have started breath therapy. Here, the focus is more on experiencing than on understanding. Or at least that's how I experience it. Personally, I find it very challenging. My back reacts with pain. I am agitated and more restless than usual. I dream a lot and sleep rather restlessly. On the other hand, I am glad that I am even willing to expose myself to this form of therapy. I wouldn't have had this strength a few months ago. It seems as if I am now ready for the next steps in development and experience. That is, in itself, something positive.

The upcoming return to my workplace stirs up old memories and feelings. I am trying to figure out what I really want. I am trying to distinguish between what my head wants and what is truly good for me. I have great respect for returning to working life. At the moment, I am still in a protected space. What will it be like when I gradually return and increase my workload? Will I lose myself in the work and its demands? What will it be like to see people from my work environment again and know that they are wondering why I was unable to work for so long? How will I react to that? What will it be like to see my boss and my team again? These questions overwhelm me, and I avoid thinking about them whenever possible. The emptiness that spreads within me as a result is paralyzing. And yet, I am inevitably approaching the unavoidable.

Fortunately, the conversation with my boss and case management goes well. I am very grateful that I have the chance to return to my previous team. Working with these people motivates me greatly, and I am now looking forward to seeing the students and my colleagues again. I am feeling so much better than just a few months ago. To feel this improvement and the anticipation of returning to work is overwhelming. I am infinitely grateful and, at the moment, don't even want to think about the fact that there is still a way to go before I am fully recovered.

I haven't even started working again yet, and my thoughts are already constantly on the school, my team, and my upcoming tasks. I remember what special to-dos came up in the current quarter and what particular challenges there were. It's not that these thoughts stress me out or that I'm afraid of returning to work. I am still very much looking forward to it. But it is sobering how quickly the mind starts running in old patterns again. I have already found it harder to fall asleep than before. Accordingly, I am a bit tense and glad that I can start very slowly with a therapeutic work trial. Now I understand what my case manager meant by the reference to pressure. It's not just the external pressure, but also very quickly the internal pressure to want to be part of a system and to perform well.

Wanting to perform was also a topic at the last self-help group meeting. We all agreed—and that is actually rather rare for the individual manifestation of a burnout disorder—that we have the tendency to want to optimize everything and every step. That definitely applies to me! I enjoy it when everything in my life goes according to plan and fits together in terms of timing. I like to optimize, even when it comes to small, inconspicuous things. I am actually quite good at planning next steps and implementing them sensibly. I have learned to deal with open sequences, but they are not in my nature, and I prefer things to be organized and under control. As I have learned especially through the burnout, that is not always possible in life, and not always sensible, even though this resource has taken me far in my professional life. This is probably the next learning step in my professional reintegration process—letting go and, in the process, seeing from day to day and step by step what comes next and what makes sense for me and my health.

The first hurdles have been overcome. I got through the meeting with case management and my boss well. I am very moved because, during the conversation, I felt joy again, especially regarding my team and the people I have worked with. I did not expect these strong emotions. Accordingly, I go home feeling buoyant but also emotionally touched. I am happy! I want to work again. I want to go back. I am glad that I can start within the framework of a work trial. That prevents me from coming under pressure again too quickly. I notice that this also brings relief to my work environment and my boss. That seems important at the moment, because no one can really predict how things will turn out. The work trial currently gives me enough freedom to allow everything that is emerging right now. Unconditionally and without judgment. I see this as a great opportunity. I am grateful that this is possible and that I am receiving the necessary support for a successful return to work.

The second hurdle has been cleared. For the first time in a long while, I am going back to my office and meeting my deputy there. I have prepared myself mentally, tried to imagine things, to set myself up emotionally, and to think through possible scenarios. I have already found my office keychain, written my first email, and taken out my work documents. From the outside, these may seem like small things, but to me, they mean the world—even if they are just small, important steps in the right direction. I want to continue to be mindful and pay attention to how these small steps feel. I neglected this before and during my burnout. For me, this is the first step toward recovery and reintegration. Mindfulness—for myself and my needs.

Today is my first half-day at work where I am alone in my office and able to get some initial tasks done. For now, it's about arriving and getting a feel for things. My plan is to be in the office about twice a week for a half-day, when my deputy is out. That's all I can manage at the moment—there are too many impressions to process. At first, I find it hard to even get into the work mindset. I am very aware of my surroundings, my office. Many memories come flooding back. Even just logging into the computer fails and causes stress. But then I collect myself and try to do everything in small steps and not put pressure on myself. And it works! I make my first phone calls, and together with the IT specialist, after several hours, all systems and logins are working perfectly again. It's amazing how much can change in just a few months. I write my first emails to my staff and professional colleagues. My pulse races when I click the send button, but after a while, I feel calm and confident. Soon, the first replies come back with good wishes. So nice! That gives me even more hope. I am on the right path. I will make it!

I feel hopeful. The past few weeks have been busier than usual. I have maintained more social contacts, and work appointments have increased again: conversations with case management, with my boss, etc. I am amazed at how well I am handling everything at the moment. Sometimes it feels like a balancing act. At the same time, I keep trying to focus on the small successes and not let myself get unsettled. For now, I am still managing that well.

The first week of the therapeutic work trial. The main goal is for me to emotionally and mentally "find my way back" and to be open to any feelings and thoughts that arise. According to my therapist, I should follow the good feelings, and the case manager also encourages me to do everything I am good at and that brings me joy. I am actually managing that quite well. I really enjoy the small things, like being able to open the door to my office for my boss and having our first conversation together. Or noticing, as I read through emails, that I am looking forward to work again, and especially to my team.

A first major hurdle is informing everyone by email that I am back and doing well so far. My heart beats noticeably faster. I am excited and very moved emotionally. Even now, as I write these lines. The burnout has truly left many marks on my heart and in my memory. But not only bad ones, because the difference compared to how I feel now is huge. And I remember so well all the small, uncertain steps in between.

Another bright spot is the reactions from my team and the many people who respond to my reaching out and wish me well. That touches my heart directly and thoroughly. Have I become an "emotional softie" during my burnout, or was I always like this? I don't know. But it's okay the way it is. I want to allow and appreciate the small joys and the growing hope. That is still all I have at the moment.

The therapeutic work trial is truly a blessing. I did not expect that. It gives me the opportunity to get back into work at my own pace and prevents me from putting too much pressure on myself. That is important, I can feel it. I am making steady, small progress. This week, I am going to our headquarters. I meet a colleague and learn to deal with the possibility that someone might "unexpectedly" ask me about how I am doing. But, fortunately, the person does not bring it up. I sense that I am stronger and emotionally better able to set boundaries than I was a few months ago. I can set boundaries when necessary. I have consciously prepared myself mentally for this scenario. I can do this! I can make it!

It's school holidays. I'm glad about that. Once again, some peace and time for self-reflection and contemplation. After the holidays, I will return with a twenty percent workload. The work trial has gone well so far. The four weeks have passed quickly. Time flies anyway. Even though I am not yet back on the hamster wheel. Honestly, I never want to go back there! Or at least not in a way that leaves me gasping for air and unable to properly perceive myself, my body, or my surroundings. I notice that I want to work again! I finally want to move forward! I am ready! My inner desire to "make a meaningful impact in the world" is coming back. That is also new! I am excited!

Figuratively Speaking—Struggle with Oneself

4 The driftwood - fighting with itself

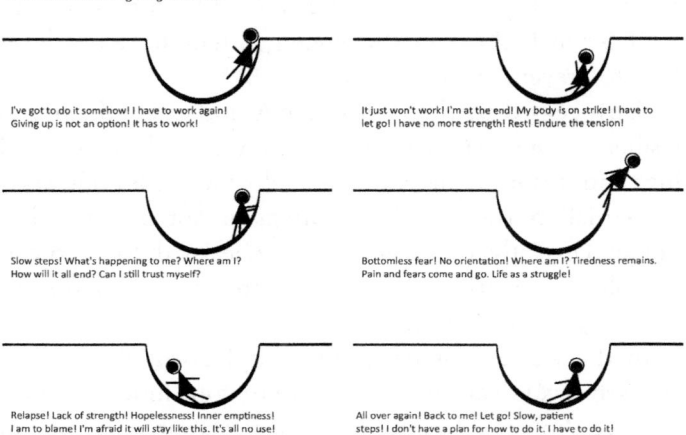

I've got to do it somehow! I have to work again! Giving up is not an option! It has to work!

It just won't work! I'm at the end! My body is on strike! I have to let go! I have no more strength! Rest! Endure the tension!

Slow steps! What's happening to me? Where am I? How will it all end? Can I still trust myself?

Bottomless fear! No orientation! Where am I? Tiredness remains. Pain and fears come and go. Life as a struggle!

Relapse! Lack of strength! Hopelessness! Inner emptiness! I am to blame! I'm afraid it will stay like this. It's all no use!

All over again! Back to me! Let go! Slow, patient steps! I don't have a plan for how to do it. I have to do it!

For (Potential) Affected Individuals—Learning Self-Reflection and Resilience

Especially with regard to a successful return to work, many questions arise about implementation and design. The fact is that there are indeed promising and diverse paths back into the working world, but these can and must be tailored individually. After all, every affected person is different and brings their own unique needs. The employer's options for implementation are also sometimes limited.

The goal is to revive existing resilience factors (see Background/Resilience) or, if necessary, to discover and develop new ones. These should become a fixed part of everyday life. It is about conscious awareness. It requires a mindful approach to oneself, one's own needs, and one's physical and emotional boundaries. Additionally, it is about reintegrating activities into daily life that are beneficial and energizing. These resilience factors can vary from person to person. It is important to secure and anchor them in both private and professional life so that they are available as lifelines in challenging situations and, ideally, help to prevent an acute crisis.

With regard to the development and strengthening of resilience, the signals from the body as well as gut feelings and intuition are good and valuable guides. However, (potential) burnout sufferers often do not perceive these signals correctly or at all, or have learned to ignore or completely override them. This presents an additional challenge when returning to work.

In this sense, it is important—and essential for recovery—that you learn to listen more to your inner voice and practice holistic awareness. Holistic awareness encompasses not only thinking, but also feeling and acting. There are three levels, often described as head, heart, and hand. I would add a fourth level—the level of spirituality. This is where hope and confidence arise. For we humans are, by nature, social beings. In this context, we are always part of a system (family/team/organization) and, in this sense, part of a greater whole (universe). In connecting with ourselves and being aware of our connection to others and the greater whole, we gain strength and power, allowing us to stay focused and make meaningful decisions.

Although my training as a psychological counselor had already taught me to incorporate my intuition and bodily awareness into my actions and decisions at work, during the recovery phase it was once again a challenge to continually make space for myself and my needs, to be consciously aware, and to remain true to myself.

The situation was also challenging in that it continued to require a great deal of patience. Just because you have discovered certain resilience factors for yourself does not mean that you can immediately apply and maintain them in the workplace context. It is a challenge to plan and gradually rebuild the bridge between the "protected space of sick leave" and the "performance-oriented work environment" back into working life. It still requires small steps, which, depending on the situation, can once again trigger fears, uncertainties, and relapses into old patterns. Thus, the path back to work is paved with many intense emotions and uncertainties, for which one can only prepare to a limited extent. Accordingly, it is advisable to continue to be accompanied by a therapist, coach, or counselor. In my case, I was fortunate that case management was also available as support. I am still very grateful for that to this day!

In addition to all the personal challenges, there may also be external changes that can cause further insecurity. For example, you may be sent repeatedly to the company doctor or case management may suggest that you be preemptively registered with the disability insurance (Note: in Switzerland, the state insurance responsible for permanent work limitations or incapacity). This is common practice and a sensible precaution, but it says nothing about your current status or the success of your recovery. This is also often the point at which the health insurance (Note: in Switzerland, health and daily sickness benefit insurance) reduces its benefits. This means that, depending on your employer, after a certain period you will only receive a certain percentage of your salary. Depending on your personal situation, this can have a direct impact on your sense of protection and security. Such changes can once again trigger pressure, a strong need for security, and/ or possibly existential fears. Depending on the case, this may lead to new topics for therapeutic work, such as a career or job change, or other personal development issues.

I wish you strength and perseverance for all that may still come. Give yourself enough time to process the impressions and emotions that arise and to work through what has passed! The time you invest will be worth it, because only in this way can your body and soul regain new energy and clarity.

For Relatives, Friends, and Colleagues—Systems Thinking

Together with the person affected by burnout, you are now entering the "hot" phase. This phase is characterized by hope and optimism. The strength of the affected person steadily increases, and noticeable improvements become visible. Nevertheless, the road ahead is still long, uncertain, and rocky. At the same time, I would also like to give you hope. As a family or team, you have probably over-come the "worst" part.

The focus now is on enabling the person affected by burnout to discover and secure resilience factors (see Background/Resilience) in everyday life. It is important to develop meaningful habits and to integrate strength-ening, stabilizing elements into daily routines and a struc-tured day. As a family, this is certainly not easy, as many different needs come together. It is neither necessary nor possible for the entire family routine to be shaped and defined by the needs of the affected person. However, it does make sense to consider together which things can be implemented and integrated with little effort. Often, after joint reflection, a few small things can have a big impact on experience, because they provide security and conti-nuity throughout the day. Even just small, regular breaks for self-reflection on what has been experienced can help to stay on a good "course." And if the affected person can already practice this at home, it will be easier for them to manage in everyday work life and the transition will be smoother.

In addition, as a family you can also benefit and con-sciously bring the topics of resilience, health, and individ-ual well-being into focus. This not only strengthens each person's self-awareness, personal responsibility, and capac-ity for reflection, but also your ability to function together as a team, to support each other, and to be consciously aware of one another. This can also be an important learning opportunity for children (perceiving, allowing, openly addressing, and learning to deal constructively with boundaries, feelings, and needs, etc.), and it can strengthen your family's cohesion and well-being.

Patience and healthy boundaries are still needed. Even now, setbacks can occur. Recovery is not a straight line that always points upward. There will be bad days, but these will most likely become increasingly rare. It remains important that the person affected by burnout receives assurance of your support during this time, but it is still their task and responsibility to find the path that suits them. Unfortunately, there is no universal recipe that always works for everyone. Small steps, patience, and sufficient time for self-reflection and the repeated awareness of one's own feelings are important and effective in the long term. The focus should be on recovery, and the needs of the employer should be considered secondary for as long as possible, even if this becomes increasingly difficult as health and energy return.

If not already implemented, I strongly recommend case management, which can provide additional support during reintegration or, if necessary, accompany a job change.

As friends, you can now hope for more contact and interaction again and also be optimistic about recovery. There is light at the end of the tunnel. Although the situation is still fragile, improvements will now become increasingly visible to you.

It remains important that you respect the boundaries of the affected person and trust that they know what is good for them. Setting boundaries and at the same time being able to accept help is something that can and should still be practiced in this phase. It helps if you offer support, exchange, or meetings with clear boundaries, but leave the decision to the other person. In doing so, you have already done everything necessary for successful recovery.

Good conversations and spending time together will probably occur more frequently again now. Perhaps you can use the framework of a good friendship to reflect together and compare different perceptions. An honest exchange can bring friends closer together and strengthen mutual trust. But perhaps it is also appropriate and fitting to simply spend carefree time together, to laugh heartily again, or to do something nice for yourselves. It may therefore make sense to ask the affected person again and to appreciate an honest answer.

> I wish you strength and perseverance for whatever may still come. There is light at the end of the tunnel! Hang in there, remain present, and focus on what is going well! Use your environment as a strengthening resource!

For Managers—Cooperate/Social Responsibility

In this phase, it is possible that there are repeated discussions about the affected person returning to work, but the actual reintegration is then postponed. I mention this again because I want to highlight how lengthy and uncertain the path back to work can be after a burnout episode.

This is usually the point at which health insurance reduces its benefits and the salary of the affected person is cut to a certain percentage after a set period. Further assessments by the company doctor may now be required to determine what the next steps in reintegration could look like. Depending on the situation, a precautionary application may be made to the disability insurance (IV) (Note: In Switzerland, this is the state insurance responsible for permanent work limitations or incapacity). Depending on the individual's personal situation, this can influence their sense of trust and protection, and may trigger an increased need for security, uncertainty, pressure, or even existential fears.

Returning to work after the acute phase of illness is another challenge that is part of the recovery process for those affected by burnout. Even if the person is noticeably better in their private life, the work environment can still trigger negative memories, fears, insecurities, pressure, and old (thought, feeling, and behavior) patterns. The affected person is therefore challenged to reclaim their health, strength, and energy in the work context, to find effective resources and anchors, and to integrate them into their daily work life. For this, your support as a manager is needed— your understanding, your trust in the person and their abilities. Expressing appreciation and support makes a decisive difference for the affected person. At the same time, these steps may require a lot of strength and patience from you during the process.

Many questions remain open, and a gradual, mutual approach is needed. What can be taken on again, and within what scope? What will the initial workload be? Which tasks and activities make sense at the beginning? How will the team be informed? How much protection is needed at the start? What do you as an employer or manager need in order to regain trust in your employee and their abilities? If there is no case management: Who will accompany the reintegration, and on whose behalf? What stumbling blocks could arise? How can these be avoided? What if new difficulties or a relapse occur? How can such a relapse, if possible, be prevented?

These and other questions are likely to arise for the person affected by burnout as well, leading to uncertainty and fear. If you as an employer or manager succeed in remaining calm during this phase of reintegration and providing as much support, security, trust, appreciation, and confidence as possible, you will have already achieved a great deal.

Ultimately, at a certain point, it simply takes some courage and trust from both sides, and a clear willingness to stay on the path together, remain in contact, and focus on the shared goal of successful reintegration into working life. It will be worth it, as people affected by burnout are usually very loyal, committed, and highly motivated individuals.

In addition, this can be an opportunity to address the topics of resilience, health, and well-being within the team or at the workplace, and to derive preventive measures from this, for example as part of a team development process.

For a team, this is an enrichment, as the reintegration of someone affected by burnout enhances mutual awareness and mindfulness, and can even bring the team closer together. Accepting personal boundaries while remaining close, maintaining social contacts, building trust and experiencing appreciation among each other, fostering mutual mindfulness and conscious awareness regarding resilience and health, establishing goal-oriented and appreciative communication—all of this can be a very sustainable, enriching, and resourceful development in getting to know each other and developing a new team culture and collaboration.

Take advantage of this opportunity and start thinking now about what a new approach to health management could look like in your company and what next steps are needed. If the affected person is open to it, consider involving them in this process as well.

I wish you strength and perseverance for everything that may still come. Openness, impartiality, and mutual appreciation provide a good foundation for new encounters. A fresh start is needed, as after a burnout, things are often no longer as they were before. It also takes time to rebuild mutual trust! Take this time and, if possible, focus on what is working and the resources that are available!

(Self-) Reflection—Steps Toward Self-Insight

For (Potential) Affected Individuals

When under stress, we often find it difficult to maintain an overarching perspective and to look at a problem, situation, or question with sufficient distance. We then feel so driven and pressured by the existing to-dos that we hardly have time to catch our breath or think clearly.

However, once the acute phase of burnout has passed, it becomes possible to think more clearly again and to view one's own actions, thoughts, feelings, and decisions from a healthier distance, to reflect on them in a well-defined way, and to make decisions. Nevertheless, everyday life remains a challenge, as the ups and downs of success and apparent setbacks, of good and bad days, emotional fluctuations between hope, confidence, great joy, and a lack of perspective, as well as a lack of motivation, are not yet overcome. In a certain sense, these ups and downs are simply part of life, aren't they?

Now is the opportunity to find out for yourself what keeps you afloat and increases the likelihood that you will remain strong and regain an overarching perspective, so you can keep your goal in sight and stay focused on it. Now is the time to set various anchors that repeatedly prompt you to pause and enjoy the rocking of the waves and simply being.

Here, I am deliberately addressing the (re-)discovery of your resilience factors (see Background/Resilience). The focus is on existing resources, strengths, and competencies, as well as the search for things that bring you joy "just because," that do you good, that help you catch your breath, and that appeal to different senses and needs.

These so-called anchors can be integrated into everyday life with little (time) effort and support you in staying healthy and resilient. Resilience factors are important in both professional and private life. They concern your own person and personality, but they can also be present in the system (family, team, organization) and be consciously activated from the outside and integrated into everyday life.

In challenging situations, these anchors are often no longer visible, so it can be helpful to confide in a good friend or family member and ask them to be mindful as well. However, it is very important that, as time goes on, each affected person is able to take on this responsibility themselves again.

In transactional analysis, this is referred to as the integrating Adult Ego State [1]. In the integrating Adult Ego State, the person is able to integrate all three structural components into the present. This refers both to the Child Ego State, with impressions, memories, and experiences from the past, and to the Parent Ego State, with memories, experiences, and influences from parents and other authority figures. The aim is to meaningfully incorporate these components into one's own experience, thinking, feeling, actions, and decisions, and thus to enjoy life in the here and now in a strengthened, conscious, and autonomous way and to be successful. In transactional analysis, reference is made here to the structural model. This model helps to make unconscious processes and structural components visible.

The integrating Adult Ego State model [1] describes how intuition can be integrated into one's own experience, thinking, feeling, and actions. In the second-order structural model, intuition [2] is assigned to the so-called "little professor" in the Child Ego State. This childlike part is particularly creative and helps to develop meaningful perspectives, viewpoints, and solutions. The more we succeed in consciously perceiving this "little professor" within us and integrating it into our perception, feelings, and daily life, the healthier and stronger we can stand in life and face emerging challenges.

Eric Berne defines intuition, in my view, very aptly: "Intuition is knowledge based on experience and acquired through direct contact with what is perceived, without the intuitive perceiver being able to explain exactly to themselves or others how they arrived at the conclusion" [3]. My experience has shown that the perception of intuition can be relearned and becomes stronger with every positive experience, as the person gains renewed trust in themselves and their own intuitive abilities.

From my perspective, intuition is an important factor when it comes to developing resilience factors (see Background/Resilience) and finding the individual path to recovery. The focus here is on your individual perception and evaluation of activities, views, places, images, etc. You know best what is good for you and what may trigger stress and pressure! You set the necessary boundaries. You determine what is good for you and what helps you move forward. So, embark on this journey of discovery and try out new things! Get in touch with your childlike, original needs that may have been neglected in the past, and be a loving, caring, and mindful parent to yourself!

The following questions can help you discover resilience factors and your own intuition regarding wishes and child-like needs:

- What gives you the opportunity in your professional life to regain a more overarching, distanced perspective and attitude?
- Which needs are neglected in your everyday life, especially when you are under stress?

- How can you proactively meet these needs and take preventive care of yourself, your well-being, and your health?
- When do you feel particularly close to your intuition?
- In which moments does your gut feeling tell you that something is not right?
- Where would you, if you were honest with yourself, need to look courageously and make a change?
- How can you regularly activate and establish this contact with your inner wisdom and balance in everyday life?
- Which activities (private and professional) help you get closer to your inner wisdom, needs, and wishes?
- Which Parent Ego State components (beliefs, assumptions, values, images, rules, etc.) still limit you today and prevent you from living your full potential?

For Leaders—With a Focus on the Organization

As a leader, it is important not only to rely on intellect, experience, and professional expertise, but also to listen to your inner gut feeling and thus consciously incorporate intuition into your own (professional and private) actions, experiences, thoughts, and decisions. It is also possible to stimulate, foster, and train this strength, power, and wisdom among employees. This not only activates the autonomy, strength, power, and resilience of the individual, but also strengthens the entire organization and the way the team interacts, focusing on the positive, the successful, and the hidden. Awareness of the different parts of the self and their integration supports self-efficacy and inner balance. Awareness of one's own intuitive abilities, in turn, enables and promotes an appreciative, nurturing, and mindful work atmosphere.

The following questions will help guide your organization closer to the topic of intuition

- How, and how consciously, does your organization use the intuitive abilities of the team or individuals in your daily work?
- How could this intuitive knowledge be utilized even better so that every employee can realize their full potential?
- Which employees already have a noticeable awareness of their own intuition and could serve as good examples for shared exchange?
- When do you, as a leader, use your intuition in your work?
- Where could you bring your intuition to bear even more strongly? In what ways would this change the process and collaboration?
- Which activities or environments inspire you and bring you closer to your intuition?
- How could you make reminders of your intuitive abilities more present in your office and daily work life (pictures, music, desktop, scents, etc.), so that access to and awareness of these resources are strengthened and recalled more often?
- In which situations do you feel restricted or trapped in old patterns? When do you react (internally or outwardly) less confidently than you would like? What would your "little professor" from your child-self whisper in your ear about this?
- Which needs are often neglected in your daily life? What first steps could you take to get closer to meeting them and thus sustainably strengthen your resilience?

References

1. Schlegel, L. (2011). *Die Transaktionale Analyse* (pp. 127–128). Deutschschweizer Gesellschaft für Transaktionsanalyse.
2. Cornell, W. F., De Graaf, A., Newton, T., & Thunnissen, M. (2016). *Into TA—A comprehensive textbook on transactional analysis* (p. 13). Karnac Books Ltd.
3. Berne, E. (2005). *Transaktionsanalyse der Intuition* (vol. 4, p. 36). Junfermann Verlag.

Phase V—The House on the Coast—Gaining Perspective and Security

Abstract The path out of burnout is a lengthy one. Even as work capacity gradually and steadily increases, this does not mean that everything is simply back to normal and running smoothly for those affected. This transitional phase on the way back to everyday life is demanding, and it is important here, too, to approach it consciously and mindfully, allowing oneself to try new paths and gather new, empowering experiences. This process involves new decisions, new encounters, and new insights, which also include the social environment. The concept of basic positions is explained simply and clearly, illustrating how people can interact with others as equals without losing sight of themselves. The concept of permissions offers a helpful approach, providing tools and pathways for self-awareness and new possibilities.

The House on the Coast

I made it. I am safe. I saved myself. No one knows how I managed it. Not even I do. The memories are blurry. The feeling remains. I wrap my arms around my shoulders and snuggle into the soft blanket that gently envelops me. I am grateful. For my life. For the chance to start over again. But first, I need to find peace. To come to terms with the new situation. To realize that I am safe. Even now, I sometimes wake up at night. Drenched in sweat. The dream is always the same. I am swimming in the sea. Surrounded by water. No land in sight. A storm is brewing. I have lost my bearings. My strength is fading. How good that it was only a dream. I want to let it go. Forget it forever. I breathe in the fresh sea air. I gaze out over the vastness and the sea. The house on the coast, which offers me a new home. Here, another tidal wave cannot reach me. Here, I am far from the water, which could carry me far out with the current. Here, I am safe. Finally. Just me and the sea in the distance. I am coming back to myself. I am regaining trust in the world and in myself. I am gathering new strength for whatever the future may bring. I am a new person. I will reinvent myself. But first, I need to rest. To regain perspective. To find orientation. To draw security and confidence. The house on the coast is the ideal refuge for this. No one will find me here. Here, I find peace to process and make sense of what I have experienced. Gratitude spreads within me. A pleasant warmth floods my body. I am safe.

My Story—Regaining Trust in Myself and the Ground Beneath My Feet

More and more often, I found myself thinking about ending my participation in the self-help group. Although I was not yet one hundred percent sure that I was over the hill, and there was a certain fear of having to endure further setbacks, I found it increasingly exhausting to keep dealing with my story and my motives, because I wanted more and more to look ahead and focus on what was going well. The framework of individual therapy provided me with enough space for self-reflection and support. I felt that it was time for me to go my own way and detach myself from the self-help group, even though most of the other participants handled it differently for themselves.

So I was ready to return and face my boss. However, the conversation at case management was tough. My boss complained that she had heard very little about how I was doing during the process. I tried to explain to her that it was not out of ill will, but simply because I was overwhelmed and couldn't do otherwise. For me, it was clear that I wanted to return to my team and, together with my deputy, work out a meaningful reintegration with a possible division of tasks. My boss was not pleased about this, but she showed herself open to looking for solutions. So I went home feeling fairly optimistic and decided that, as difficult and upsetting as this first contact with my boss had been for me, I wanted to count it as a success. I managed to clearly express in the conversation how I envisioned my return. The idea of a therapeutic work trial still did not motivate me, but I probably had no other choice. We then arranged a three-way meeting, where I would meet my current deputy. I did not want direct contact with my team just yet. I did not feel ready for that.

Contrary to my expectations, at the next meeting with case management, my boss confronted me with the fact that she would not approve or support a return as I had envisioned it. My world fell apart. I was so looking forward to returning to my team that I had no idea how on earth I was supposed to motivate myself otherwise, if, as my boss planned, I was only to take on individual areas of knowledge management. Here, I would have to completely retrain, take on unfamiliar tasks, and be in constant contact and exchange with my boss. But I wanted to return to my old office, to work independently and autonomously on my original tasks and duties. Here, two different ideas collided, and at first, I truly did not know how to deal with it. My boss's reaction deeply unsettled me. It was challenging that my wishes and needs apparently carried no weight and that my boss alone had decided what my return would look like. My case manager had not been prepared for this either. As so often, with my own expectation of myself to react as openly and unprejudiced as possible, I took the idea with me and tried to sort out my thoughts in peace. Over time, I realized that I had no other choice. I was dependent on my boss in this situation, and the last thing I wanted was to get into an open workplace conflict. I wanted to return to my original position, I wanted to return to my team. By the next school year at the latest, if my recovery and reintegration were successful, I would be entitled to my original position. My boss offered me this as an alternative. At least this prospect gave me a longer-term perspective. Until then, I would have to adapt to the circumstances on site, whether I liked it or not.

After another consultation with the company doctor, it was clear what my return would look like. After an initial phase in the therapeutic work trial, the gradual reintegration would follow, first at twenty percent, then forty percent, and so on. The workload was to be increased monthly, which would give me enough time to slowly get used to the demands. In the therapeutic work trial, you are still officially on full sick leave and start with simple tasks, so that the pressure to perform and time pressure can be kept as low as possible. This gives you the chance to get a sense of the situation on site and to mentally and emotionally settle back in. This way, both you and the employer have the opportunity to rebuild mutual trust, without running the risk that the situation on site will get completely out of hand if the return is scheduled too early, and of course also to avoid a possible relapse of the affected person. In my case, case management really made an important contribution to the reintegration process. Having an outside perspective, a neutral discussion partner, helped me a lot in some situations. The tensions, misunderstandings, and differing ideas between my boss and me were certainly not always easy for my case manager to endure. But it was precisely here that she was able to make an important contribution to understanding in her neutral mediating role.

The return proved more difficult than expected. But not because I lacked energy or because I was not mentally or emotionally stable enough. I struggled to find motivation for my work again. I no longer had a leadership role and was therefore only challenged to a limited extent. As a result, I found the content and tasks my boss assigned me interesting, but it was something completely different from my previous duties in a leadership role. Suddenly, I hardly had any contact with people, which was very difficult for me at first! And somehow, with these changes, I seemed to have lost my sense of purpose. I couldn't really explain it to myself. So, as before, I tried to focus on what was going well, the small successes, and my resources. I still had plenty to deal with myself outside of work.

I attended therapy sessions weekly, which helped me make sense of things. It was still the case that I was dealing with both physical symptoms such as severe exhaustion, sleep disturbances, back and headaches, as well as feelings of shame, guilt, fear, and strong self-doubt. It wasn't that I couldn't handle the tasks and topics at work, but that I was still overthinking everything and letting my own thoughts, my physical symptoms, and my experience of weakness and personal limits throw me off track, which made me strongly doubt myself and my abilities. The therapeutic work trial challenged me on many levels, both with myself and my situation. The goal was for me to be able to settle back into my office. But only when my deputy was not present. That was important to me! Regular contact and working together in the office would have overwhelmed me at first. Fortunately, I was also able to alternate working from home.

The gradual return to work with the new role was really very bumpy and was a real feat of strength for me. At the beginning, I still made some mistakes at work, which were directly related to this feeling of insecurity and inadequacy. I was determined to make a good impression and put myself under a lot of pressure. Yet my tasks and work were really not demanding. But even just the daily routine and finding my way around with more to-dos was a completely new challenge for me. In addition, I had the impression that everyone in the company, not just my boss, was paying close attention to how my return was going and how I was doing. I felt like I was constantly being watched, which in all likelihood did not correspond to reality. However, my perception showed very clearly how much I still had to deal with myself and how much my world still revolved around me and my own experience. I put an enormous amount of pressure on myself. I remember that my first contact with my team colleagues took place at an online event. I was so nervous and at the same time very happy to be back. The high level of nervousness and my still rather isolated and self-focused lifestyle led to me sitting in front of the computer a day too early, that is, on a Sunday at eight o'clock, trying to log in. Because of all the nervousness and insecurity, I had mixed up the day of the week. I was really very embarrassed and as a result doubted my abilities and skills even more.

The new department I had to take over was structured around various projects, for which I could organize my own time and work from home as needed. Since I no longer had my own office, this suited me very well. Also because I still had to manage my energy meticulously throughout the day and was glad to be able to take breaks again and again. Due to the new tasks and projects, I was not able to build on previous experiences from my work as a school principal as planned. Although I enjoyed working on different projects, the difficulty now lay in rebuilding trust in myself and my abilities. I had no comparison to how things were before my burnout. On the other hand, I noticed that the gradual re-entry was really good for me and that I was already accomplishing quite a bit, but also reaching my limits. Even just a thirty percent workload pushed me to my limits at that time. I had trouble structuring my daily routine and getting used to the new weekly schedule. I became more restless inside and, depending on the situation, found it difficult to concentrate. On the other hand, interactions and encounters with people went very well. These no longer tired me out as much as they did during the acute phase of the illness. That was already a big step forward, which made me personally very happy.

I was still in regular contact with my case manager and had recurring meetings with her and my boss. These meetings were always very exhausting for me. My boss did not have the same perception as I did and often confronted me with criticism. Among other things, she said that I was asking too many questions during the process. It took some time before I was able to distance myself enough from her perspective and evaluation to confront her and ask for concrete examples. I had expected her to notice my positive changes and small progress. That was not the case, which initially threw me off balance. In discussing this with my therapist, I realized that this was understandable to a certain extent, because my boss only had the comparison from before my burnout. She had not witnessed all the hurdles and progress in between. Another step in my development was that I began to receive her comments openly, examine them mindfully, and compare them with my own perspective. In this way, I was increasingly able to regain my self-confidence and no longer let external evaluations throw me off or make me too dependent on them.

Over the following weeks and months, I worked steadily and increased my workload in four-week increments. However, this was not always straightforward and not as easily implemented as planned by the company doctor. Even just an increase of ten percent in my workload was really difficult for me and triggered new fears, pressure, and insecurities. Often, I needed more than four weeks to get used to a new workload. On the other hand, my mind and willpower wanted nothing more than to leave everything behind and move forward as quickly as possible. My case manager once confronted me with her impression that, from her point of view, I was having trouble accepting my illness because I was demanding too much of myself too quickly. Was that possible? In the subsequent reflection with my therapist, I realized how much I was clinging to the idea of getting well quickly and leaving the burnout behind. This expectation regularly led me to take on too much too soon. I still struggled with changing routines or situations in which I had to be fully present for too long. One to two hours of intense concentration was no problem, but after that I needed another break. If I missed it, I would then feel stressed, frustrated, and emotionally and energetically completely drained. This feeling sometimes lasted for several days, which frustrated me even more and put me under pressure, because I would have liked to have accomplished "more." Accordingly, I had to acknowledge at this point that my case manager was probably right in her assessment. The tendency to overextend and overstep my own limits was still present, and in many cases I was probably not sufficiently aware of this danger.

Deliver perfect work! Be well organized! Finally be able to achieve something again! These were themes I knew well and which still acted as drivers for me in everyday life. However, I thought I had already overcome these tendencies. The issue of overexertion and high performance orientation was especially central in the work context. At least, that's what I thought. In my private life, I wanted to express myself creatively, advance my projects, pursue my hobbies, simply finally live a normal life again! I would never have thought that "I want to... I should be able to... I just have to... When I can again..." would also be so present here. Through social exchange, I realized how much wanting and personal progress were also at the forefront in my private life. Instead of being completely in the here and now and satisfied with what is and what is revealed to me. "Relaxing without wanting to achieve" was the new magic word, and in this sense, I saw myself challenged to find out for myself what would make this state of "just being" more and more possible for me.

Making decisions was also a major challenge during this phase. It sounds trivial. But over time, I could actually gauge how I was doing by my ability to make decisions.

If I was stressed or under pressure inside, I tried to weigh things logically in my decision-making, gather all the information, and then make the right decision. If I was doing well, I was calm and relaxed. Then I could look at the problem in a well-defined way and also tolerate not having a solution ready yet. I then had the patience to simply wait until my gut feeling balanced out with the facts and showed me what I needed to do. Over time, I also realized that there was often not just one right decision. I was allowed to decide for myself. Step by step, I learned to weigh not only the hard facts but also my intuition, and to consciously give myself more time when making decisions. It was once again a personal learning process, about returning to myself and my inner wisdom and strength. When I was truly in touch with myself, I knew I could trust my own judgment. I knew that at a later point I would always have the chance to reassess the situation and make new decisions. I realized on a deeper level that no one has all the answers to all of life's questions, and that it is part of life to face these questions, to find the answers that are right for oneself, and to find trust in oneself.

With the return to working life, I at least had the impression of getting a little closer to a normal life and making a contribution to society. I had been socially isolated for a very long time, even though I was in a relationship for a while. In the meantime, I was single again. That was okay for me, because with my return to working life, I still had a lot to deal with myself. I had wondered what it would have been like if I had already been living with someone before my burnout. In my view, single life further intensified the social isolation. The increasing withdrawal kept me from really allowing a critical outside perspective. Maybe a partner would have confronted me at some point with the fact that I had sleep problems or was out and about in working life at impossible times and with too much pressure and stress. Maybe, just maybe, everything would have turned out differently then?!

The return to work is still very difficult. But things were moving forward step by step and in the right direction. Again and again, I was confronted with my fears and worries. I still sometimes worried about what other people would think of me if they knew I had suffered from burnout. This was also occasionally a topic in the self-help group. But it was no use. I could not undo what had happened. I had to look forward, focus on the good.

With this newfound self-confidence, I once again had the courage and energy to go out, meet new people, and perhaps allow myself to form new acquaintances. This opened up a new field of learning for me. Dealing with new situations, with getting to know people, with closeness and distance, and the question of when I should confront someone with my burnout diagnosis—all of this was a major challenge for me. I was deeply afraid of prejudice. I still disliked talking about my illness, as it made me feel especially guilty and weak. On the other hand, I hoped that it would do me good to have someone by my side and to live in a partnership. A relationship can offer a great deal of security and comfort, and so I gradually dared to open myself up to meeting new people again. Hidden within all of this was the realization that I could never fully predict how others would react to me and my story. Accordingly, it was only possible to protect myself from being hurt to a limited extent. And I learned from this to set better emotional boundaries and not let myself be defined by the opinions of others. That was a long, but very healing part of the recovery process.

When it came to doubting myself, I was still a world champion. I wouldn't say that I was naturally an insecure or doubtful person. But with the burnout and the realization that it had affected me so insidiously in this intense form of self-alienation, it triggered a very strong, all-encompassing insecurity within myself. I was also very worried about my professional future. I was still unsure whether the leadership role was really the right thing for me. Although this work still brought me great joy, I knew that I would once again be taking on a lot of responsibility and that I could only control and manage the stress level and workload to a limited extent. I also still had physical complaints in certain situations. I noticed that my ability to concentrate was no longer the same as before the burnout. Depending on the topic, the problem at hand, and my stress level, I would immediately get back pain again. I was still far from being back at the performance level I had before my burnout, and I didn't know if I would ever get there again. I often wondered whether I would ever find my place in society again and regain solid ground under my feet. Here, too, no one could give me a clear answer or make a prognosis.

Burnout Diary—Snapshots

"Burnout is like a gray veil that imperceptibly settles over your life and experience. Only over time do you notice how many shades of gray there are. In the meantime, you have simply forgotten how colorful life can be. Lifting the veil is often frightening, but it is worth it. Because life has so much more to offer than gray, black, and white."
Rebecca Petersen

At the moment, things are going well with the start of my first small workload of twenty percent. I usually look forward to the content and tasks, but I notice that I miss the leadership role. In consultation with my boss and case management, it was decided that, due to the change process, I will only take this on again from the next school year. This makes the onboarding easier for me and is certainly a sensible solution for the employer. Mentally, however, I am often with my team. I miss the direct contact and the responsibility I had taken on in that role. It is hard for me to "just" let go of this, and I wonder whether I can really "find my way back" to my old life. Or whether, here too, a kind of letting go is needed. Again. Letting go sometimes really seems like a virtue to me. As does patience. Neither was probably given to me at birth. But I learn every day and with each personal insight in different areas of life, and I integrate what seems meaningful to me.

I work from home. The therapeutic work trial is over, and I am completing assignments as part of a regular twenty percent workload. That's a good start! Although somehow, the in-between is difficult for me. I have major motivation problems. It's hard for me to get active for "only" twenty percent and to get going at all. Before the burnout, I had such a huge work overload that I had no choice but to force myself to work. I don't want that anymore. I know that now. Before the burnout, it was, in a sense, a survival mentality. I only realize this now that I have the comparison. No wonder I was always so stressed. It's actually a shame, because I always really enjoyed my work. At least the content and the contact with people. Having a systemic impact always gave me a sense of meaning. That also drove me to achieve top performance. Now I sit here, and somehow I miss both—the external pressure and the sense of purpose in what I do.

I still have great difficulty making decisions. Or at least, this is particularly evident in the professional context. The gradual return to work means that I am supposed to work "only" twenty percent. So should I work two half-days? Or one full day? Although, with my current capacity, I can't really manage that anyway. Then there's the question of whether to attend a training course. Should I participate for "only" one day, or skip it entirely because just half wouldn't be worthwhile? I don't know. I notice that I miss contact with people and look forward to the input from the training. So I decide to participate, but only on the first day. Making and implementing this decision is very difficult for me! I feel the stress it causes throughout my body. And all this just because of such a small, seemingly unimportant decision. Setting boundaries and letting go is the magic formula. It takes courage and energy to let go of my ideas and expectations here and to be happy and content with what is possible and what will emerge for the moment.

Oh dear, will this never end? I sit in front of my computer, completely agitated. My first training via Zoom with many people I haven't seen in a long time due to my absence. I want to log in, and it doesn't work. I try again. It doesn't work. I first write an email to a colleague, then to my boss, to ask if the training is starting late. No answer. So I write to the secretary who sent the invitation. I wonder what's going on. In my head, I think: Great, I'm making a great impression again, being the only one who's late. At some point, I look at the date on my computer. Sunday? Today is Sunday?! Oh no. How embarrassing! I'm a day early! How could that happen?! I try to recall the messages. With one, it doesn't work anymore. Out of necessity, I write a funny email with the sentence "I guess I was a bit too early." I try to take it lightly. But honestly, it's not easy for me, because it brings back memories of the first phase of my burnout. Despite everything, I want to use this "free" day meaningfully for myself. In a sense, it's a "gifted" day. I'll make the best of it and treat myself to a coffee first.

"Do you actually notice how often you use the phrase 'I have to '...' again?" a colleague asks me in a friendly conversation. "Excuse me?" I thought. "Could that really be true?" In the subsequent self-reflection, I realize how, apparently unnoticed, I have once again started to schedule and plan everything in my free time with increasing energy and motivation. Yes, I want to advance creative projects, pursue my hobbies, finally live a normal life again. That gives me energy and fills me with a sense of purpose. But am I not at risk of missing out on some of the power of the present moment? This irrepressible desire to move forward leads me to constantly remain in a thought bubble instead of simply relaxing mentally and internally and letting go. This realization runs deep and really gets me thinking.

A friend asks via WhatsApp: "When do you want to meet? What time in the afternoon? At which café? Should we go for a walk afterwards or have something to eat together?" So many, actually simple and logical questions. But they always tend to overwhelm me. It's the same, for example, with opening the mail or reading emails. It feels like everyone wants something from me. It is still the case that, depending on my stress level, I find it difficult to process such everyday things in a sensible and well-bounded way, or to make seemingly trivial everyday decisions in a forward-looking manner. That, too, is still part of it and is often a good indicator of how I am currently doing.

I am single and currently getting to know someone. That, too, is a challenge. Dealing with new situations, with closeness and distance, and the question of when to share with someone my own burnout diagnosis. I am afraid of prejudice. In general, I don't like talking about this topic. On the other hand, I think it would do me good to have someone by my side and to be in a relationship again. A relationship can offer a lot of security, support, love, and important feedback. And I think the likelihood of developing burnout would have been lower if I had had someone at home who might have reflected back to me that something was wrong and that I had changed. Perhaps, however, I would have tried to hide it at home. I don't know. I think the social environment and how one deals with being ill, the subjective evaluation of oneself, and the attitudes within family and friends all have an influence. In any case, I am grateful for all the people who respond to my burnout openly, mindfully, and without prejudice, and who ask interested questions without making hasty judgments. With every positive experience of opening up, I feel lighter and stronger.

Returning to work continues to be difficult. I am unable to increase my workload by twenty percent each month as planned by the company doctor. Often, even a ten percent increase overwhelms me, and I have to slow down on various levels. Through all this, I am very grateful for the support of my case manager. I wouldn't have thought so at the beginning, but it really helps to have someone neutral to talk to and reflect with, who can mediate in difficult situations and point out boundaries and opportunities. Someone who is not emotionally involved and has no personal interests at stake.

I still feel insecure because I simply don't know what my professional future will look like. As an organization, we are in the midst of a change process, and understandably, I have existential fears. I am firmly convinced that I will be fully capable again in a few months. But I am just not there yet. I feel a certain pressure to prove myself anew: to myself, to those around me, and to my employer. That is not easy to endure. My motivation to achieve and produce is still dormant within me. But it is difficult to channel this energy in moderation and not overstep my limits again. It's as if I have to learn to walk again in certain areas, right from the beginning. My confidence in my own abilities has been damaged. This is part of the recovery process—finding my place in society again and feeling solid ground under my feet.

My relationship with my new supervisor is still tense. I think the reintegration process and the long period of uncertainty about my condition have been a burden and a source of insecurity for both of us. Since we hadn't known each other long before my illness due to the change in leadership, it is probably difficult for both of us to properly assess each other in the process and to build trust. Of course, this affects my reintegration process. Supervisors play a crucial role and bear significant responsibility in this process. Leaders who provide support and encouragement are very important and helpful. It's about focusing on success and existing resources, having patience, and expressing appreciation. However, if the relationship of trust is severely shaken, among other things due to a very long period of illness, it takes a lot of openness and goodwill in mutual contact. If, in addition, the affected person has strong fears, worries, and performance pressure, or if the relationship of trust between employee and supervisor is strained, it may make sense to consider a fresh start and possibly reorient oneself professionally. Changing jobs can be an opportunity and help to leave behind the identity of "I am ill" and to dare a new beginning in another organization and role. Depending on the situation, this step requires a lot of effort and can be unsettling. I know I want to stay. I want to return to my team. Even if I can't always understand my supervisor's reactions, I want to remain optimistic and benevolent.

I feel a great deal of insecurity—my other inner voice, which has arisen from the exhaustion depression, is making itself heard. A more pronounced, doubting voice that

I now recognize and can consciously set boundaries for. After reflecting with my therapist, I realize that this inner voice usually paralyzes and frightens me more than it helps. Therefore, I want to find a new way of dealing with myself.

I am currently entering a job application process after all. This is very exhausting and nerve-wracking alongside the recovery process. But I think it is important to keep possible options open and to see how the option of changing jobs feels, even though I still want to return to my team. I quickly start sleeping restlessly again and having night sweats, and my body reacts during the day with enormous fatigue, renewed headaches, or muscle and joint pain. I also become quickly overwhelmed in relationships and once again have great difficulty making both big and small everyday decisions. I notice setbacks in my recovery. Just the question of a possible job change immediately gives me sleepless nights. I am probably not ready yet. Once again, it takes patience and the ability to endure not knowing.

I am practicing doing things that distract me, bring me back to myself, give me courage, and restore my self-confidence. I have discovered sauna bathing as a great resource for myself. There, I can switch off in just a few minutes and feel my body again. Going for walks and having a coffee somewhere in peace, feeling the energy of the city around me without really being part of it or having to actively interact with anyone, reading a book or writing a blog post, booking a massage, etc.—all these things do me good in everyday life, and I try to integrate and plan them regularly whenever possible. My experience has shown that otherwise I run the risk of "forgetting" them and then once again focusing "only on work." This personal tendency scares me, even though it has gotten me far in life over the years. Here, I probably have to learn to protect myself from myself.

Figuratively Speaking—Slowly Back to Life

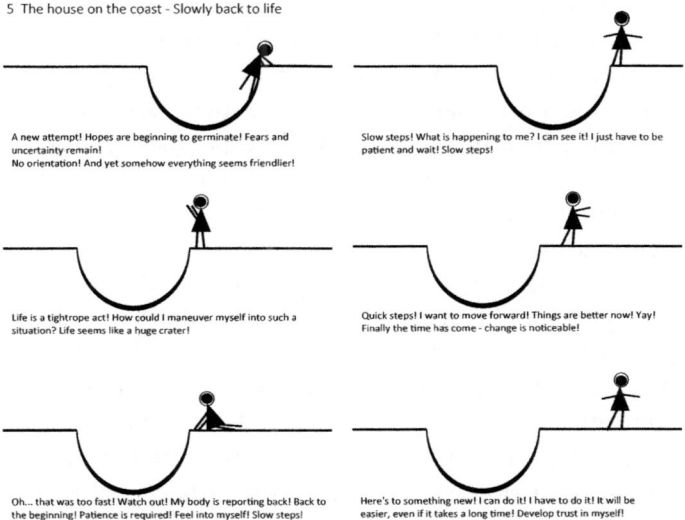

5 The house on the coast - Slowly back to life

A new attempt! Hopes are beginning to germinate! Fears and uncertainty remain!
No orientation! And yet somehow everything seems friendlier!

Slow steps! What is happening to me? I can see it! I just have to be patient and wait! Slow steps!

Life is a tightrope act! How could I maneuver myself into such a situation? Life seems like a huge crater!

Quick steps! I want to move forward! Things are better now! Yay! Finally the time has come - change is noticeable!

Oh... that was too fast! Watch out! My body is reporting back! Back to the beginning! Patience is required! Feel into myself! Slow steps!

Here's to something new! I can do it! I have to do it! It will be easier, even if it takes a long time! Develop trust in myself!

For (Potential) Affected Individuals— Learning Self-Reflection and Resilience

How does one move from shaky footing to a stable stance and foundation with greater self-assurance and self-confidence? What might the fine-tuning for returning to the working world look like in detail? How can one manage personal setbacks well and learn from them? What are realistic expectations during this entire period, and how can one maintain a positive attitude and motivation? Such questions, among others, become central in this next, fifth phase, when it comes to re-entering working life.

As I have described repeatedly in the previous chapter, I felt insecure, lost, and powerless in so many moments during the recovery phase. This feeling persisted for a long time and was intensified by the planning and actual return to work. Fortunately, over time, the uncertainties noticeably diminished, and I cannot say exactly how the feelings of insecurity and fear eventually balanced out with anticipation and drive. At some point, it was simply the right time, and until then, I tried to face new experiences and thought experiments and observe what they triggered in me. I still had no choice but to keep moving forward step by step and to learn to deal with whatever arose in these new situations.

Accordingly, I unfortunately cannot tell you exactly how you should shape this phase in order to reach your goal. Burnout is highly individual, and so the path back must also be tailored individually and requires gradual adjustment throughout the process. For this very reason, it makes sense to seek professional support from a therapist, coach, counselor, etc. For a long time, the actual goal was not really visible or tangible to me and stood in contrast to my wishes and, depending on the situation, unrealistic expectations. I could only live day by day and try to focus on what was going well.

For me, it remained central and vital to orient myself to my physical limits, to focus on my inner needs, and to repeatedly give myself enough space and time for self-reflection. This allowed me to be more present in the moment and to be content with what was possible at the time, so that I could then take the next small steps with renewed strength. Again, it took an enormous amount of strength and patience in so many moments to deal with internal and external resistance and to process and make sense of all the impressions and experiences of the day. My goal was to gain as realistic a perspective as possible on returning to work, one that also included setbacks and stumbling blocks. I considered this an important factor for success. But this required a lot of preparation time and sufficient understanding and mindfulness on my part.

Over time, I realized that, alongside the great respect I had for returning to work, I was also very much looking forward to rejoining my team and returning to working life. However, I never expected this to happen immediately. By then, I had reached a point where I simply hoped with confidence that the "right" feelings and developmental steps would emerge at the "right" time. What I want to say is: Give yourself time and observe without judgment what is happening to and within you. The time will come when you will simply sense what the next steps are! Give yourself this time and space to explore and wait for it, even if it is often difficult for you.

Just as burnout can manifest in different ways, so too is the path to healing different for everyone. What I can say with certainty is that it took much longer than I had anticipated and required an immense amount of patience, strength, and understanding from everyone involved. If you are increasingly able to (re)act from this positive attitude of acceptance, then you have already achieved a great deal and contributed to your personal healing. So, be as appreciative and loving with yourself as possible, and celebrate all the small and large successes you have already noticed and achieved on your way back!

Perhaps you will even manage to invite feelings of uncertainty and not-knowing as powerful companions on your journey and see them as positive support?! In a positive sense, uncertainty can lead us to look more closely and check for ourselves whether something truly fits us. Not-knowing (or not being able to know) may bring us closer to spirituality and an awareness of our human limitations?! Both are areas that, in retrospect and in relation to my (past) experience with burnout, have given me a great deal of clarity, confidence, and strength.

I now sincerely wish you much strength, confidence, and flexibility for your journey back into a more colorful (working) world and an enriching everyday life with your family and friends! It is worth sticking with it. You can do it! Focus on what you have already achieved. Every further step is a success and brings you closer to your goal!

For Relatives, Friends, and Colleagues— Systems Thinking

Breathing a sigh of relief without losing respect for potential stumbling blocks ahead and maintaining mindfulness throughout the process? How can a family move forward now? How does a sense of security develop in daily life together, and how can new energy for the recovery of the person getting well be generated? Where is individual and/ or shared processing and time for making sense of the past needed? How can this process of making sense be implemented meaningfully?

In this Phase V, the affected person may already be feeling somewhat more optimistic and the situation has somewhat stabilized. However, many questions remain unanswered. Fortunately, progress in the recovery process is becoming increasingly visible.

Emotional detachment from the workplace and from restrictive (thought, feeling, and behavior) patterns is becoming increasingly successful, and it is getting easier for the affected person to set boundaries, perceive their feelings, and follow their true needs, allowing for deep healing to take place. Nevertheless, this phase is also a kind of trial run. The return to the old or a new work environment is imminent. Old fears and limitations may resurface. And yet, courage and openness are needed to take the next step forward.

You, as relatives, friends, and professional colleagues, play an important role in this phase! You can be a vital support and provide encouragement. Still, sufficient mindfulness is needed so that the affected person feels supported while also feeling empowered in their autonomy. I recommend, whenever possible, initiating a conversation in advance to offer support but also to inquire about needs. It may be that the affected person wants to handle many things on their own and seeks the necessary support elsewhere (e.g., through therapy, coaching, counseling, etc.). Nevertheless, it can help to reach out and make an open, proactive offer of connection, thereby showing appreciation and presence. Even now, a protected, safe, nonjudgmental space for exchange and interaction is important.

It is possible that the affected person is still suffering from various symptoms such as sleep disturbances, limb, back and/or headaches, exhaustion, etc., and that these may even intensify at times. It is important to remember that the long break and absence from working life have naturally left their mark, and the entire organization (physically and mentally) must readjust to the new circumstances and demands (pace, daily structure, workload, etc.). This adjustment and adaptation are part of the recovery and reintegration phase. Total relaxation would be out of place here, while pressure and tension should still be avoided. This creates a field of tension that makes the process challenging and requires sufficient mindfulness, (self-)reflection, and flexibility from everyone involved.

A therapeutic work trial, in which the affected person is present on site but does not yet have to perform under (time) pressure, can be a sensible first step. After that, a gradual return to work is recommended. A combination of a work trial and a set workload is also possible. Here, too, setbacks and new challenges may arise, once again burdening the life of the affected person. In addition, there are people who return directly with a higher workload. The design of the return to work depends on the condition of the affected person, but also the context, prognosis, personal circumstances, history, available options, and measures in the workplace, etc., all influence the successful implementation of the professional reintegration. Therefore, it continues to make sense to maintain therapeutic support, even if the temptation for the affected person to stand on their own two feet again and be fully functional is great.

A great deal of patience, mindfulness, and understanding is needed for the experiences, thoughts, feelings, and actions of the affected person. He or she must find their own way, and this can sometimes be a very challenging situation for outsiders. The goal is to strengthen the autonomy (in the sense of the definition from transactional analysis, see Phase III—The Sea—Recovery and Setbacks), self-efficacy, and thus the self-confidence of the affected person, and to recognize and meaningfully process any uncertainties. Emerging fears and setbacks are, so to speak, part of the path to healing—this must be endured together.

This requires a great deal of patience, openness, and understanding from you as relatives, friends, and team members. It is therefore advisable that you seek direct communication and, if necessary, obtain support for yourself through counseling, coaching, etc. This is about you and your needs! Remember that you, too, are an important part of the system and should therefore take good care of your own strength and needs! A prolonged period of illness and a partial return to working life can demand a lot from you as a family and as a team. It is important that you give space and attention to these thoughts and feelings and any possible sense of being overwhelmed, and do not simply swallow them or take them too lightly!

I wish you much strength and confidence in this challenging phase of adjustment and finding your way! Don't forget: you can only be a strong support if you take sufficient care of yourself. The same applies to you: take your own needs and feelings seriously and, if necessary, express how you are feeling in the situation. If needed, seek support from a professional!

For Managers—Corporate/Social Responsibility

Depending on the course of events, many months may have passed in which your employee was wholly or partially absent due to illness. The time may seem endless, and it is possible that it is still not clear when and how the affected person's return to work will take place. The only thing you can do in this phase is wait, show patience and understanding, and from time to time send a signal of solidarity, appreciation, trust, and empathy.

Depending on the needs of the affected person and the operational possibilities, your employee will start with a therapeutic work trial, which can last several weeks. The advantage here is that both sides, employer and employee, can gradually see, without pressure regarding performance and time, how the contact works, which tasks seem meaningful, and how the affected person can handle taking on responsibility and increasing external demands. I myself was initially very skeptical about such an approach using a therapeutic work trial. In retrospect, however, I must say that I was ultimately very grateful for this opportunity to re-enter gradually. The period of absence can indeed be very long, so that at the beginning it is really a kind of mutual "getting to know each other" and an internal adjustment process for both the affected person and the environment. As a result, it is very likely that the workload can be increased in small steps, first by ten percent, then perhaps by twenty percent, e.g., over one to two months each, until the employee is back at their original workload, if that has been agreed upon. The phase of gradually increasing the workload, possibly in combination with a work trial, can be drawn out and depends on the condition of the affected person, as well as on operational circumstances (possibilities for adjusting tasks, workplace, working hours, etc.) and the flexibility available on site. So, once again, a good deal of patience, confidence, mutual trust, and perseverance is required from everyone involved. You yourself can best support this challenging time and your employee by highlighting what is going well, honestly naming positive aspects, and pointing out successes. Usually, due to the great uncertainty, the affected person's self-perception is still impaired, so they will be grateful if you offer support and an outside perspective in this regard. Be lenient at first and hold back on too much criticism until the relationship of trust has stabilized. I assume that your employee will already be critical enough of themselves. As a manager, you must therefore weigh up how honest your feedback should be and whether and when it is actually necessary and appropriate to address important points of criticism. It is not about excessive coddling or special treatment, but about making it as easy as possible for the affected person, after a long and very unsettling period of illness, to regain solid, secure ground under their feet. Ideally, case management has already taken over the case leadership and serves as an advisory, mediating, and connecting link in the upcoming or already ongoing process of reintegration.

If you have not yet found the time, now would certainly be a good moment to familiarize yourself with the facts surrounding burnout. This will undoubtedly help you in communicating with the affected individual and foster mutual trust and understanding. Depending on the personality of the affected person and the context, the need or openness for a personal exchange about their own well-being may be rather low. Do not take this personally! You may recall that people affected by burnout often struggle with feelings of shame and guilt. This considerably hampers social contact and open exchange. It therefore makes sense for you to at least have some knowledge of the facts about burnout and to inform yourself accordingly. This can, depending on the situation, serve as a door-opener for clarifying conversations with your employee.

In my view, the success of reintegration depends largely on you as a manager. The central question is the attitude with which you approach the affected person, what demands (explicit or implicit) you place on the individual or the situation, what adjustments and support you can offer in terms of workplace, tasks, time management, and assumption of responsibility, how much appreciation and trust you are able to redevelop towards the affected person, and how much you trust them to cope with the existing circumstances. All of this significantly contributes to the successful resumption of work by the affected individual. Any form of pressure (e.g., time, performance, workload, flexibility, teamwork, etc.) or generally excessive expectations is particularly detrimental. There may be setbacks and stumbling blocks during reintegration! Realistic expectations on both sides contribute to success and also minimize pressure on everyone involved. It is therefore all the more important to sufficiently and carefully reflect on and, if possible, discuss in advance with the affected person and case management any fears, anxieties, feelings of disappointment, etc., as well as possible (challenging) scenarios and next steps.

Not every company can afford to allow for a lengthy reintegration process and/or implement a therapeutic work trial. Nor is case management established in every organization. This makes me all the more an advocate for active workplace education and prevention regarding potential burnout, because when burnout occurs, the entire system is heavily challenged and the financial consequences are significant. Any efforts to prevent burnout are worthwhile on various levels. However, burnout cannot always be prevented, as the interconnections are complex and multifaceted. On the one hand, a healthy sense of boundaries and a realistic view of the issue are needed; on the other hand, openness and willingness are required to reintegrate affected individuals into working life. People who experience burnout are usually highly committed, disciplined, and experienced. It is therefore worthwhile to actively support these individuals in their return to work! This requires, in the initial phase of reintegration, adapted and supportive working conditions! At the same time, I believe it is legitimate to openly communicate your own concerns, fears, (organizational) limits, and any emerging overwhelm as an employer, supervisor, or colleague, and to include these in the design of the reintegration process and in necessary strategic decisions. If needed, seek professional help and support through coaching, supervision, case management, etc.! It is not solely your responsibility as a manager or organization to ensure that a reintegration measure is actually successful. In my view, the employer or supervisor is entitled to set appropriate boundaries, without shifting or neglecting their own responsibility. If you succeed in shaping the reintegration process and making your contribution, I see many opportunities for team and personal development, as well as for strengthening a supportive and appreciative organizational and leadership culture.

People affected by burnout are usually highly committed, professionally competent, and conscientious employees. They shape a team with their high motivation, dedication, and personal skills. If these strengths and resources can be integrated into the organization and the team in such a way that unnoticed self-exploitation by an individual is prevented, then a burnout incident appears in a new light and can serve as an "organizational kick-start" and as an opportunity to strengthen organizational health and resilience, leading to greater mindfulness, trust, mutual understanding, and successful communication within the team.

The fact is that people affected by burnout often do not notice what is happening to them. This may also apply during reintegration if they fall back into the same patterns. The relapse rate is correspondingly high. Therefore, sufficient caution, appropriate expertise, mutual mindfulness, and, if possible, an objective, external perspective from people who feel able to address such issues directly with the (potentially) affected person and provide honest feedback are needed.

If, as a manager, you succeed in building a secure, supportive relationship with your employees based on trust, openness, and appreciation, and you are also sensitized to the topics of burnout and resilience and can respond in a targeted, conscious, and mindful way if you suspect something, then I believe the likelihood of a relapse or of another employee developing burnout is much lower.

This effort is worthwhile in any case, because, as mentioned, burnout involves a long period of absence, illness, and recovery. By educating yourself and deepening your knowledge about burnout and resilience, you not only protect yourself but also your employees, thereby strengthening resilience and well-being throughout the organization. This is therefore an investment that pays off not only financially, but also in human and organizational terms.

> If necessary, seek support yourself during the reintegration process, and if you ever feel uncertain, simply focusing on what is going well and expressing appreciation can be a good next step and a door-opener for collaboration!

(Self-) Reflection—Steps Toward Self-Knowledge

For (Potential) Affected Individuals

With regard to burnout, I find another concept from transactional analysis particularly helpful. This is the basic attitude [1], also known as the OK-OK stance or basic position, which describes how I relate to myself, others, and the world. At first glance, this concept may seem somewhat trivial. However, upon closer examination, it becomes clear how quickly and unconsciously we slip into a Not-OK position (toward ourselves or others) in everyday life, thereby sabotaging ourselves and devaluing ourselves or others.

The OK-OK stance comprises four positions:

+/+ I am OK. You are OK.
+/− I am OK. You are not OK.
−/+ I am not OK. You are OK.
−/− I am not OK. You are not OK.

The OK-OK stance enables autonomous thinking, feeling, and behavior. It assumes that both people inherently possess value and dignity as human beings, regardless of their actions or attitudes. Possible statements might be: I accept myself as I am. I accept you as you are. You have your story. I have my story. I am worthy of being loved. You are worthy of being loved. These beliefs and statements refer to the essence of a person, but not necessarily to a person's specific behavior. It may be that I do not agree with what someone does and cannot or do not want to accept it. I may and should communicate this. Ideally, I do so with a respectful and appreciative attitude toward myself and the other person, which becomes evident in communication. In the encounter, I accept who the other person is as a person. Their essence as a human being is acceptable to me, even if their behavior may not be. I do not place myself above the person, nor are they above me. As human beings, we meet on the same level and communicate and act as equals. I accept that the person has their own story and has become who they are today because of it. I also accept my own story, which has made me who I am today. I allow myself to have my own needs, feelings, and opinions, and I allow my counterpart to have their own needs, feelings, and opinions. With this awareness, I accept and respect the existing boundaries—my own, but also those of the other person. All these statements demonstrate a clear and appreciative OK-OK stance. A Not-OK stance, on the other hand, would be if I judge or belittle myself (even just in thought), or if I verbally or mentally attack, devalue, ignore, exclude, or judge my counterpart.

It is interesting here to observe oneself in contact with others and, over time, to discover which situations tend to lead you into Not-OK positions (toward yourself or others). Only when we act from an "I am OK—You are OK" position can we act and decide for ourselves and others in a way that is beneficial, drawing on our own strength and power. Unfortunately, a Not-OK stance is often adopted unconsciously. This, in turn, affects how we interact with others and how mindfully and nonjudgmentally we, for example, listen and engage with the concerns or perspectives of others. A Not-OK stance influences how we relate to ourselves, our experiences, and our needs and views, without reacting to others and their perspectives in a devaluing, irritated, angry, or confrontational manner.

Questions for Reflection

- Can you relate to the statements above? If so, which ones resonate with you in particular and why? In which situations are you able to approach people with an OK-OK stance? Where, when, and with which people do you find it more difficult?
- In which situations do you tend to slip into a Not-OK position (position of inferiority)—toward yourself or others? How do you recognize this?
- How do you manage to admit your own weaknesses and limitations and still (or perhaps because of this) adopt an OK-OK stance?
- What is your view on the statement that every person deserves respect and appreciation, regardless of their achievements, success, or actions? Justify your position!
- What does it mean to you to be successful in life? What is your personal definition of success, happiness, and well-being in life?
- Which of the four basic positions do you tend to prefer when you are under stress?

- In stressful situations, do you feel superior, inferior, or on equal footing? How does this manifest for you (in behavior, thinking, feeling)?
- With which people are you particularly able to remain in the OK-OK position? Why? What new perspective or action (regarding yourself) could change or diminish this?
- With which people do you find it especially difficult to remain in the OK-OK position? Why? What new perspective or action (regarding yourself) could change or diminish this?
- In which situations do you adopt an "I am not OK" position? How does this show itself? What new perspective or action could change or diminish this?
- Which position did your mother/father often take? This refers to themselves and/or toward you. How did this manifest and/or change in stressful situations? What change/insight/action would have been good for your parents or for you? What would this have changed?
- From which OK position were you most often approached as a child? How did this manifest? What conclusions did you draw from this as a child? Where would it be important today (regarding your health and well-being) to distance yourself from this and take new paths?
- To what extent does this childhood experience still shape your interactions with people/supervisors today? Where would a new perspective or experience be helpful in order to take new paths?
- Do you perhaps have a certain expectation of how someone will usually interact with you? To what extent do you influence the interaction with your counterpart through your actions/behavior? Where might a different approach be needed? How would this change your behavior or that of your counterpart?

- In which situations (professionally or privately) could you perhaps adopt a new, positive attitude? How could you behave completely differently for once? What impact would that likely have on you, your counterpart, and the situation?

Especially in the case of burnout, as in life in general, it is important that I approach myself from an OK-OK stance. Healing can only occur if I allow myself to adopt an OK-OK stance. Only in this way can I adequately care for myself and my needs.

Permissions (Schlegel 2002) are another concept from transactional analysis that helps us to achieve greater autonomy. This concept was explained and described in more detail by Pat Crossman [2]. Permissions were not, or not sufficiently, given by parents or caregivers in childhood. As adults, we can later grant these to ourselves. Permissions serve to open doors for people, enabling them to take new paths and have new, positive experiences that strengthen their own OK-OK stance, broaden their perspective, and allow and enable new experiences and ways of seeing things. For each of the five drivers (see Phase VI—The Lighthouse—Classifying Uncertainty), which indicate a Not-OK stance toward oneself, there is an antidote, which is referred to as a permission.

Be perfect!	You are good just the way you are!
Make it right for others!	You are allowed to do what is right for yourself!
Be strong!	
Try harder!	You are allowed to be weak, to feel and express your needs.
Hurry up!	Do it as you can! You are allowed to relax!
	Take the time you need.

The following questions can help you discover possible permissions

- Where in your life do you need permission for change?
- What permission would benefit you in terms of your health and resilience?
- What prevents you, as an adult, from granting yourself these permissions, even if you may not have received them from your parents as a child?
- What do you need in order to give yourself these permissions here and now?
- What could be the next meaningful steps towards autonomy in this regard? What is the next small step you will take as soon as tomorrow?

For Leaders—With a View to the Organization

These considerations also lead to interesting questions for reflecting on your organization

- Which of the four basic positions is your preferred one (the one you mostly take) as a leader? How does this change when you are under stress?
- Which basic position do you take when a particular employee comes to you with a problem or concern? Are there employees who tend to trigger a Not-OK position in you?
- From which position do you interact with which people? Analyze your team and write down your corresponding OK position for each person. What do you notice?
- Now add to the list the OK-OK positions you suspect the others hold! What do you notice?

- With which people would you like to bring about a change in the OK-OK position? How would your OK position need to change to make this possible? How could you succeed in encouraging these individuals to change without overstepping boundaries? How could you positively support the strengthening of the other person's autonomy?
- Which of the four positions is predominant in your organization? What are the reasons for this?
- How does this change when you or the team are under stress? Is there then a favorite position, or are you able to maintain the OK-OK position?
- How could the general attitude in your team be improved or changed? What next steps would be necessary for this?
- What would your team need to sharpen awareness of mutual appreciation in communication? What next steps would make sense? How could you introduce your team to the importance and impact of the OK-OK attitude?
- What permissions would benefit you as a leader and help you gain more autonomy and self-efficacy? What next steps would be necessary for this?
- What permission would benefit your team and help it gain more autonomy and self-efficacy? What next steps would make sense?

References

1. Schlegel, L. (2002). *Handwörterbuch der Transaktionsanalyse* (2nd ed., pp. 91–95). Herder Verlag.
2. Schlegel, L. (2002). *Handwörterbuch der Transaktionsanalyse* (2nd ed., pp. 63–64). Herder Verlag.

Phase VI—The Lighthouse— Making Sense of Uncertainty

Abstract In this phase, it becomes increasingly easier; strength and vitality gradually return. Confidence in one's own body and self grows. Viewing things from a distance, from a safe remove, helps to gain new perspectives. The strength and courage to shape and act increase. Yet, recovery is still not complete, and healing takes time. It becomes clear how persistent and protracted burnout can be, and how much effort is required to reclaim a healthy life. The theories regarding drivers and injunctions may initially seem somewhat sobering or even restrictive. However, as one delves deeper, resources and insights emerge that allow for a new, nonjudgmental perspective. This is the preparation for new, unknown paths and discoveries. The way forward is open and free, once again allowing new strength, hope, and confidence to blossom in the observer.

© The Author(s), under exclusive license to Springer Fachmedien Wiesbaden GmbH, part of Springer Nature 2025
R. Petersen, *Tsunami in the Head – Better Understanding and Coping with Burnout*, https://doi.org/10.1007/978-3-658-49737-8_7

The Lighthouse

A wonderful place to orient oneself and look out in all directions. Admittedly, the climb was exhausting. Setting out on the journey required courage and energy. Still, I am glad to finally be here. What a view! I feel free! This place, where hardly anyone ever comes, is beautiful. The tower, accessible to only a few. I made it. I survived the catastrophe. I have become a different person. Richer in experience. Shaped and reinvented. A second life has been given to me. Now I realize that I can actively shape things. That nothing and no one can dictate how I have to live my life. That I am allowed to find out for myself which direction I want to go and where I want to find my happiness. And at any time, I can reorient myself, set a new focus. I decide where the beam of light should shine. I decide. I find my way between solitude and contact with the outside world. I have the choice. I can invite people into my life if I want. But it is also legitimate to stay by myself and wait. To enjoy the moment. To look in all directions and wait with anticipation for a ship to appear on the horizon. I am allowed to stay where I am or set out on new paths. Just as I please. I am allowed to ascend, withdraw, or travel to the nearby village. I am allowed to feel, reflect, and reorient myself, without pressure or the compulsion to adapt to someone else. I am allowed to lose and find myself again, knowing that the light on the lighthouse will keep turning. This point of orientation remains and is visible even in the greatest storm. I am safe and keep my bearings. I am myself, and that is good. I have new strength again and reach out my feelers. It still takes a bit of courage. I move forward step by step and dare more and more to follow my heart. My trust in the world and in myself grows every day, and I am increasingly daring to actively shape my dreams and put them into action. Step by step. Without being overwhelmed. Life gains meaning. I feel effective. I look forward to what is to come. I am happy.

My Story—Feeling Sun and Wind on My Face Again

The increase from sixty percent employment just over a month ago to now eighty percent was once again a small milestone for me. I noticed that the thought of soon having to be on duty four days a week filled me with great fear and anxiety. At the same time, I was very much looking forward to it, because the planning was moving forward step by step toward returning to my team and my original leadership responsibilities.

During this time, I felt the need and the courage to increasingly confide in my family members about my illness. I continued to create this space for encounters very mindfully and did not set myself a deadline by which I wanted to have told whom. But I noticed that with every positive reaction, my courage and confidence grew, and I became accustomed to talking about my weaknesses and what I had experienced without feeling weak, guilty, or inadequate. I did not always succeed, but I became more practiced at dealing constructively with the feelings and possible self-doubt that arose afterward, so that they no longer burdened and drained me for as long.

Over time, I developed a clear daily routine that helped me stabilize and take mindful care of myself and my health. At first, this still felt a bit rigid. For example, I started each morning with meditation and found it difficult to cope if I could not do this as planned. I continued to integrate exercise into my daily life several times a week.

In addition, I had gotten into the habit of walking home from the office in the evening. On weekends, I often went hiking. I also continued to try to integrate writing into my free time. It was my way of expressing myself, organizing my thoughts, and being creative. Over time, I hardly had any days when I felt completely beside myself and my plans for the future seemed to go down the drain.

I again paid more conscious attention to incorporating social contact as a resource and welcome break in my daily life. This could be a phone call in the afternoon, meeting a friend for coffee, or going for a walk together. I came to value such encounters again. Here, I could consciously work on my perception and learn to read my physical signals better while "being in contact." I was now better able to consciously use my bodily signals and sensations as orientation in my perception and (experience of) life. In the early phases of burnout, this was still completely impossible, because I could not really feel myself or perceive my needs at all.

Over time, I adjusted certain routines or shifted them throughout the day. Healthy nutrition had always been important to me, and I incorporated intermittent fasting into my daily life. At times, I still meditated daily, but at different times. This change became less of a problem over time, although I was very careful not to fall back into the same patterns as before the burnout. I exercised several times a week. I drank enough fluids and supplied my body with sufficient electrolytes and minerals. I consciously and regularly took time for myself and for "just being." I deliberately pursued positive thoughts and focused on the positive. I let self-doubt throw me off less and less. I kept a regular journal and made a point of writing down three things I was grateful for each evening. All this may sound a bit banal and over-structured, but overall it helped me to keep sight of what was going well during difficult times.

It gave me a sense of control and orientation. I still remember exactly how, at the beginning of my burnout, even just implementing these individual, seemingly banal routines was a feat of strength for me. Now I was working eighty percent. That was an additional challenge, requiring me to adjust certain routines or implement them more flexibly. But over time, I managed this better and better.

What was also new was that I had learned more and more to listen to my gut feeling and follow my intuition. This was beneficial not only in my private life but also in my work as a school principal. It meant that I was increasingly able to come home to myself and trust that I would find the necessary answers in due time. Every day, I followed my heart as best I could and listened inwardly so as not to neglect my needs. Depending on the situation and the decision, this still required a great deal of courage, mindfulness, and self-confidence. But here, too, I was on the right track and noticed with every small step, with every further success, that I was on the right path.

When it came to decisions, I was able to integrate a new kind of lightness into my life. I did not have to know all the answers immediately, and by now I knew that there was often no right or wrong. That took some of the pressure off me. Working with inner parts in talk therapy also helped me to properly classify my critical voices. From my youth, I knew both a self-assured, encouraging inner voice and a very critical, insecure one. As a result of the burnout, a third, especially critical and unsettling voice had developed, constantly reminding me that I could no longer trust myself. After all, I had not recognized the alienation that came with the burnout and had walked straight into my own misfortune. Only when I realized and properly classified this inner third voice and its origin as a result of my illness was I able to respond more relativistically in situations of uncertainty and put this voice in its place. That was another breakthrough for me! Overall, I became increasingly able to trust myself and my abilities and competencies again. If, in stressful situations, I tended to let this critical voice gain the upper hand, I could consciously take a short break, breathe, encourage myself, and suddenly my rational thinking would work again and I would find solutions to my problems without much difficulty. The more I was able to recognize and break this negative thought cycle in the moment, the faster I found my way back to myself, my self-confidence, and my existing abilities. This had a very positive effect on all areas of my life and greatly strengthened me and my self-confidence.

Burnout Diary—Snapshots

"Burnout is like a blow to the bow that tears you out of your life. As a result, you have to intensely confront the consequences and yourself. Improve your maneuverability. Repair the damage to the ship. For the moment, just let yourself drift. Endure the feeling of being at the mercy of things. Surrender control to the sea until the bow is repaired. Only in harmony with the tides is it possible to pick up speed again and find your path and your purpose."
Rebecca Petersen

I feel better. Much better than a few months ago. Fortunately! Things are looking up. And that's not just a premonition—more and more noticeable, small signs are appearing. However, so many intense memories remain. The good thing is that at least I am having more contact with friends again. It's still easier for me to be one-on-one than in a group, but that's okay. I can actually enjoy time with friends again and no longer feel threatened or so stressed that I can't really be present, listen, or stay in touch with myself and my needs. That's a big step forward.

I can do this. I'm managing to work on the different projects well. I'm accomplishing a lot and occasionally receive praise from my new boss. That's progress. I'm also really looking forward to being able to work with my team again soon. Preparations for the handover with my deputy are underway. I'm a bit nervous because it's an important next step and I can't say exactly how it will turn out. But I'm optimistic. I will manage!

Today it's happening again. I'm meeting a friend for a walk. I'm looking forward to it. The meeting goes well and I come home cheerful and strengthened, even though I'm still a bit tired from the exchange and all the impressions and now need to recover. I'm once again paying more conscious attention to integrating social contact as a resource in my everyday life. Even if it's just a phone call or a WhatsApp message. I've managed to consciously work on my perception and learn to better read my physical signals during "being in contact." I'm now better able to consciously use my bodily sensations as a guide in my life. In the early phases of burnout, that wasn't possible. Social contacts were a burden and a stressful situation for me back then.

I'm currently making an absolute change of direction in my life. Every day, I follow my heart as best I can. Depending on the situation and decision, that takes a lot of courage and self-confidence. But it's working better and better. I want to continuously build and strengthen this ability to be connected to my inner wisdom! I feel I've never been closer to happiness, satisfaction, and well-being than I am today. That makes me optimistic! I don't have to have all the answers right now. I can let go of control. I can take small steps and notice with each one how energy and motivation flow back into my experience. Maybe this is exactly how I imagine the "breathing of spirit" that's often referenced in spiritual contexts. I was raised

Christian, which certainly made access to the spiritual easier for me in many moments. In so many phases of my
burnout illness, I still want to push through with my head.
Then I learn the hard way that this doesn't (any longer)
work, because my body rebels and sets limits. So I'm
forced to try new and different strategies. In the moments
when I manage to allow weakness and fully surrender to
the moment, I feel this strength and wisdom within me,
as a contrast to the uncertainty and the recurring fears and
self-doubt. Both are allowed to exist. At the very beginning, this feeling and the confidence are almost impercep-
tible, and yet I sense a budding trust within me that I am
being carried, without needing to intellectually categorize
or understand it. In precisely the moment when I can let
go and allow it, this feeling of "being carried" becomes all
the stronger. The inner wisdom, as I like to call it—the
good, comforting feeling inside me that's hard to describe.
We all know it and carry it within us! If only we allow
ourselves to listen inward and then, for once, simply let go
of thoughts and attempts at explanation.

I enjoy my work. I'm still in the process of gradually
rebuilding, and that remains a major challenge. It's very
frustrating and sobering to experience how little energy
I sometimes have, how quickly my body reacts to overload or upsetting topics or encounters, and then sleep or
my back immediately suffer again. On the other hand, I
can slowly but surely accept that I still need to be patient
and can't control everything! The exchange with my school
leadership colleagues helps me with this. I notice that they
struggle with similar problems, are often overloaded themselves, and that certain structures are not ideal. For better
understanding: the organization is in a multi-year change
process. In the future, the integration settings for students
will be managed by the regular school. This is a good and
important step in terms of integration, and I'm pleased

about this development! The regular school is creating a full-time position for this new responsibility and task. That also makes sense in the implementation process! On the other hand, it's sobering for me, as I realize that over the past six years, I've taken on the workload of two full-time positions. Is it any wonder that I ended up with burnout?!

Another visit to the company doctor is coming up, even though I'm almost back to my original workload. That irritates me at first! But somehow I understand that my employer wants to know from a neutral person once again where I stand and how I'm doing. At the beginning of the conversation, I'm still a bit uncertain. But I quickly gain trust in the doctor. That also has to do with the fact that I'm generally feeling better again. It's easier for me to engage in social interaction. I'm honest and open! I share everything that seems important to me, trying to give a good overall picture from the beginning to the present moment. The company doctor asks questions where she feels it's important. She encourages me, is appreciative and open. Occasionally, she confronts me with her perceptions and assessments. I really appreciate that, as it gives me new hints and input for self-reflection. The doctor takes a lot of notes during the conversation, and yet I feel that we are well connected. I'm amazed myself at the long, rocky road I've traveled and am now describing in detail. I think I can really be proud of myself! And yet I still feel this uncertainty. I simply can't yet really assess what all will come my way. I still have major hurdles to overcome, things that challenge or exhaust me daily. I haven't fully regained complete trust in myself and my body. From my perspective, it's still possible that everything will turn out differently than I planned. So I'm extremely cautious. I want to protect myself from unrealistic hopes and disappointments. I remain vigilant—toward myself and my environment. That seems to me the safest way.

Figuratively Speaking—Something New Emerges

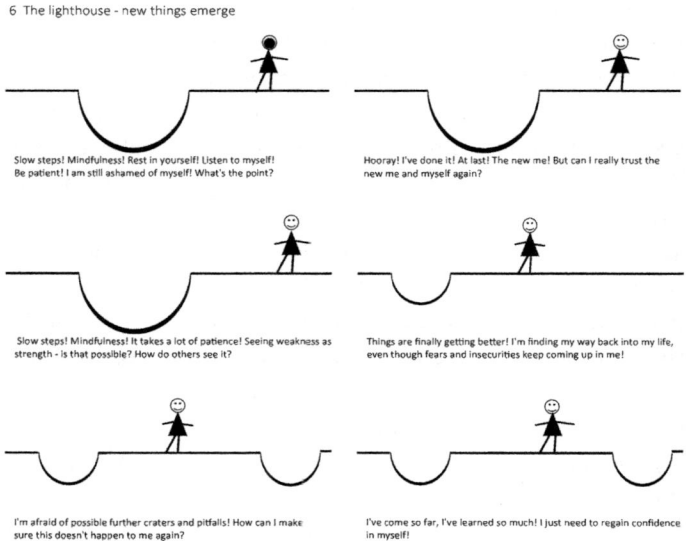

6 The lighthouse - new things emerge

Slow steps! Mindfulness! Rest in yourself! Listen to myself! Be patient! I am still ashamed of myself! What's the point?

Hooray! I've done it! At last! The new me! But can I really trust the new me and myself again?

Slow steps! Mindfulness! It takes a lot of patience! Seeing weakness as strength - is that possible? How do others see it?

Things are finally getting better! I'm finding my way back into my life, even though fears and insecurities keep coming up in me!

I'm afraid of possible further craters and pitfalls! How can I make sure this doesn't happen to me again?

I've come so far, I've learned so much! I just need to regain confidence in myself!

For (Potential) Affected Individuals— Learning Self-Reflection and Resilience

As already mentioned in Chapter IV, I see intuition as an important tool on the path to recovery and returning to life. Intuition is a vital companion because we cannot always explain with reason why we interpret or decide something one way or another. Trust that you know what is good for you and gradually rediscover your inner, primal trust! In my experience, it is possible to acquire this trust in yourself even later in life! You are your own expert! You decide what your path to recovery should look like. Your intuition will know, at the right time, what is good for you. You can openly and courageously embrace whatever comes your way. With the help of your intuition, you will recognize which impressions and cues from outside are important for you and which you can safely forget. In my experience, this distinction is not always easy, especially if we rely solely on our intellect. Intuition (colloquially: gut feeling) is the ability to make a decision or gain insight very quickly, without consciously using reason or rational conclusions. The insights come from the subconscious, from "implicit knowledge"—without lengthy deliberation or weighing of options. Sometimes this is referred to as the moment of "simply knowing." This is an important aspect of the learning process, both in relation to life itself and in terms of strengthening your resilience and intuitive abilities!

We are almost at the end of our journey, and so, alongside all the progress and successes, there can always be setbacks and a return to old patterns. This is not a problem, because the direction in which you are moving, and have moved so far, is right. As long as you can see setbacks as pointers for your next steps in development, everything is truly fine!

Such setbacks and relapses into old behavioral, emotional, thought, and belief patterns can be an indication that the behavior in question is deeply rooted in your script and that change has not yet become sustainable. You may recall the topic of scripts, which was already discussed in Chapter II. If not, you can briefly review it there.

If change is to be sustainable, it is important to create and reinforce new (neural) pathways, i.e., to gather new experiences and be patient until a new "good and stable" habit—like a highway lane—has developed, making relapses less likely. It is not the case that your personality and personal traits have simply been given to you since birth and you must accept them as they are. You can change and further develop yourself and your personal traits, with all your thinking, feeling, behavior, and beliefs, at any time. You may be wondering how this is possible? Well, you have most likely done this, sometimes consciously, sometimes unconsciously, over the past months and throughout your life. The reason we seemingly cannot change in certain areas is only because we believe that the thought or personal trait is a part of us. However, it developed during the formation of our script and can therefore change again. As mentioned, this can happen consciously or unconsciously, through aha moments, self-reflection, experiencing new things, and through personal insights that come from within, from your inner wisdom and your heart.

One reason you may still find it difficult to create new pathways could be the drivers and injunctions that are part of your script. It is important for me to mention that these are human-made, subjective theories and models. Therefore, it is always important, in these considerations, to decide for yourself what seems helpful and right for your own understanding and experience. Theories and models are new perspectives, and you, as the expert on your own life, can decide what is relevant and helpful for you.

Therefore, I would like to return to the topic of drivers and injunctions, which are part of script theory. You will find a more detailed explanation in the section on self-reflection below. In addition, a test regarding drivers may help you recognize why you still maintain certain behaviors or what drives you excessively, even though it is not truly beneficial for your health and recovery. This can then lead to new insights and more mindful, healthier behaviors.

Learning resilience means finding the right path for yourself, with your own values and judgments. Depending on the situation, this can be a great challenge, but it can also be very exciting. It is important to keep in mind that there is not just one right way. Moreover, you can always decide anew and take a new direction at any time. Your intuition is an important guide in this process. It is worthwhile to learn to use it better and better. I wish you much joy and exciting insights as you discover and deepen this ability!

For Relatives, Friends, and Colleagues—Systems Thinking

You made it! Yes, you too! Because through your support, patience, and understanding for the affected person, you have made a significant contribution to successful recovery. The burnout illness has been overcome, at least for the moment.

Unfortunately, the relapse rate for burnout is relatively high. That means it makes sense to consider which strategies, attitudes, and perhaps habits have helped, and how you, as a (family) system, want to protect yourselves from a relapse in the future.

But first, it is time to take stock together and appreciate what you have achieved! Take your time and "celebrate" your shared success! Burnout is one of the most challenging illnesses because it affects the entire system and brings with it such diverse manifestations and complex symptoms.

For joint reflection in the sense of taking stock, I have put together a few questions for you:

- Where were you able to overcome stumbling blocks and challenges together, and how did you grow from them?

- How did these shape your life together (positively and negatively)? What do you want to keep, and what do you want to let go of?
- Which habits, rituals, insights, images, "aha" moments, anchors, etc., do you want to maintain in the future?
- What could still be optimized or changed in your daily life together? Where might it also be necessary to let go and simply "be"?
- Which values have newly emerged for your life together, or have gained in value and importance for you as a family/team? How are these lived, and how do they manifest?
- How has your communication and perception of each other, in your relationship and in your interactions, changed?
- How do you show and practice mutual appreciation in everyday life?
- What are you especially grateful for?
- Where might special recognition or a conscious closure and letting go of old thoughts, fears, anxieties, and expectations be needed?
- Is it possible that the experience of burnout has even created opportunities for change? If so, which ones?

All these questions for reflection can help you actively use the coming phase and view the experience of burnout from a new, positive perspective. Here, too, the affected person will again rely on your support. As a (family or work) system, you are only as strong as your individual members! Just as each person is fundamentally responsible for their own well-being and health, you can still support each other in daily life and actively practice mindfulness and mutual appreciation in your interactions. That makes a difference!

It is therefore time to take a deep breath and breathe freely! It is time to enjoy the view and recognize what you have achieved as part of the journey, drawing joy, pride, and confidence for the future from it!

You have become richer and stronger through what you have experienced—the experiences during the burnout illness have shaped you (and your environment and system)! Consciously carry this strength and energy into your daily life. Rejoice that life can finally pick up speed again, without immediately throwing you off track! Even though the risk of relapse remains, a new awareness, intensity, and joy of life can enter your life!

> Enjoy carefree joy in life whenever possible to the fullest, and be consciously present in each moment! Have the courage to leave the past behind and look forward with confidence! This, too, is an important step for relatives, friends, and colleagues to return to a carefree togetherness.
>
> I sincerely wish you a healthy, fulfilling, and successful future!

For Leaders—Corporate/Social Responsibility

It is of great importance to me, within the framework of this book, to address you as a leader and your team regarding your (shared) responsibility in the recognition, prevention, and successful reintegration following a burnout illness. Your support matters, as in my view, preventing and/or early detection of burnout is crucial and can avert much suffering and harm. As a leader, you play a central role in initiating meaningful, effective, and supportive preventive measures and protective (organizational) structures and processes. You are probably already aware of this yourself, but perhaps you are not quite sure where and how to start?!

Burnout is a highly complex illness that depends greatly on the personality factors of the affected individual. As social beings, people are connected to others (and their environment and system) and mutually influence each other. They depend on one another. This applies not only to collaboration and family life but also to social life in general. Social connectedness has a direct impact on an individual's well-being and physical and mental health. Fundamentally, evolutionary survival depends on other people and successful social contact.

Corporate/Social Responsibility is therefore a central aspect in relation to burnout prevention and recovery. The point is that, as mentioned, those affected by burnout often cannot realistically perceive themselves or the course of their illness. Moreover, direct, honest confrontation with observations and assessments within the team is usually not easy for various reasons, or it is blocked, not heard, or not taken seriously by the person affected by burnout.

If a burnout illness and withdrawal from working life due to illness and exhaustion have occurred, the recovery phase can last several months to over a year, which is not uncommon in cases of burnout. You are very likely already aware of this as well. This not only has significant financial consequences for the company, but also a direct and not to be underestimated impact on the team and the entire organization. On the one hand, this relates to social effects triggered by short-term and unpredictable changes that influence team dynamics and collaboration structures; on the other hand, it also means that the system is thrown out of balance by the resulting personnel gap and must adapt. A team may suddenly face pressure and staff short-ages and must perform the same or even more work with fewer employees over an extended period, as redistribution and more coordination are now required. In addition, important expertise is temporarily missing, which may be lost entirely if reintegration is unsuccessful.

It is therefore worthwhile for the organization as an employer to actively participate in the prevention and avoidance of burnout, to protect employees, and to fulfill its shared responsibility or corporate/social responsibility.

So how is it possible to avoid burnout as a team? In my view, four factors play a decisive role:

- Communication within the team (openness, space and time for community, sociability, and exchange).
- An appreciative attitude and culture (resource- and solution-orientation, a positive error culture, viewing weaknesses as potential for development, utilizing and focusing on the resources and strengths of individuals, mutual appreciation, openness, trust, mindfulness, and awareness of corporate/social responsibility), which is actively practiced, continually revitalized, and discussed.
- Preventive and regular sensitization to the topics of burnout and resilience, recurring discussions about individual health and successful team interactions, as well as topics such as workplace conflicts, differing values, the shared WHY, and the organization's goals, etc. The exchange should not just be implemented on paper, but should enable and promote genuine, real encounters.
- Fostering and jointly developing openness to change (seeing change as a learning process and learning to deal constructively with emerging feelings and thoughts;

viewing mistakes made and challenges encountered as opportunities for change and learning; valuing the perceived resistance and irritation of individuals; strengthening individual autonomy; experiencing the benefits of collective action, which strengthens the system/organization and shared values and attitudes; regularly reflecting on the organization's "blind spots" with external support or with a professional/coach/consultant).

In addition to all these ongoing development topics, it should not be forgotten that the person affected by burnout must make significant changes to themselves, their attitudes, and their behavior during the recovery period. This is often an exhausting, emotional, and challenging personal development and change process. Moreover, despite all efforts, it is not certain that the affected person will actually return to the company. However, addressing the topics of health, resilience, and burnout is worthwhile for the team and the entire organization in any case.

Accordingly, I hope that as a leader you can see a possible burnout case among your employees, despite all the hardship it causes, as an opportunity for change, and that a new awareness of the importance of resilience and health can emerge in your team and organization as a result.

I wish you and your team all the best for the future and for your shared pursuit of strengthened health and resilience, a supportive and appreciative team culture, as well as supportive and protective organizational structures and processes! In addition to the personal responsibility that everyone bears for themselves, this is probably the central contribution to preventing burnout!

(Self-)Reflection—Steps to Self-Awareness

For (Potential) Affected Individuals

Drivers [1] (also called counter-injunctions) and injunctions [2] (also known as ban or witch messages) are part of the script, which was explained in more detail in Chapter II. According to the theory of Mary and Bob Goulding, there are twelve injunctions, some of which we are very likely to have internalized during our childhood. The drivers are unconscious "helpers" (not always implemented positively), which represent the supposed, childlike attempt to weaken, unmask, or disempower the injunctions as untrue. Since drivers and injunctions were mostly "decided" and internalized unconsciously as processes in early childhood, it is all the more difficult to recognize and combat them. This is especially true for the injunctions, as they originated non-verbally and in early childhood, and their origin can therefore often not be determined with certainty. Becoming aware of drivers and injunctions in adulthood can help to weaken and sustainably change the routine, often destructive and solution-avoiding (driver) behavior in a positive way. Becoming aware of the injunctions is not always possible and not necessarily required. Even just weakening the drivers can enable a positive change towards autonomy and enhance well-being.

The twelve injunctions

- Don't be! (Don't exist!)
- Don't be a child!
- Don't be yourself!
- Don't grow up!

- Don't succeed!
- Stop that! Don't do it! Don't do anything, don't do anything at all!
- Don't be important!
- Don't belong!
- Don't be close!
- Don't be healthy! (Don't be normal!)
- Don't think!
- Don't feel!

The five drivers

- Hurry up!
- Please others!
- Be perfect!
- Be strong!
- Try hard!

The drivers originate in early childhood and were conveyed verbally and actively modeled by parents and caregivers. They drive us in the sense of "I must ..." because we unconsciously feel inferior and classify ourselves as "not okay." Injunctions point to an "I am not okay" attitude. To avoid this feeling of inferiority, we have submitted to the drivers. The goal was to restore our value as a person. Becoming aware of (overly) active drivers can help to recognize, gradually dissolve, and weaken limiting mechanisms, destructive beliefs, and unconscious restrictions in (experiencing) life.

To identify the drivers, there is a corresponding self-assessment questionnaire from Transactional Analysis, which is available for download on my website. For injunctions, it makes sense to reflect on them more closely in the context of self-reflection or therapy, counseling, or coaching.

As already mentioned, the exact origin is not always traceable and is not always absolutely necessary for successful development and change towards autonomy.

Once you have recognized a driver or injunction as restrictive and formative for yourself, you can specifically try to weaken it or counteract it step by step in everyday life. In Chapter V, you have already received some examples in the context of the theoretical concept of permissions. Often, simply becoming aware is enough to begin to detach yourself from script-bound behavior, thinking, feeling, and beliefs, moving towards a healthier, more balanced, and freer expression and development in everyday and professional life. The more autonomously (script-free) you are able to act and decide, the stronger you will become in terms of your resilience and recovery. Strengthening autonomy leads to being able to think, feel, act, and decide more consciously and freely overall, which enhances general well-being.

Questions for Self-Reflection

- What especially drives you in everyday life? Which drivers are particularly strong? How do these specifically manifest in your daily life?
- Where do you find it particularly difficult to let go of or change your previous (driver) behavior? What unconscious beliefs or injunctions might be hidden beneath this?
- What beliefs or injunctions might be hidden in your parents? Which of these have you perhaps adopted and internalized yourself? How could you distance yourself from them? What permission would you need for this?
- What fears or insecurities do you encounter in everyday life? How do you deal with them? What new approach

or insights would help you take the next step towards strengthening and autonomy?

- How would a caring mother or father likely react and deal with it if his/her child had this problem or challenge? How could you treat yourself with such care in this situation? What permissions would you need to implement this beneficially?

- If you had no knowledge of your injunctions, what permission or magical message from your unconscious would still help and enable you to take new steps towards greater health and resilience?

- What resources and competencies do you notice in yourself in everyday life that have enabled you to confidently and successfully overcome hurdles and challenges so far?

- How would a good friend likely answer this question? Alternatively, how would your boss answer this question? How would you like to answer it?

For Leaders—With a Focus on the Organization

In teams and organizations, it is also evident that they have internalized certain beliefs, assumptions, rules, and structures in their (team and collaboration) culture, and possibly also (script) patterns and processes, which in turn—consciously or unconsciously—affect collaboration and task execution. Drivers can also shape everyday professional life, shared interactions, and teamwork. Drivers are not inherently negative, as long as they do not cause a person to constantly exceed their resources and limits, leading to personal depletion and health risks. Becoming aware of restrictive beliefs, assumptions, and expectations within the team and organization can already achieve a great deal, which in turn can strengthen autonomy, self-efficacy, and well-being for oneself, within the team, and across the organization.

The following questions can open up helpful perspectives in reflection with your team

- Which (behavioral) patterns, beliefs, or rules do you perceive as being effective in your team? Where and how do these manifest?
- Which (behavioral) patterns, beliefs, or rules do you view more negatively? Which have a positive/negative impact on resilience and health in your team? Why? What risks could arise from an excessive focus and implementation? How do these influence teamwork? Where might a weakening or change be needed?
- Which drivers do you, as a leader, particularly exemplify? Where are you a (negative or positive) role model? What changes might be needed to reduce the impact of these drivers in yourself? How would this positively affect your resilience and health?
- Which restrictive beliefs, expectations, or assumptions (about life, about yourself, or about others) have you internalized that unconsciously influence and perhaps even hinder you in your role as a leader? How can you counteract these? What permissions would be needed for this?
- Do you perhaps have a motto or saying that comes to mind particularly often and drives and shapes your thinking, actions, and decisions at work? Do we perhaps have a motto or saying in the team/organization that we would put on our banner? What does this

motto/saying drive us to do? What opportunities and advantages arise from it? What disadvantages or stumbling blocks could potentially result? Where would it make sense to integrate new ideas or insights?

- Which drivers do you perhaps recognize in your employees? Are there certain drivers that are particularly common in your team/organization? Is there perhaps a preferred driver in your team/organization that is unconsciously adopted by most and perhaps highly valued and encouraged? How could you contribute to a possible change and/or reduction of these drivers? How can you achieve this without overstepping boundaries? What permissions could be helpful for reducing the drivers? What advantages would such a reduction have—especially regarding resilience and health?

- Which (unconscious) patterns do you follow as a team or organization? Do you perhaps have a motto or guiding principles that (unconsciously) drive you and set a certain direction? What advantages and opportunities arise from this? What risks or disadvantages could result?

- What are you convinced of as a team or organization? What guidelines and/or rules exist in your team/organization? Which guidelines and rules are explicit? Which guidelines or rules are implicitly effective? What advantages/disadvantages result from this? What changes might be sensible?

- Which areas of internal structures or procedures should you as a team/organization question more and not regard as "the one truth"? Where would it benefit your team/organization to try new approaches and become more flexible? What positive effects might these changes have on the team/organization?

- Where could you, in the spirit of creative development, engage with new areas, behaviors, ideas, guiding principles, visions, etc., and see what emerges? Where might courage be needed to take the first steps into the unknown and only over time recognize the opportunities that can arise from these new discoveries/steps?

References

1. Schlegel, L. (2002). *Handwörterbuch der Transaktionsanalyse* (2nd ed., pp. 5–7). Herder Verlag.
2. Schlegel, L. (2002). *Handwörterbuch der Transaktionsanalyse* (2nd ed., pp. 84–90). Herder Verlag.

Phase VII—The Great, Wide World—Integration Internally and Externally

Abstract How can the final phase of burnout be recognized and classified? Is there ever any certainty that the danger has passed? When can one speak of complete recovery? When do setbacks finally become noticeably less frequent? What hurdles still need to be overcome even in this phase? Theories on symbiotic relationships and fundamental psychological needs offer clarifying insights into the topic of relationship formation—with oneself and with others. The in-depth sections for (potential) affected individuals, relatives, managers, and teams once again invite (self-)reflection. Change and further development are once again at the center, along with an attitude that integrates a holistic approach, promotes the strengthening of autonomy and personal responsibility, and especially focuses on resilience and health within organizations.

© The Author(s), under exclusive license to Springer Fachmedien   **223**
Wiesbaden GmbH, part of Springer Nature 2025
R. Petersen, *Tsunami in the Head – Better Understanding and Coping
with Burnout*, https://doi.org/10.1007/978-3-658-49737-8_8

The Big, Wide World

Just a few months ago, it was unclear to me whether I would ever find my secure place in the big, wide world again. And now here I am. The lighthouse has receded into the distance. But it is still there. I can feel it. I have integrated it into my thinking, feeling, and actions. It has become a part of me in my memory. But without the feeling of uncertainty or weakness. I have grown beyond myself. The big, wide world lies before me. I am ready to discover it anew. I am ready for new, positive experiences. Confidence, clarity, and strength have spread within me. I can't quite explain it. But it feels good. It was worth staying near the lighthouse for so long until I found this inner strength and power again. I would not have thought it possible. But it was possible. I can feel it, even though many people are afraid that another tsunami will level the world to the ground. Now I am wiser. I have learned. I know the warning signs. My antennas are still in use. But not in a way that throws me into fear and panic when another small tremor comes. The antennas are simply there. As my support. Just for me. Now I am in this world with more strength, clarity, and confidence. I have been given a new life. At least that's how it feels. I will enjoy it to the fullest! Even though I don't yet know exactly what that will look like for me. But I will find out. I am looking forward to this journey of discovery. Life is good.

My Story—Knowing Again that Life will Turn Out Well

The planned increase to eighty percent of a full-time position was once again a small milestone for me. I noticed that the thought of soon having to be on duty four days a week filled me with great fear and concern. At the same time, I was really looking forward to it, because the plan was moving step by step toward returning to my team and my original leadership responsibilities. Unfortunately, my supervisor was out sick for an extended period, which further strained the situation in our organization. In contrast, I had regained new strength and self-confidence. I was already regularly in contact with my deputy, and together we autonomously organized the gradual handover of the various areas of responsibility. I had more energy and interest again in participating in school development topics and other overarching issues from the management team. My life was finally picking up speed again.

This last phase of burnout felt like the beginning of a new life! I was productive again and could, in certain situations, even go beyond my limits without having to pay for it in the days that followed. I was motivated. I had successfully returned to my team. I was able to reestablish myself as a leader and could feel for myself that I was doing so much better than just a few months ago. What a relief. I really enjoyed my job. Admittedly, a lot was still in flux for us. My boss was still absent due to illness. In the meantime, a new interim overall manager had been appointed. I was able to handle this leadership change well, as I could once again take on and fulfill my original area of responsibility. I realized that I was indeed capable of working as a leader again. The first weeks after starting back with my team were already very turbulent. I had to deal with several staff absences. This meant that my core tasks and the daily duties had to be put on hold for the time being and caught up on later. There was no way around it. I passed this first stress test with flying colors. After two weeks of intensive work and days when I worked up to eleven hours again, it was clear proof to me that my health had sustainably improved. I was very relieved and a little proud of the path I had taken and my regained resilience!

At the same time, I still noticed the physical effects of my burnout. My back pain was still present from time to time. I also occasionally had the impression that my memory performance had suffered and deteriorated. For me, however, this was always related to the level of sufficient sleep and tiredness, for example after a concentration-intensive task or a long meeting with friends. Then I noticed that my concentration and memory reached their limits. My sleep was a sensitive commodity. If the work at school was particularly intense and long during the day, I sometimes had trouble falling asleep or staying asleep again. These were the few physical signs that still reminded me of my intense burnout.

How often had I asked myself in the past whether I would ever be able to perform again? For how long could I not even imagine being able to deliver peak performance for an entire day and then maybe go out with friends afterward? For how long did I carry this small quantum of uncertainty within me—a voice that kept trying to prove to me that I probably couldn't fully trust myself? Because deep down, I was still very aware that I hadn't recognized my burnout at the time! That shock ran deep! But now it seemed as if I had also left this last phase of uncertainty behind me. Or at least I was able to put this inner voice in its place and assess it correctly more and more quickly. This back and forth and this uncertainty about my resilience would accompany me for a long time in the final phase and beyond, and were repeatedly a topic in therapy sessions.

After more than a year, I had made it. I was once again responsible as principal for my original team and solely in charge of all matters. I was finally able to leave the ongoing sick notes behind me. My deputy had stopped working at the end of the month. The handover went well, though at times it was very demanding. I was amazed at how well I had managed this phase and the increasing complexity of onboarding with the various challenges. I once again felt great motivation for my work as principal. The planning day with my team during the summer holidays had shown me that it was the right decision to return to my original workplace. That was not a given. I was afraid that my employees might behave differently and perhaps no longer trust me with certain tasks, even though I had never made it public that I had suffered from burnout and that this was the reason for my long absence. My team responded straightforwardly and seemed pleased that I had returned safe and healthy. They had already noticed months earlier that I had returned to the organization for onboarding with other tasks. But now it was finally clear that, as their supervisor, I could pick up where my deputy had left off. In my interactions with my employees, I realized once again that the leadership role suited me, that I thrived in this position, and that it brought me joy to be there for a team and to provide important structures, orientation, and support for the staff. I was especially happy to be in contact again with parents and students and the team in the regular school setting. I noticed how interacting with people once again mobilized new energy within me. Previously, during my burnout, all of this had only drained my energy. That was a major step forward, which made me optimistic and inspired me. However, I would like to note here that many things were still not as they had been before my burnout. Fortunately, I could now say that this was no longer my goal. I now saw the changes I had made as positive. My development was not yet complete. But I had found a new quality of life in everyday life, which allowed me to experience calmer times and to consciously enjoy and engage in encounters with other people again. I allowed myself a lot of rest and sleep and paid attention to getting enough exercise, sports, and healthy nutrition. My back still determined my daily schedule on some days, and so I oriented myself more than before to my bodily sensations and the energy I had. At work, I made a point of taking enough breaks and tried to follow my drive for achievement and perfectionism less. I was increasingly able to strike a balance between head (thinking), heart (feeling, sensing), and hand (doing), and that filled me with great satisfaction.

Dealing with breaks was another aha moment and learning process for me in personal self-reflection. Unconsciously, I had equated breaks with something unimportant, secondary. This did not apply to my employees, but only to myself. I believed that I didn't need breaks! Let alone was I really able to perceive or pinpoint when I actually needed a break. Accordingly, I was quick to fall back into my old pattern at work in the office, especially under stress, simply skipping breaks. Once I started working, I was so absorbed in a task that I was reluctant to mentally detach and allow an interruption. Just two hours later, my body would signal me with back or headaches. I learned from this that when my body speaks to me, it's actually already too late and I had crossed my limits several times. Over time, I realized that these very interruptions through a break were especially important and valuable for me, even though I often found it difficult to take a break at all. So I started setting the alarm on my phone to force myself to take a half-hour lunch break. Over time, especially after moving into my new office, I even suddenly found joy again in taking a short walk to the grocery store, buying something for lunch, and then eating with other teachers in the staff room. A new ritual developed from this, which allowed me valuable social contact and at the same time provided distance from work and fascinating insights into the everyday lives of others. I now even saw the back and headaches as a resource and wake-up call—a clear sign that it was okay to take things more slowly and with less effort.

The burnout illness had deeply shaken my fundamental trust in life and in myself. After a long period of illness and recovery, I had finally found my way back to myself and my inner strength and power. I could even say that I now stood stronger and more grounded in life than ever before! If there was one thing I now saw clearly, it was that after the intense and prolonged illness, I was no longer the same person as before. And that was a good thing. Certain parts of me had been left behind, others had been added! That is probably the case in every crisis, in one way or another! But with a burnout illness, I could say from my own experience that the shocks and effects are profound and highly complex, and in my case, at their root, felt existentially threatening, identity-robbing, and very frightening for a long time.

So I had found my way back to myself, and with that came the certainty that I wanted to take care of myself and was able to do so again! I had decided for myself that I never wanted to fall into such overload again and would do everything to prevent a relapse. The burnout illness had helped me, in a rough way, to get out of the hamster wheel and recognize the overload. I hadn't been able to do that before. I really did not want to experience a relapse under any circumstances. Unfortunately, there was no guarantee for that. By now, however, I rated my resilience quite highly. I now knew much more precisely what I wanted and what I didn't, and how it felt when I acted against my inner voice and intuition. Conscious awareness had become an important benchmark for me. I now seemed to have truly arrived at myself and had thus regained trust in myself. Through personal reflection and exchanges with others, I had realized that my experience could be an important resource for other people! That was the reason why I wanted to write this book. Even if I was sometimes unsure whether and how many people I would reach with it. Fortunately, I had learned that it is not crucial to always know and control everything in advance. Sharing my experience was therefore an important next step on my developmental path. I wanted to be able to stand up and openly talk about my experiences with burnout. Knowing that what I had gone through could not define me as a person. And because I knew that it is possible to recover from burnout and emerge stronger! With this, I wanted to encourage others and break the social taboo! In my view, individually experienced weakness and suffering can thus become a societal strength!

The topics of burnout, depression, and mental illness are still equated with weakness and inadequacy in our society. They are stigmatized and often associated with prejudice, even though, fortunately, more and more people are openly speaking about their experience with burnout. On the other hand, many do not talk openly about their experience, which I can well understand. I sometimes wonder how people will react to my disclosure and what influence it will have on their perception of me. At the same time, I now feel this strength in me again, not to let it unsettle me. I want to encourage everyone to believe in themselves and to prioritize their own health and resilience early enough. Nothing else is worth it! Only in this way can a lot of personal suffering, as well as family and societal harm, be avoided. Every case of burnout inevitably affects the entire system, and in this sense, each of us bears a responsibility toward our environment.

The burnout illness had taught me that I was worth taking care of myself and my health, and that I would be of no use to anyone if my health suffered and I became unable to work. Our health and well-being are directly linked to our innermost wishes and ideas of a happy life. I knew that even before my illness. Meaningfulness, feeling valuable, loved, and accepted, being part of society, is important for every person, regardless of status, education, professional or work ability. Every person is valuable, regardless of what he or she achieves or can achieve! Unconsciously, however, we are often convinced of the opposite, so that we let ourselves be pushed into withdrawal by feelings such as shame, guilt, and inadequacy. Very few people can claim to be completely free of self-doubt and to have received an invulnerable fundamental trust from their parents for their personal life journey. Each of us has our own personal story with experiences that bring insecurity, discouragement, and patterns of adaptation. Perhaps we believe that we were negatively shaped in our childhood and therefore cannot change. But change is possible, at any age and at any time! At the latest as adults, we can autonomously decide which path we want to take. We can show ourselves an appreciative and loving attitude and take sufficient care of our body, mind, and soul. That is exactly what I was able to learn and recognize for myself in different ways during my burnout illness. It was a rocky road that often threw me off balance and challenged me personally. From my experience, there is no way to successful recovery without a holistic approach that integrates intuition and spirituality. There are many different ways to design and discover one's own preferences and needs. My broad expertise and professional experience had taken me far. Accessing things through thinking and my intellect came easily to me. Accessing through feeling, experiencing, and my intuition was something I had to partially relearn and further develop for myself during my burnout illness. Realizing how much I had become alienated from myself would probably shape and influence me for the rest of my life. And that was a good thing, because I had the impression that through my personal development and experience, I had become an even better counselor and leader. In life, it was always about finding one's own suitable path and answers to central questions. Detours and setbacks were not failures, but opportunities for further development. In this sense, I now saw the courage and ability to admit weakness as a strength, because I had so often experienced that this very admission opened up unexpected opportunities for personal encounters (with oneself and others). For that, I was infinitely grateful!

Burnout Diary—Snapshots

"Burnout is like an avalanche of demands crashing down on you. Whether these demands come from yourself or from outside. Your reaction time is too short either way for you to get yourself to safety. The snow swirls you around and presses you down with full force. Every movement hurts and makes your breathing slowly become shallower."
Rebecca Petersen

I am back in life! Sometimes still a bit unsteady on my feet, but stronger and more aware than ever before. And that's a good thing. I have fought my way back to my place in the organization and in life. I am content. A gradual return makes sense. I still have many personal issues and questions I want to work on. I am still grateful for the support of a therapist. Certain routines are becoming established, others are falling away. Things I used to hold onto with all my strength (mentally and emotionally) are now becoming less and less important. My health is increasingly improving, without me having to actively do anything or even being aware of it. I notice that helpful routines and anchors integrate or change in my everyday life quite naturally, without effort. I can let go of control more and more and trust that things will turn out well.

I have stopped writing my book! I urgently need a break. I am not sure where the journey should go or what I should do with my original plans for this book. All I know is that constantly dealing with my burnout illness has recently been costing me a lot of energy. It's not worth it to me. I will no longer put myself under pressure! That's what I've learned in recent months! I know that it is counter-productive for my health. I will simply remain open to the possibility that this original desire—to generate meaning for myself from my suffering and experiences with burn-out—will once again change for the better. I am confident that I will find my way, including with regard to a possible book publication. For now, that simply requires some time, patience, and, obviously, a conscious letting go!

In everyday life, I still deliberately use strategies from positive psychology, coaching, transactional analysis, and personal development, as well as from spirituality and mindfulness teachings. I have learned to build in stabilizing structures and habits and to notice more quickly when I am overstepping my boundaries. The question remains whether and how I will manage to maintain these helpful anchors and resources even when my workload and professional stress increase again. Time will give me the answer. What I really enjoy, though, is that I have discovered for myself that there is not just one meaningful strategy, but that I intuitively notice again and again what does me good at any given moment. I have noticed that my needs can change over time and throughout the development process. With this realization, a new kind of flexibility and lightness has entered my everyday life, because I no longer have to cling so tightly to planned structures.

Today I managed it again! Another milestone has been reached. I told my mother and my brother about my burnout illness. I am getting better and better at talking about it. Even though my pulse still rises with every revelation to people who are important to me, and I am close to tears. So I am gradually letting more and more of my family members and friends in on what I have experienced in relation to the burnout. It takes courage, and here too I am giving myself time. I listen to myself. I don't set any specific goals. I decide in the moment, based on my gut feeling, and listen to my heart. Many people react positively, sharing their own experiences, fears, and moments of weakness. My mother and brother do as well. I notice in these exchanges that my own strength increases as a result. I observe myself and recognize how much better I am doing since the collapse caused by my burnout. I am in a completely different place than before the burnout. I have certainly carried some scars and injuries with me, but they are healing, step by step, and even seem to be manifesting as evidence of new strength, wisdom, and confidence. I am often overcome by a deep sense of gratitude. Sometimes the feelings of guilt and shame return, as do sadness and fear. But I am increasingly able to see in this process that they have less of a paralyzing effect on me, or that I can leave them behind after a short time. That gives me a sense of security. I still feel that I must not become too euphoric too quickly and that I still need to give myself time with everything. Or perhaps better said, I am allowed to give myself time. Especially in enduring emerging emotions and being aware that I do not have to put myself under pressure, there lies a great resource. Also because I am not only trusting myself, but also the connection to something greater, and trusting that things will work out somehow. Strength can develop from weakness. I have now experienced this myself, both physically and emotionally.

I have finally adopted a new, more flexible daily routine that keeps me mentally afloat and can be reconciled with my new workload. I hardly have any days anymore when I feel completely beside myself and as if my future plans are going down the drain. I use strategies from positive psychology, sports and nutritional sciences, and spirituality. In recent months—or at least since I was mentally and physically able to do so again—I have worked on myself intensively and purposefully. I have engaged in personal development. Not only within the framework of various therapies and treatments (physio, talk therapy, breathing therapy, TCM, coaching, etc.), but also through delving into literature, further education, etc. I notice that this combination of "mind, body, and soul" and different approaches, as banal as it may sound, does me a lot of good, and that I have found my own individual, suitable path. At least for the moment. The question remains whether and how I will manage to maintain this rhythm and positive focus. I wonder what my workload should be in the future. Do I want to aim for a full-time or part-time position in the long term? I cannot answer that definitively at the moment. And that's okay! One thing at a time, I tell myself!

Lately, I find myself wondering more and more often whether I am already over the worst and can feel safe from a possible relapse. Have I really overcome the burnout? Can I trust myself enough again to actually notice if I were to fall back into old patterns of overexertion and overwork? At the moment, I still have support and regular therapy, for which I am still very grateful. But what will it be like when I am fully on my own again? When will I be ready, and how will I notice? I don't know the answers to any of these questions yet. I still don't know what the future will bring.

But that's okay. In my reintegration process within my organization, case management still proves to be an important resource. Even now, as I have been working at eighty percent for quite some time, partly from home. Although I now need less support and fewer conversations from case management, it is reassuring to have a neutral person who knows my story by my side. I am truly grateful that this support is available at my workplace.

At the moment, we are seeing a lot of absences among employees at the organizational level. Not all of them are due to overload, but some are. In such moments, I sometimes relive the self-doubt and exhaustion of the acute phase of my illness. Sadness, anger, and helplessness spread. And then the thought returns that maybe it does make sense to publish the book after all. It could be an opportunity to point out the mutual responsibility we have for each other in an (organizational) system and in society, and which, in my view, we should actively acknowledge. I am not saying that my illness or someone else's burnout could have been prevented in this way. But precisely because burnout can lead to a strong sense of self-alienation and the symptoms manifest so individually and diversely, exchange and education are important. Togetherness and social encounters are valuable, because in trusting interactions, people can look out for one another. With targeted team development and prevention, awareness of the dangers of possible burnout can be promoted. This topic of prevention is truly very close to my heart and gives me new confidence. Yes, maybe I will decide to publish the book after all, if possible.

I have more energy again to actively contribute to management tasks and take responsibility for overarching projects. I can lead, shape, and guide, just as I did before my burnout. This feeling is indescribable. We still have many processes and procedures that need to be clarified and worked through. But that's a good thing. I feel that I can make a difference in the organization and contribute my skills and strengths to good effect. That motivates me.

On bad days, I still doubt myself and my abilities, like today. When will this uncertainty finally end? I have several staff absences to deal with and therefore have to find substitutes. I have to put aside all the core work of my school leadership role for weeks because I am busy with recruitment. Even the best organization and planning can't help with that. Now it's a matter of setting priorities. Eleven-hour days are becoming more frequent again. The good thing is that I have the strength to manage them. I never thought that would be possible again with this intensity. On the other hand, I wonder whether I want to keep this up in the future and whether the organization as such is the wrong workplace for me. I see this as a conscious decision for myself. I have a responsibility to myself here. A responsibility I bear for myself and my health. In this context, my therapist confronted me with the possibility of a relapse and the fact that the "data highway" in the brain quickly finds its way back to old patterns. She asked me directly whether I really want to take that risk. Of course not! The confrontation helps me realize that, while it is gratifying that I am so productive again, I am at risk of slipping uncontrollably back into old habits and overwork. I will do everything I can to prevent that. I owe it to myself!

Similarly, I am looking around the job market and considering what else, besides the school leadership role and consulting work, might be an option for me. At the same time, I notice that I simply enjoy the leadership job very much and can derive a great deal of meaning and motivation from it. At some point, this question will probably be resolved for me. I am open to new things and, in the meantime, I am trying to set healthy and sufficient boundaries for myself. No more excuses!

I still make use of the opportunity for talk therapy. It never gets boring, and I believe that I benefit enormously from it every time. I am grateful for the many insights I am able to take away for myself each time. For example, there is the realization that in recent years I have identified too strongly with my job as a school principal. That's true, even though I never really wanted to admit it! In addition, I wanted to do my work as perfectly and efficiently as possible. As a single person, my life at times consisted only of work, sleep, eating, and a bit of exercise. I was already aware of this back then, but at the same time, I didn't really know how I could actively change this situation. During the time of Covid and the lockdown, I used the social isolation as an opportunity to spend even more time working in the office or at home. I started working earlier in the morning and finished later than usual. I also wanted to be sufficiently available for my team. All of these are tendencies that, from an outside perspective, need to be critically assessed. However, I would not have believed the actual extent of my overwork if I hadn't looked more closely at my work time notes from a year ago at a later point. I felt completely taken aback! In half a year, I had unknowingly accumulated an incredible number of overtime hours and, over the course of the day, had apparently just skipped all breaks. I started working earlier and earlier in the mornings, sometimes before six o'clock, and would also work from home at the most impossible times. But I never consciously noticed or realized these changes at the time.

It still happens that I occasionally become insecure and ask myself whether I am up to the demands of being a school principal. In times of crisis, I perform at my best and simply function. That is a real strength. It becomes problematic when I overthink possible shortcomings or view my performance very self-critically. However, I am now able to regulate myself much more quickly in this regard. This is because I have realized that if, when feeling overwhelmed or inadequate, I can remain calm and allow myself to take a short break, the problem or question usually resolves itself, and my abilities and self-confidence return effortlessly. Here, "Strength lies in calmness!" applies, because as if by magic, I can then suddenly solve the issue or make the decision without any problems and think and act with newfound clarity.

It remains a challenge to focus on and actively shape both my private and professional life. I simply enjoy working and therefore tend to focus on it too much and define myself by it. Somehow, I can't change that. In many moments, I simply enjoy being so focused and professional, shaping the workday with my team, and seeing how the students flourish and make progress. I am very convinced of my team and their abilities and competencies. I still have high expectations of myself when it comes to my work as a school principal and leader. At the same time, I now notice much more quickly when I and my body are reaching their limits. I can react more quickly. I now know very clearly that it is absolutely pointless to push myself beyond my limits too often. That serves neither me, nor my team, nor the organization as a whole. As a result, I have to prioritize much more and learn to live with the often very large, unfinished pile of to-dos without feeling pressure or guilt. Especially when it comes to the concerns of my staff, I still often struggle with this. And yet I now know that this is precisely where an important personal vulnerability lies, one that challenges me and that I must repeatedly work on and, if possible, learn to overcome for my own protection.

I pay attention to healthy nutrition! Cooking has become a new, rediscovered passion. Even when I sometimes come home late in the evening. I have also rediscovered fasting for myself. I meditate daily. I exercise regularly and spend time outdoors in the fresh air. I drink enough fluids, consciously take time for myself and for "just being." I consciously follow positive thoughts! I keep a journal and deliberately note things I am grateful for. All of this may sound a bit trivial. But it helped me tremendously during difficult times. And just establishing these simple routines was a real feat of strength at the beginning of the burnout illness. And now, as I am doing better, these routines have become an important support in my everyday life. I notice that I still have to work on maintaining them. That is not always easy alongside work. I have already changed some of the routines again and adapted them to my new daily life. But overall, they give me stability. I have even written down certain insights and routines in a small notebook, which I keep in front of me in my school principal's office, as a reminder and personal prompt! I used to think that these routines were akin to an inflexible life. Today, I see these routines as positive, strengthening anchors and resources that are good for me personally and help me take care of my mental and physical health. They have become an important resource, without me having to perform them compulsively.

I still go to the sauna for inner balance. A resource for body and mind. Hiking also helps me clear my mind in a good way and allows me to feel my body intensely. I have started writing again. Suddenly, I knew that I now felt the strength and motivation to devote myself to my previously shelved book project. The feeling of having made significant progress in my recovery encouraged me in this. This is a wonderful development, and I am glad that I was able to consciously take and use this writing break for myself without doubting myself too much.

I still go for a massage from time to time. I notice what a big difference there is in my experience when I lie on the massage table today. I am able to calm my mind much more quickly, engage in a brief conversation with the masseuse, laugh together, and then just switch off, relax, and enjoy. It is no longer absolutely necessary for my well-being, but it is incredibly pleasant. That was different before my burnout illness. I had practically rescued myself onto the mat. My thoughts would race throughout the entire treatment, and I could hardly relax at all. The change is therefore actually physically noticeable, and I am pleased that I am now in a different place than I was back then.

I have now been working successfully in my company again for more than a year and a half, the last half year almost one hundred percent without sick leave. I have reached a milestone! I have returned to my team at my original workplace. Unfortunately, my wish to reduce my workload will not be possible so quickly, but I hope that my employer will accommodate me in the long term. I am aware that, at the moment, it is still about building and consolidating mutual trust. Every month in which I successfully do my job and both I and those around me increasingly notice that I am capable again gives me further confidence and energy for life. I am proud to have managed the re-entry with my team! They welcomed me back well after my long absence. We are now functioning again as a well-coordinated team. I have the impression that mutual trust in our collaboration can now grow.

I am actively fighting to finally be able to go on vacation again. Fighting in the sense that I want to bring it into my awareness. I tell practically everyone in my organization that I am going on vacation for a full two weeks. As if I want to protect myself from backing out and starting work earlier than planned. I have already made a long to-do list that I want to tackle after the vacation. Letting go is hard for me. But I manage it and travel to the mountains as planned. It takes a few days for my mind to unwind and for me to stop thinking every few hours about something I still need to do for work. Eventually, these thoughts become less frequent. I have arrived. Hiking in the mountains does me good. I am, in the truest sense, "over the mountain." I am finally "vacation-ready" again, and I am only now realizing it. That's how it started back then with the burnout illness: that I was no longer able to recover during vacations and create distance from everyday work. Another milestone has been achieved. What a relief!

Figuratively Speaking—Finding Security Within Myself

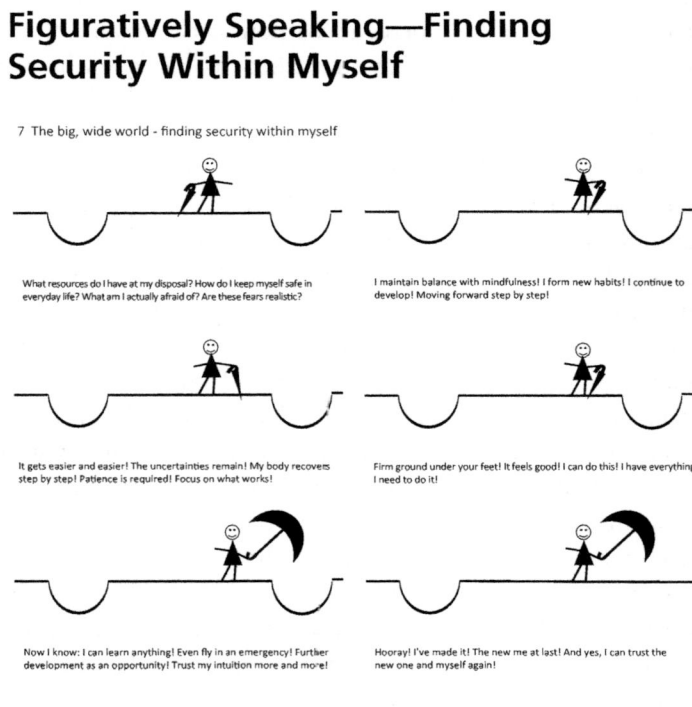

7 The big, wide world - finding security within myself

What resources do I have at my disposal? How do I keep myself safe in everyday life? What am I actually afraid of? Are these fears realistic?

I maintain balance with mindfulness! I form new habits! I continue to develop! Moving forward step by step!

It gets easier and easier! The uncertainties remain! My body recovers step by step! Patience is required! Focus on what works!

Firm ground under your feet! It feels good! I can do this! I have everything I need to do it!

Now I know: I can learn anything! Even fly in an emergency! Further development as an opportunity! Trust my intuition more and more!

Hooray! I've made it! The new me at last! And yes, I can trust the new one and myself again!

For (Potential) Affected Individuals— Learning Self-Reflection and Resilience

In the final phase of burnout, the focus is on integrating what has been learned, whether on an emotional, cognitive, or behavioral level. All aspects are important! We humans are a unity of mind, body, and soul, and thus recovery also requires the most holistic approach possible. If we focus on only one area, we run the risk that another aspect will be neglected. If we do something good for one aspect, we can assume that this will benefit our entire organism and the other aspects as well.

In this final phase, the goal is to integrate helpful processes, habits, and routines into your personal and professional daily life. In an earlier phase, the focus was on identifying and becoming aware of these personal resources and new habits in the first place. Now you have already made significant progress! Many of these new habits have likely already become part of your actions, thoughts, and feelings. Others may still require more attention depending on the situation and your stress level. That is perfectly fine for now and will probably remain the case in certain areas for some time, as it is part of the personal development journey to achieve long-term recovery from burnout. Development means constant change (in thinking, feeling, and acting) as well as apparent setbacks.

A new attitude and a new perspective on yourself and the illness are needed. By this I mean that you must mentally get used to the idea of no longer being ill! You have developed significantly over the past months, and it is possible that you have only partially noticed these changes yourself. We often continue to dwell on old issues because we are used to it; dealing with these topics has become a habit and seems to provide us with security and orientation. At this point, it is important once again to recognize that you are not your burnout illness and that you can leave it behind!

It is time to appreciate the experiences, insights, and learning steps you have made, to record them in writing if necessary, and then to let go! Writing things down helps you to mentally implement the idea of letting go of still being ill and to give it form and expression! Ultimately, this includes letting go of the doubting thoughts that remind you of a possible relapse and consciously releasing the many uncertainties that were present in so many areas of life for a long time. It is about letting go of those thoughts that prevent you from making a powerful new start. At the same time, there may be countless thoughts and insights that have given you courage, strength, and confidence. Of course, you should keep these and consider which thoughts are encouraging for you and should continue to accompany you. Let your intuition guide you here!

Conscious letting go is not always easy! It can be helpful to perform a kind of ritual in which you name all those thoughts, fears, and worries once again, perhaps even write them down on a piece of paper. It is important to acknowledge their value in the past. Every thought, every fear, etc., has contributed to your development. Now it is time to let these thoughts, fears, etc., go with gratitude. They have fulfilled their purpose. You no longer need to hold on to them. For example, you might write down these thoughts and burn them, bury them, or literally let them drift away in a stream or lake. Take this idea with you and consider what might be helpful for you in this process of saying goodbye and letting go. There is no right or wrong here! Your intuition will show you the right way and the right time for you!

During the course of your burnout illness, you were at times intensely focused only on yourself. This focus on your own person was very important and purposeful at the time. In the meantime, you may have more energy available again to connect with other people and be present in the outside world. At this point, I would like to draw your attention to another important concept from transactional analysis.

This concerns symbiotic relationship patterns. According to the theory by Schiff et al., a symbiosis occurs when two or more individuals behave as if they together form a single person. This is also referred to as "psychological togetherness," in which there is an over- and under-responsibility. The person who takes responsibility for the other(s) activates only their Parent and Adult ego states within the relationship. The Child ego state is excluded. The other person, in turn, will activate their ego states in the opposite way. In such a relationship, those involved do not use their full range of ego states. Both people have access to only part of their ego states. Accordingly, both tend not to make autonomous decisions or take autonomous actions. This is evident, for example, when one person assumes responsibility for the other without being asked. As a result, a mutual dependency arises with a lack of boundaries [4].

The concept of symbiotic relationship patterns is closely linked to the concept of the three basic needs, which is described in more detail at the end of this chapter under (self-)reflection. On the one hand, I would like to encourage you to take a closer look at your relationships and friendships. It is also worthwhile here to consciously "sort out" and reflect on which contacts are truly good for you and give you energy, and which are rather draining, demotivating, or constricting, or even intrusive and overstepping boundaries. Health and resilience are directly connected to autonomy, self-efficacy, and self-responsibility. Actively shaping your own life path and taking care of your own needs is possible when you maintain a supportive relationship with yourself and energize all your ego states. This is not the case in symbiotic relationships, so a process of detachment toward autonomy is necessary. Such a process of detachment can be very unsettling and exhausting depending on the situation and relationship, so it may be helpful to seek professional help from a therapist or counselor.

It therefore makes sense to examine whether possible symbiotic relationships exist in your network and to reflect on how strongly they affect you. For your final recovery, it is important that you increasingly take responsibility for your own thinking, feeling, acting, believing, and decision-making, and that you are sufficiently attentive to your individual needs. This is entirely in the spirit of strengthening autonomy and personal responsibility, which, as mentioned, will benefit your overall health and resilience.

So, take a critical look at yourself again in reflection, so that you can directly address and, if possible, resolve deeper patterns of unhealthy dependencies and symbioses in relationships! It does not have to be the case that symbiotic relationship patterns are present. Sometimes relationships can simply feel paralyzing or draining. Then it is important to find out where your own boundaries lie and what might be the trigger for discomfort and unease in your interactions with that person. A therapist or psychological counselor can provide helpful support here and accompany you on your path to greater clarity. It is also important for me to mention that there are temporary symbioses that can make sense and be supportive and nurturing. Just think of a mother and her infant, or a person who has broken their leg and needs help getting dressed and cooking. In such cases, support from another person makes perfect sense, as long as the development and expression of autonomy are not restricted and the person can still energize their three ego states (see Phase IV—Integrative ER-Ego) with energy.

If this is not always possible for you at the moment and you still have phases in which you feel unwell and need additional support (e.g., for decisions about your next development steps, etc.), this does not mean that you are not fully functional in your life or are not acting responsibly. It may be more of an indication that you are still relying too much on others and have handed over responsibility for your happiness (and, depending on the case, your health) to someone else. This carries the risk of dependency and a lack of boundaries.

If this supportive person is no longer available or acts and reacts differently than expected or desired, this can lead to relationship conflicts, insecurity, and possibly relapses on your path to recovery. Therefore, for sustainable recovery, it makes sense to get to the bottom of the issue of supportive, nurturing, and energizing relationships sooner or later and to gain clarity for yourself. This will further increase your resilience! In addition, you depend on your environment trusting you to handle things again and allowing you to regain your autonomy, if that is not already the case. Be mindful here and encourage your environment when you notice that people close to you are giving you more and more space, encouraging you to make your own decisions, and no longer preventing you from pushing your limits. You can trust yourself more again and allow yourself to make mistakes or cross boundaries along the way. Do not be afraid! Step by step, you will notice what is good for you and where it may have been too much.

I wish you strength and perseverance, knowing that you have already come a long way! Resolving relationship issues takes time and patience. So do not overwhelm yourself with it. There is no rush! Let what you have read sink in for a while and then decide which next steps you want to take.

For Relatives, Friends, and Colleagues—Systems Thinking

Life has, in all likelihood, regained a sense of calm and composure, and perhaps a bit more speed and stress has crept back into your daily routine. At the very least, you are increasingly experiencing yourself on solid ground, with familiar processes and routines—whether in your partnership, family, or organizational team. That is a good thing!

Nevertheless, there may still be a lingering aftertaste and the awareness that things will never be exactly as they were before. The experience of burnout has likely left its mark—not only on the person affected, but also on the family or the team.

It is now important to take another step forward and draw a line. This requires a conscious act of letting go and turning toward the new and the carefree. This is essential in order to fully leave the illness and its memory behind. It marks another milestone in the recovery process—for the entire system.

Give the affected person the chance to truly be themselves again. Trust that they are capable of accurately assessing themselves. Do not be afraid if the person occasionally takes on too much and reaches their limits. This is part of the learning process and is an important component of recovery and the strengthening of the affected person's autonomy.

Refocus your attention more on yourself! The former burnout sufferer is now healthy again, autonomous, independent, and responsible for their own health, needs, and for maintaining their boundaries. This distinction and separation are important. There was a phase when your support was helpful and absolutely necessary. That is no longer the case. Let go! Start anew with trust in life and your shared daily routine.

Consider how you can handle this new freedom and lightness. Is it easy for you, or do you catch yourself asking again, observing critically or anxiously, and/or wanting to add your opinion to a topic?

Depending on your situation, it may be time for you to adjust to these new circumstances and begin your own process of working through and letting go. Depending on how close you were to the affected person, this may be an intense personal process. Perhaps you still have fears or concerns about a possible relapse that are weighing on you? Or images from the past that you cannot let go of? Do not hesitate to seek help and support through counseling or therapy if needed.

Perhaps, however, you find it easy and are simply looking forward to finally returning to a normal, carefree life! Maybe you were not so deeply affected by the whole situation and events, and over the past months you were able to take good care of yourself and maintain healthy boundaries. Wonderful!

In that case, my suggestion is: Enjoy life to the fullest! Do something good for yourself! Laugh together and savor the newfound energy! Relax and allow lightness and newfound joy to enter your professional and family life!

You did it! The experiences surrounding the burnout can now gradually fade into the background! Let go now and take a deep breath! You have made it through the period of greatest uncertainty!

For Managers—Corporate/Social Responsibility

The affected person has, in all likelihood, been working again for several months in accordance with their position prior to the burnout illness and is no longer on sick leave. Over time, you have noticed that a few uncertainties still remain. However, it is becoming increasingly clear that the employee truly feels better and is once again able to take on full commitment and full responsibility in the company.

Perhaps you feel relieved about this positive development?! It was a challenging time—for yourself, the affected person, and the team. Maybe you empathized along the way and had to learn to deal with the uncertainties and setbacks of the affected person. There may have been tensions or conflicts between you as a manager and the employee during this period that you had to resolve. Perhaps case management was involved, which was able to provide support but also meant additional effort for you?! Let's be honest: a burnout illness does not leave the organization and the team unaffected! But together, you made it through!

Perhaps, during the reintegration process, it was necessary for the person to change their workplace and thus they are no longer part of your organization or team. This, too, leaves its mark in addition to the vacancy that needs to be filled, and creates a gap that, depending on the situation in the company, should be addressed and discussed within the team.

From my perspective, a burnout illness is always a symptom of a very complex, multi-layered problem that affects and can impact an entire system. In most cases, internal company structures and leadership culture play a significant role. It is therefore important not to simply shift all responsibility onto the person affected by burnout, but to assume personal responsibility in the sense of corporate responsibility and to critically examine the structures and conditions within the company.

Questions arise such as: Which local structures can foster, prevent, or avert a burnout illness? How do you design sustainable and holistic health management in your company? How do you handle workplace conflicts? How do you ensure successful communication and a culture of appreciation and trust within the team? With what attitude do you approach someone affected by burnout in general and/or after their return? Where do you locate the reasons for a burnout illness within your team? What are you willing to actively contribute to prevention and strengthening resilience in your team? What prevents you from taking a clear stance and moving forward with the next steps?

I am convinced that organizations fundamentally care about the well-being and health of their employees. However, in the demanding day-to-day business, they are often overwhelmed when it comes to implementing and establishing a sustainable and holistic approach to health management, as well as to team, leadership, and corporate culture. In my view, this is where money, time, and other valuable resources are being saved in the wrong place.

I am aware that not every manager or team member can or wants to change the entire organization right away. It takes courage to engage with company issues in the long term in the spirit of corporate responsibility, especially regarding health and resilience, and to take a clear position.

I firmly believe that every (leadership) person in the company can make an important contribution. The small things make a decisive difference. Positive feedback from a supervisor can work wonders and provide relief. It is about making enough time for team interactions, establishing appreciative encounters, and consciously creating time slots in your busy schedule for exchange, organizational topics, and (self-)reflection. It is about meeting a former burnout sufferer with openness, appreciation, and respect. Ask interested and open questions instead of giving unsolicited advice or voicing prejudices and judgments—this makes a difference in your interactions and fosters mutual respect. I would like to remind you that burnout has so many facets and manifestations that no one can truly know what the formerly affected person has gone through or what challenges they may still be facing today. Be open and interested in genuine encounters and exchanges at eye level. Build trust and approach difficulties and emerging conflicts with an open, solution-oriented attitude. Trust the person to take on responsibilities again! Do not expect everyone to talk about their experiences. Dealing with the illness and the experiences is highly individual. Respect boundaries here as well, but be open and signal your willingness to engage in dialogue. This greatly contributes to a trusting relationship!

I have deliberately chosen the term "formerly affected" here. Because even here, your support is needed! A formerly affected person can only fully recover if their environment gradually restores trust and believes that they can assess themselves correctly and perform. This requires openness, appreciation, and tolerance from everyone involved. If you feel uncertain, express it and address your concerns and fears with the person in a calm moment and in a protected setting. Dare to openly discuss feelings such as sadness, anger, helplessness, etc., or thoughts and concerns about stress and being overwhelmed. This enables the person to reflect on themselves and take personal responsibility for their position. Trust your counterpart with your observations and assessment! In my view, this is the royal road to appreciative and respectful interaction, leading to a supportive, open, and understanding relationship!

This very sense of "we" is so important for a good working atmosphere in the team and the entire organization! Then it becomes possible to talk openly and honestly about burnout or one's own limits and weaknesses without fear of being judged or considered incapable of coping. This is another important step toward a strengthened organization that employs healthy, motivated, and high-performing staff and operates sustainably, respectfully, and successfully. In my view, investing in corporate responsibility and sustainable health management is always worthwhile!

> I wish you much success in implementation! If necessary, seek support from an external expert! It is worthwhile to establish supportive structures in the team and organizational structure that strengthen and focus on the health and resilience of employees. This requires long-term processes and solutions.

(Self-)Reflection—Steps Toward Self-Insight

For (Potential) Affected Individuals

On my path to recovery, transactional analysis—and in particular, the theory of the three basic needs [1]—has repeatedly helped me to consciously do good things for myself and pay attention to my needs. When I was in an emotional or energetic low, I sometimes simply forced myself to take action (e.g., getting a massage or going for a walk, etc.), because I knew it would do me good and I would feel better afterwards.

The basic needs [1] according to Eric Berne describe, in contrast to physiological basic needs such as sleep, food, and shelter, the psychological basic needs of a person. These are recognition/stroking (stroke), stimulation (stimulus), and structure/time management (structure). I could go into detail about each of these areas here, but that would go beyond the scope of this book. Therefore, I will try to summarize them for you as briefly and clearly as possible:

Recognition/Stroking (stroke): This can be either negative or positive attention, which is expressed by another person or by oneself. If positive recognition is not possible, people settle for negative recognition [2]. According to Spitz, an Austrian developmental psychologist, a lack of recognition or contact, especially in childhood, can even lead to physical or emotional disorders [3].

Examples: praise, a smile, touch, discussion, argument, conversation, SMS/WhatsApp message, etc.

Stimulation (stimulus): Your five senses (smelling, tasting, feeling, hearing, touching) are stimulated in different ways, which can lead to greater well-being. In addition, it can be helpful in everyday life to promote a holistic approach and implementation, for example in problem-solving or structuring the workday. It can be useful not only to activate thinking (head), but also to include feelings and sensations (heart) and actions (hand). Besides thinking and analyzing, it can also help to consciously include intuition in the process.

Examples: spices/scents, sauna, walk, shower, flowers, massage, etc.

Structure/Time Management (structure): You structure your time at work and in your private life with routines, familiar processes, and specific time slots such as breaks, meetings, etc. This creates security and fosters variety and enjoyment of small things in everyday life. Psychological games (e.g., simmering conflicts), small talk, activities/hobbies, or intimacy in relationships can also be forms of time management and provide structure and security in daily life.

Examples: morning meditation, meals/breaks/apéro with colleagues, regular weekend hikes or walks, church service, phone time with a good friend, etc.

The psychological basic needs are closely related to the theory of symbiotic relationships according to Schiff et al. [4], since in symbiosis we transfer the satisfaction of our psychological needs such as attention, stimulation, and structure to another person.

In transactional analysis, symbioses [4] are said to occur when people consciously or unconsciously experience themselves as incomplete (see Phase VII—symbiotic relationships) and thus enter into a dependency on others.

You have heard about the script in Chapter II. All parts of the script essentially serve the attempt to move others to provide help, support, and/or expressions of love and affection. The aim is to finally obtain what was missing in one's own personality development. In this sense, other people serve to take over precisely those missing abilities in relationships and to satisfy unfulfilled (relationship) needs. Therefore, it is understandable that especially during a burnout episode, which is accompanied by great insecurity and stress, communication and relationship patterns increasingly take on a symbiotic character [5].

Accordingly, examine which relationships give you strength or drain your energy. Critically consider where you may be taking too little responsibility and leaving your own satisfaction and fulfillment of needs to others or burdening them with it. Once again, pay attention to how your psychological basic needs are being met and find new habits and routines to meaningfully and regularly incorporate them into your personal and professional life!

The following questions can help you with self-reflection

- Which areas related to the three psychological basic needs (recognition, structure, stimulation) do you already actively and mindfully implement in your daily life?
- Which areas are currently being neglected?
- How could you reactivate and revitalize the area of structure/time management (structure) in your personal life?
- How could you reactivate and more consciously incorporate the area of stimulation (stimulus) in your personal life?

- How could you reactivate and more consciously enliven the area of recognition/stroking (stroke) in your personal life?
- How could you also more consciously incorporate, activate, and enliven the three areas of psychological basic needs in your professional life?
- Which friendships and contacts from your professional or personal life give you strength, confidence, and enable you to experience self-determination and autonomy?
- Which friendships and contacts from your professional or personal life drain your strength, confidence, and tend to limit your self-determination and autonomy?
- How do you deal with defeats, setbacks, and mistakes? Which inner voices become loud within you then? What do they express?
- How do you deal with personal successes and progress? How could you redesign and implement this behavior in relation to the basic need for attention (strokes)? What kind of attention could you give yourself as a result of a success? What does this idea trigger in you?
- Where would it do you good, in terms of satisfying the three basic needs (stroke, stimulus, structure), to open yourself to new perspectives, possibilities, and ideas? What new, empowering, and fulfilling experiences would you thereby make possible for yourself? To what extent would these have a positive influence on your personal development?

For Leaders—With a Focus on the Organization

The three basic needs and the theory of symbiotic relationship patterns can also provide an exciting basis for reflection regarding your organization! Here are a few ideas for implementation and (self-)reflection:

Recognition

- How and for what do you give each other feedback, comments, or praise within the team? In your view, what is the balance between praise and criticism?
- Do you maintain a conscious feedback culture? If so, what do you pay attention to? How is this recognizable?
- What characterizes the way people interact in the organization? How is this visible, audible, and tangible?
- Which values (consciously or unconsciously) shape the culture of collaboration? What forms of recognition are common in your team?
- When is the culture of collaboration lived and put into practice? How is this recognizable? How is it defined? Who has shaped it?
- Are there (sub-)groups/departments, etc., in your team where special "rules" or "values" apply? For example, regarding closeness/distance? Type of communication? Appreciation? Values? Work quality? Collaboration? Definition of leadership?

Stimulation

- How do you implement creativity and the activation of different senses in your team/organization? Are there places that invite relaxation and rest, physical activity, or social exchange and lingering?
- How do you ensure variety in the daily work routine in your organization? What opportunities do employees have to implement this? In your view, what impact does this have on the resilience and health of team members?
- How important is the integration of intuition to you personally/in your organization? How do you manage to integrate it into your and your team's professional routine?

- How is a holistic approach (thinking, feeling, acting)— if already present—recognizable in your organization? What advantages are/would be accessible as a result— especially regarding strengthening resilience and health in the team?
- How are team events organized? How do you enable regular exchange and encounters within the team? How do you manage to create a noticeable difference from the often head-heavy and stressful workday?
- What changes regarding the stimulation of different senses would your team particularly enjoy? What do you think? What would your team probably say if you asked each person about it?
- What advantages do you see in stimulating the senses and taking a holistic approach in your organization's daily work—especially regarding strengthening resilience and health? What conclusions do you draw from this for yourself and your team?

Structuring

- What rituals and rules exist in your organization? (explicit/implicit, conscious/unconscious?)
- How important are structure and security in your organization? How do you justify this assessment?
- How are structure and security ensured and maintained in your organization? How is this recognizable?
- Where is there potential for change and why?
- What role do you take on as a leader in this regard?
- How could awareness of the importance of structure and security be increased among leaders? What impact would that have on the organization?
- Which structures are more conducive to strengthening resilience and health? Which are more inhibiting? Where would change be necessary?

- Where, in your view, is the most energy and motivation lost for you/your team/your organization? Where would change make sense?
- What particularly enables and consciously fosters energy and motivation for yourself/in the team/in the organization? Where would change be necessary?

Symbiotic Relationship Patterns

- Which employees tend to act symbiotically in their behavior and often take on too much responsibility for others? What benefit do these individuals gain from this type of cooperation with others?
- Which employees behave more passively? What benefit does passivity have for the person concerned? What need might be behind it? How could you, as a leader, encourage these individuals to take on more responsibility? What impact would that have on you/on the team?
- How is autonomy and personal responsibility generally in your team? To what extent does your behavior as a leader influence this? Where might change be needed to strengthen autonomy and personal responsibility in the team?
- How could you specifically encourage greater autonomy and self-responsibility in your area of leadership? What concrete changes would result from this? How would your attitude as a leader then have to change? How would you recognize this? How would your employees recognize this?
- What advantages do you see in promoting autonomy in your team/organization? How could you encourage greater autonomy and self-responsibility in your team? What next steps would make sense? What small

next step will you implement concretely in the coming weeks?

- How could you encourage greater autonomy and self-responsibility, especially with a view to strengthening resilience and health for yourself/your team/the organization? What next steps would make sense for you and your team? What might implementation look like in concrete terms?

References

1. Schlegel, L. (2002). *Handwörterbuch der Transaktionsanalyse* (2nd edn., pp. 83–84). Herder.
2. Schlegel, L. (2002). *Handwörterbuch der Transaktionsanalyse* (2nd edn., pp. 356–358). Herder.
3. Spitz, R. A. (1992). *Die Entstehung der ersten Objektbeziehungen* (Vol. 5, pp. 112–113). Klett-Cotta.
4. Schlegel, L. (2002). *Handwörterbuch der Transaktionsanalyse* (2nd edn., pp. 313–320). Herder.
5. Schulze, H., & Sejkora, K. (2015). *Positive Führung – Resilienz statt Burnout* (pp. 83–84). Haufe.

Afterword

What remains is a profound life experience that has changed me permanently. What remains is gratitude for my successful path to recovery. What remains is my commitment, as a school principal, psychosocial counselor, coach, supervisor, organizational consultant, and teaching transactional analyst PTSTA-C, to help prevent others from having to go through such an experience.

What remains is the certainty that a burnout illness can be an opportunity for change. What remains is the conviction that a burnout illness has nothing to do with failure. A burnout illness means much more! It is a sign that a person has repeatedly ignored and disregarded their own boundaries and, in this sense, has failed to respect themselves and to show sufficient appreciation and respect for their own person and needs.

Burnout is particularly dangerous because the hormonal changes caused by high stress levels have a major impact on one's own perception and, quite literally, can cloud the

R. Petersen, *Tsunami in the Head – Better Understanding and Coping with Burnout*, https://doi.org/10.1007/978-3-658-49737-8

senses as a "tsunami in the head." As a result, one can no longer properly assess oneself and one's situation, so that physical symptoms are misinterpreted or recognized too late, which can lead to long-term and lasting physical and psychological damage.

The good news is that there is a way out, even if it can be very long and arduous and you are repeatedly confronted with new, often unimaginable challenges. But successful recovery is possible! I am an example of this, even though it took a very long time before I trusted myself enough to accept this emerging hope as a fact and to consciously leave the burnout illness behind me.

I am once again fully capable, my memory and cognitive abilities have improved, my hormonal balance is back to normal, so I can sleep through the night, and my body can adequately handle a minimal to sometimes even very high level of stress. For a long time, this was unthinkable for me. I was very afraid that I would never again reach such a high level of performance and resilience. With a lot of patience and confidence, which I developed through my counseling skills and existing coaching abilities, combined with my acquired knowledge of nutrition, exercise, and relaxation techniques, as well as the conscious integration of spirituality and intuition into my daily life, I have managed to reach a new level of health and well-being. At the same time, none of this would have been possible without the help of various people from outside.

This is possible for everyone, and I am pleased if I can make an active and lasting contribution to the education, prevention, and recovery from burnout with this book. In my various roles and responsibilities, I can also make an active contribution to the prevention, support, and assistance of (potential) burnout sufferers, as well as to the development of organizations, teams, and leaders. This fills me with great satisfaction and gratitude.

Transactional analysis offers many helpful concepts and perspectives. It was not easy for me to limit myself in this book to a few selected concepts. At the same time, it was important to me to give you access, to present helpful new perspectives, and to provide practical tools that you can apply directly in your professional and personal life. The knowledge of transactional analysis has enriched my life both professionally and personally, and there is still so much more to discover! I want to continue sharing this knowledge and my experience with others and thus contribute, through counseling, supervision, organizational development, and training and further education, to empowering and strengthening autonomy.

Thank you at this point for your personal interest, the time you have invested, and the courage to engage deeply with the topic of burnout and resilience, both with yourself and in your professional and personal context! In doing so, you are making a direct contribution to prevention and to the promotion of mental and physical health!

Conclusion and Outlook

In this book, I have tried to provide as broad and diverse an insight as possible into the burnout disorder, addressing different perspectives and, through the variety of approaches, enabling a holistic view. I am aware that this work is by no means complete or definitive, nor can it do justice to all those affected by burnout.

At the same time, I have tried to let my ideas, knowledge, and intuition guide me, in the hope that you, dear reader, will find yourself directly and personally addressed by an aspect or description, and will be able to establish a personal connection to the topic of burnout and resilience. This is the first important step toward a better understanding and an unbiased attitude toward burnout and those (potentially) affected.

It was important to me to incorporate personal events and experiences while also presenting different perspectives and possible solutions. I also wanted to shed new light on this multifaceted and complex topic, to depict it as

© The Editor(s) (if applicable) and The Author(s), under exclusive license to Springer Fachmedien Wiesbaden GmbH, part of Springer Nature 2025
R. Petersen, *Tsunami in the Head – Better Understanding and Coping with Burnout*, https://doi.org/10.1007/978-3-658-49737-8

holistically as possible, and to emphasize that it cannot be about finding someone to blame, a specific trigger, or an isolated cause. In my view, the question of blame and possible parties responsible is rarely truly helpful! In my opinion, we all share part of the responsibility—as a society, and in this sense also as organizations, as leaders, as team and/or family members, as friends and acquaintances, and of course as individuals and (potentially) those affected.

Corporate/Social Responsibility is therefore, for me, the key word in burnout prevention and successful treatment. A term that goes hand in hand with a new attitude characterized by mindfulness, respect, honesty, openness, as well as mutual trust and appreciation. If we manage to view burnout not from the perspective of blame and an admission of weakness, much has already been achieved! Here, as a leader, team or family member, or as a friend/acquaintance, you can already make an important contribution to a re-evaluation and a more nonjudgmental attitude!

Thank you for your interest in this book. I hope you have found some answers and insights that motivated you to pick up this book in the first place.

Recommendations

As already mentioned, my perspectives and approaches to the topic of burnout and resilience are only a first step toward personal deepening and clarification. On my website www.triflect.ch you will find numerous free materials for individual deepening, including the letter to those affected (appendix). In addition, I have created online courses on the topics of burnout and resilience as well as transactional analysis, in which you can learn step by step and at your own pace, accompanied professionally by me. There are many other books and sources that you can explore afterwards, focusing on personal development and professionalization. I have compiled and described some of them for you in more detail. More detailed references can be found in the bibliography below.

R. Petersen, *Tsunami in the Head – Better Understanding and Coping with Burnout*, https://doi.org/10.1007/978-3-658-49737-8

Transactional Analysis (TA)

1. Transactional Analysis: A helpful book if you are generally interested in transactional analysis and want to get an initial overview. It provides a good introduction to the most common topics in TA and offers exciting exercises for (self-)reflection at the end of each chapter [1].
2. Positive Leadership: A great book for deepening your knowledge, especially for leaders who want to explore resilience and burnout within the framework of transactional analysis and recognize and resolve restrictive patterns [2].
3. The Constructive Conversation—A Guide: A helpful read if you want to further familiarize yourself with the concepts of transactional analysis, especially in a professional context. The book is enriched with many valuable and practical examples from work and private life, which makes for an easily accessible approach [3].
4. Systemic Professionalism and Transactional Analysis: An exciting approach for consultants and coaches, but also for leaders who would like to integrate systematic thinking and are open to critically questioning their own actions and professionalizing themselves [4].
5. Transactional Analysis: This classic offers in-depth connections and explanations for all those who want to know the details and are looking for various sources and references. However, this book is not as easy to read as the foundational work "Transactional Analysis," which was presented first in this list [5].
6. The Dictionary of Transactional Analysis: This is a very compact work that provides a quick overview and easily understandable definitions of the most important terms in transactional analysis [6].

Burnout—Professional Articles

1. Hochstrasser, B. (22.06.2016). Burnout-Behandlung Teil 1: Grundlagen. *Swiss Medical Forum.*
2. Hochstrasser, B. (29.06.2016). Burnout-Behandlung Teil 2: Praktische Empfehlungen. *Swiss Medical Forum.*
3. Hochstrasser, B. (February 2023). Burnout und Erschöpfungsdepression. *Zeitschrift für Psychiatrie und Neurologie*, pp. 2–7.

References

1. Stewart, I., & Joines, V. (1990). *Die Transaktionsanalyse – Eine Einführung.* Herder Verlag.
2. Schulze, H., & Klaus, S. (2015). *Positive Führung – Resilienz statt. Burnout* Haufe Verlag.
3. Gührs, M., & Nowak, C. (2014). *Das konstruktive Gespräch – ein Leitfaden.* Verlag Christa Limmer.
4. Schmid, B. (2008). *Systemisches Coaching – Konzept und Vorgehensweisen in der Persönlichkeitsberatung.* EHP-Verlag.
5. Schlegel, L. (2011). *Die Transaktionale Analyse.* Zürich: Deutschweizer Gesellschaft für Transaktionsanalyse.
6. Schlegel, L. (2002, 2nd ed.). *Handwörterbuch der Transaktionsanalyse.* Herder Verlag.
7. Welter-Enderlin, R., & Hildenbrand, B. (2006). *Resilienz – Gedeihen trotz widriger Umstände.* Karl-Auer Verlag.
8. Buchenau, P., & Nelting, M. (2015). *Burnout – Von Betroffenen lernen!* Springer Gabler Verlag.

Appendix

Letter to those affected—A simple way to make contact

I spent a long time considering how it might be possible both to raise awareness about the topic of "burnout" and to reach potential sufferers with my book. Looking back, I can admit that there were many signs of burnout in my own case. At the time, however, I simply did not want to see or acknowledge them. I vehemently dismissed and did not take seriously the critical comments from friends.

So how is it possible to reach someone in the early stages of the illness and encourage them to reconsider? This led me to the idea of a personal letter, which you can easily copy and send to the person concerned. Of course, it is also possible to simply address the affected person in a quiet moment. In my experience, someone suffering from burnout will rarely listen and will initially adopt a defensive attitude. From my experience, this is almost a classic symptom of the illness and corresponds to the personality

R. Petersen, *Tsunami in the Head – Better Understanding and Coping with Burnout*, https://doi.org/10.1007/978-3-658-49737-8

structure that even favors burnout. That is why I came up with the idea of a letter, which the affected person can read in peace and thus have time to process the information both intellectually and emotionally. It may take several attempts before the information can penetrate the person's consciousness. In any case, a letter that you hold in your hand is less easy to "ignore" or "deflect" than a hint or advice from a good friend.

I hope that this book and this letter will serve to shake up as many affected individuals as possible at an early stage and encourage a "radical" change in thinking. Or, as a first step, act as a door opener to further inform oneself about the topics of burnout and resilience.

My wish is that (potential) sufferers do not fall into burnout in the first place and therefore do not have to endure such a long and intense recovery process. At the same time, I hope that (potential) sufferers can learn from my experiences in their own personal situations, so that they can benefit as much as possible and draw a little hope, strength, and confidence from my story.

In this spirit, I sincerely wish you all the best on your personal journey and, if necessary, sufficient courage to take a closer look and take your own observations seriously, so that you can offer them to the potential person affected as support or an offer of help, and honestly communicate what you observe, without attaching any expectations to it.

You can also find the materials for the "Letter to those affected" available for download on my website.

With best regards
Rebecca Petersen
www.triflect.ch

Part 1—Initiating Contact

Date: _____

Dear _____

You are receiving this letter from _____,
because he/she is concerned about your health and your
current well-being.

From my own experience, I know how difficult it is to
take time during a stressful period to reflect on your own
well-being and tune in to yourself. The problem is that
this very difficulty in finding calm is a sign that you have a
tendency to fall into the burnout trap. I speak from experience! I went through the same thing! I was so caught up
in the hamster wheel of work, stress, pressure, and constant performance that I didn't notice the wheel spinning
faster and faster, and that the only real way to survive
would have been to get out immediately. Instead, because
of my high expectations of myself, I chose to just run even
faster and ignore feelings like overwhelm, weakness, and
inadequacy. That was at the beginning. Over time, I simply stopped feeling anything; I had no access at all to my
emotions and needs. I was just functioning! But until the
very end, I was firmly convinced that I would never experience burnout myself!

You might be thinking now: "What is she talking
about? She doesn't even know me!"

That is correct! However, I know from personal experience that suggestions from people who know you well
and are especially close to you are all too quickly and very
effectively—almost reflexively—deflected and ignored.
This is also called denial.

Exactly such a person is now trying, with this letter,
to give you the opportunity to honestly reflect, in a quiet

moment and without denial, on where you currently stand, how you are feeling at the moment, and what you truly want from life. Find a quiet place for this, take your time, breathe deeply, and try to simply endure—and, if possible, even enjoy—the silence, the idleness, and being alone with yourself for about ten minutes. If you already find this difficult, it is quite possible that you are already caught in the hamster wheel of stress and overload, and that you can no longer bear it when the wheel slows down a bit or even comes to a brief stop.

You might be thinking now: "Yes, that's true. Actually, I do feel extremely exhausted. But honestly, I can't just step out of my system! Impossible! What would my children do then, what about my partner, my supervisor, my colleagues and my team, my clients, etc.?"

I can very much understand this concern as a justification as well! I felt exactly the same way! But at some point, I reached a stage where I simply no longer had the strength to think about alternatives and feasible ways to get out. Whenever such thoughts briefly surfaced, I immediately dismissed them as foolish ideas because I was overwhelmed by the prospect of thinking any further about them. Honestly: With burnout, there inevitably comes a moment when you crash the system into the wall! Just like that, out of nowhere, and with total destruction! I have experienced this myself! And then you no longer even have the strength to resist the fear, uncertainty, and insecurity about possible alternatives. Then there is only emptiness, and you are no longer able to think for the supposedly "oh so" important system, let alone be there for the people who matter to you and fulfill your previous role!

Then you are simply at the end of your strength. You have given up on yourself and the world! You are a physical and emotional wreck. Accordingly, the alternative—to take a brief moment right now for an initial (self-)reflection—is truly a meaningful and good idea! Perhaps, on your first attempt, you will succeed in identifying next steps to improve your current situation. Or you may calmly decide that you are overwhelmed, see no possible way out yourself, or simply cannot make any "life-changing" decision at this time. In that case, it is best to seek professional help. That means making an appointment today with your general practitioner, a psychologist, or a counselor, just to make sure you are assessing your situation correctly and are well supported throughout the process. This is certainly the better alternative than simply leaving your current situation as it is! Believe me! As I said, I speak from experience, and I would not wish a single person in this world to have to experience this kind of physical and emotional "collateral damage" or "total breakdown" themselves!

The topic of burnout is multifaceted, complex, and the symptoms are highly individual. As a result, the symptoms are often misunderstood and underestimated. Even I, as a psychological counselor and coach, did not correctly interpret my own symptoms and the first clear warning signs at the time—or, as already mentioned, I successfully ignored, suppressed, and misclassified them. In addition, I simply had no idea what everyday life could look like otherwise, or how it would feel to live with less stress, uncertainty, and (performance) pressure. Moreover, my work simply meant a great deal to me. Receiving recognition and being able to contribute my strengths and resources brought me great joy, and I viewed my ambition, assertiveness, and my physical and mental strength as entirely positive qualities. I never would have thought that, in the long run, this could have such disastrous consequences for me, or that things could turn around so quickly.

For you, however, it doesn't have to end this way!

I therefore have a request for you: Afterwards, please take a free online burnout test for yourself and familiarize yourself with possible symptoms and early warning signs of burnout. Of course, it is possible that in an advanced stage of burnout, even this will be of little help, as you may no longer be able to properly perceive your own situation and existing symptoms. This is a consequence of prolonged stress! Due to the increased concentration of stress hormones, self-perception becomes increasingly difficult, and individual physical symptoms are often downplayed or misinterpreted. An external assessment could provide you with additional and important insights here.

So if you have the courage to ask someone close to you (perhaps the person from whom you received this letter) for an external assessment, then the second part of this letter may be the next right step for you. Simply let the person know that you would like an external assessment and ask them to complete Part 3 and return it to you.

I am sure the person in question will be pleased about your inquiry and about being able to support you in your self-reflection and throughout the process.

With the external assessment, you can once again take your time to reflect and decide whether you might want to proactively seek professional help from a psychologist or a physician. Perhaps it will also help you to read my book "Tsunami—Burnout in the Mind" and gain insight into my story and my experiences with the topics of burnout and resilience. Or maybe you would like to visit my website www.triflect.ch and make use of the resources available there (e.g., online courses, driver test, etc.) and the information for yourself.

Decide calmly and entirely for yourself! Consciously choose what seems right to you as the next step. There is not just one correct path!

The decision is entirely up to you! No one can really help you with it. And that's a good thing! Because ultimately, you are responsible for your own happiness and health! You know best what is good for you and what is right for you!

In any case, briefly write down here what thoughts spontaneously come to mind, even without much prior consideration or meaningful explanations, and what next steps you would like to take for yourself:

With or without burnout symptoms, it is wise to regularly take time to pause and reflect, to assess your current situation, and calmly consider where you stand in your life, whether you are truly (still) happy, feel comfortable, where you want to go in your life, and what personally gives your actions and daily life a sense of meaning.

You are, in any case, worthy of living a happy, healthy, and content life without pressure, stress, shame, or guilt— you do not need to achieve anything special or change yourself to deserve this!

I sincerely wish you all the best, as well as much courage, strength, success, and good health!

With best regards

Rebecca Petersen

www.triflect.ch

Part 2—External Assessment

Date: _____

Dear _____
External assessment of: _____
External assessment for: _____

You are receiving this letter at your own request from _____, because you wish to reflect on your health and current well-being regarding the topic of burnout with the help of an external assessment.

I congratulate you on this first, important, and courageous step!

Below (Part 3) you will find a detailed list of possible signs of burnout. The markings indicate the assessment of _____, which you can use for your personal reflection.

Important: The external assessment is merely an observation by a third party! It is now entirely up to you to reflect for yourself and decide which symptoms and early signs you can actually identify in yourself.

Proceed as follows:

1. Briefly skim through the external assessment. Then cover the left side so that you can no longer see the external assessment.
2. Now, using a different color, check off the symptoms that you believe apply to you! Don't spend too much time thinking about it, and if possible, cover the marks in the front (those made by the other person) so that you can form as unbiased an impression as possible.

3. Remove the cover on the left side. Now compare the two assessments and relate the differences to your own self-assessment.
4. Take a moment to let these impressions sink in and, if necessary, take a moment to calm down. Create some distance!
5. Then decide whether you might want to seek professional support from a psychologist or physician. If you are still unsure about making a realistic initial assessment, a consultation with a resilience or burnout coach, therapist, or your general practitioner can also be helpful, especially in the case of diffuse physical symptoms. The (external) assessment (Part 3) can already serve as an initial helpful orientation and a basis for discussion.
6. In any case, briefly write down here any thoughts that spontaneously come to mind, even without much prior consideration or explanation, and what next steps you would like to take for yourself.

You did it! I am pleased that, unlike me back then, you have consciously chosen this brief, honest self-assessment and reflection, and that you have taken the time to put your health and well-being at the center, if only for a moment.

Perhaps you now even feel compelled to take a closer, personal look at the topic of burnout?! In that case, my book "Burnout—Tsunami in the Mind" could provide you with helpful insights and an initial overview. Alternatively, take a look at my website www.triflect.ch. There you will find useful materials and resources on the topics of burnout and resilience.

I sincerely wish you all the best on your future path, along with much courage, strength, success, and good health!

With best regards

Rebecca Petersen

www.triflect.ch

Part 3—External Assessment
Date: _____
External assessment of: _____
External assessment for:_____

Possible Early Signs and Symptoms of Burnout
Check the symptoms that apply to you and add keywords, if necessary, indicating how you recognize them. You can also add to the list under "other."

Psychological Symptoms

- Emotional exhaustion
- Emotional lability
- Irritability
- Aggressiveness
- Insecurity
- Anxiety, panic
- Depressed mood
- Loss of motivation
- other: _____
_____

Physical Symptoms

- Fatigue
- Inability to recover
- Sleep disturbances

- Autonomic symptoms (digestive disorders, multiple pains in abdomen, back, neck, teeth, head)
- Susceptibility to infections
- other: _____

_____

Cognitive Symptoms

- Attention disorder
- Concentration disorder
- Memory disorder
- Difficulty making decisions
- Reduced mental flexibility
- other: _____

_____

Behavioral changes

- Increased or decreased activity
- Social withdrawal
- Addictive behavior
- Decreased performance
- Absence from work
- Tendency to accidents
- Reduced resilience
- other: _____

_____

Source: Hochstrasser, B. (29.06.2016). Burnout Treatment Part 2: Practical Recommendations. *Swiss Medical Forum*.

Important

An external assessment refers to the observation by a third person! It is up to you to decide which symptoms and signs you can actually identify in yourself! It is important not to view the symptoms in isolation, but to also consider a possible psychosomatic connection. You do not have to take any potential next steps alone! You are allowed to seek support! This is not a weakness, but a strength! Even if it is difficult for you at times to consult a professional. Take your situation seriously! It is worth it!